THE
FIGHTING
ILLINI
A Story Of Illinois Football

THE
FIGHTING
ILLINI
A Story Of Illinois Football
by
Lon Eubanks

THE STRODE PUBLISHERS, INC.
HUNTSVILLE, ALABAMA 35802

"We'll have the will to win, and if we go down, we'll go down fighting...hard and clean. That's the Illinois way."

—Ray Eliot

To
Laurine Eubanks,
In Memoriam,
And For My Wife,
Kathleen

Contents

Foreword

Football at the University of Illinois has been my life's passion since I first became associated with it as a young freshman player. That is why it is such a pleasure for me personally to see the traditions of the Fighting Illini set down in a book, written with such understanding. Lon Eubanks has done a superb job of capturing the inner spirit of football at Illinois in the era when I was head coach and in the other periods as well.

Those of us who have been associated with Illinois for such a long period of time take special pride in the greatness of this university, whatever the endeavor. We take joy in the football victories and we agonize, if only briefly, in the defeats. But in the final analysis, we know that the important thing is that we have strived to achieve the height of our ability, as athletes and as men.

Those of us who have been a part of Illinois football believe there is something special at the heart of it—the spirit of the Fighting Illini. This book helps immeasurably to put it into words.

Ray Eliot
Honorary Associate Athletic Director
University of Illinois

Prologue:
The Illini Tradition

The measure of college football is in its timelessness; the days seem to crawl by, and then suddenly they are swept away, as if in a jetstream.

The past blends quickly into the present, and tomorrows rapidly become yesterdays. For the player, the soreness of angry muscles in winter conditioning is replaced by the sweat of spring practice. Then, there is the waiting, the almost endless waiting of the summer. Finally, when it seemed like it would never come, it is fall. The trees, which once were green, have turned into a kaleidoscope of the season, multicolored hues of auburn, orange, and brown.

For the fan, nothing quite can match being in a giant stadium in September, a delirious celebration of sight and sound, a wonderland of stunning color and blaring cacophony.

It is a retreat from the regular, the routine—a rendezvous with a particular brand of excitement that can strain voices, drain emotions, and build a feeling of pride in a way that few other such forms of relentless devotion can.

Almost as soon as a season begins, it seems, it is over, leaving behind countless memories for everyone. Yet the pages of the calendar turn, and there is always "next year." The faces change, but the games continue, piling one upon another to make seasons, then eras, and eventually the blur of history.

The days whir past. "Stop," you say. "I want to get off for a while. I want to savor this day. I want it to stretch beyond the dusk and the dawn. I want to sip it, like a fine old wine."

The University of Illinois has long been a part of the phenomenon of college football, from a day in 1890 when its first team led by a student, Scott Williams, traveled to Bloomington to play Illinois Wesleyan, and the fans broke out with this cheer:

Rah, hoo rah, zup boom ah!
Hip, zip zaazoo, Jim Yim Bazoo—
Ip, siddy, ay ki
U of I, Champaign.

It became evident in the beginning that Illinois was establishing high standards for its football program.

"A new step has been taken in our athletics," the student newspaper, the *Illini*, reported on October 17, 1891. "It is one worthy of praise. The football players are required to sign an agreement that they will abstain from liquor and tobacco and will keep early hours."

Stories are still retold about the legendary spirit of the late Arthur Hall, who was a star player for Illinois before the turn of the century and its first man to serve as Illinois coach for more than three years. Hall guided the Illini from 1907 through 1912, before becoming an attorney and probate judge in Danville.

They tell how Hall, as a player, had to be dragged from the field by his own teammates whenever he was replaced in the lineup. A yellowed old newspaper clipping remembers, "It usually took four huskies to hold him down after he had been pulled out."

Thus it happened in the game with Purdue in 1900, the year he was captain:

"The Boilermakers led the Illini 5 to 0, and the rooters from Lafayette were getting ready to strike up the paean of victory. Six minutes were left to play, and Captain Hall was tottering in his tracks at halfback. He was hardly strong enough to give the signals. Coach (Edgar) Holt ordered Hall out of the game, and he was dragged to the sidelines. Someone else started to give the signals.

"Hall darted out on the field, claimed the right as captain to play, pushed the substitute aside and gave the signal for himself to carry the ball. He carried it right over Purdue's goal

12

line and fell beneath the goal posts. They had to pry the ball out of his arms. He was unconscious, dead to the world and the storm of cheers."

And from those early days a tradition of Illinois football emerged, rich in both fact and folklore.

That tradition is Bob Zuppke, for example, introducing one innovation after another, including the huddle.

Some will argue that Zuppke first got the idea of the huddle when he watched the players at the Jacksonville School for the Deaf assemble close together after each play so each man would be able to see the sign language they all used.

Rune Clark, who played under Zuppke in the early 1920s, always insisted that the idea actually was born in a practice in 1922.

"In practice that fall," Clark once said, "we complained to Zup how in scrimmage the other team always knew what we were going to do because they knew the signals. So Zup told us to gather around him a few yards back and tell him what play

Bob Zuppke (left) congratulates Ray Eliot, his successor as Illini coach.

we were going to use.

"He tried it first in the opener against South Dakota, and it worked fine. Hardly anyone commented on it. But when we started the game at Iowa the following week, Howard Jones immediately protested. The game was held up five minutes or so while we discussed the huddle with the officials, who could find nothing in the rule book against it."

Illinois used the huddle from then on, and most other teams quickly adopted it.

But not all of Zuppke's inventions worked out as well.

Harry Gamage, who was an assistant coach under Zuppke in the 1920s, remembers: "Zup used to make a lot of his own equipment, and I remember once he designed a thigh pad that slipped down into a one-piece pant right below the belt. In those days, the padding was felt, and Zup's thigh pads were about seven inches wide and a foot long. The problem was that when they were in your pants, you couldn't get down in a stance very comfortably, so the kids all unlaced them and took them out before they went on the field. Zup called the sportswriters out to see the new thigh pads he'd invented, and he called some of the kids over to show them. There wasn't one in a pair of pants out there. Was he ever mad.

"I can remember another time when Zup went on a trip to the South with the baseball team and saw some greens on some golf courses covered with cotton seed hulls. So Zup decided he'd make a football practice field out of cotton seed hulls. He had a couple of carloads shipped up from the South, and just north of the stadium, to the east, he built a cotton seed field. It looked good, and the idea was good; but the first time it rained, that cotton seed smelled so bad it made everyone sick, and that field was done away with in a hurry after that."

Zuppke's hallmark as a coach, as much as strategy, was his psychological buildups before a game.

A tale which has become another legend is how Zuppke stepped before the squad and said, "The only man who comes out of the game today is a dead man."

Late in the game, one of the Illinois players was flat on his back on the field, and Zuppke sent in a substitute.

The young reserve quickly hurried back to the sidelines. Zuppke stopped him and asked him why he had not stayed in

Red Grange roars toward the goal line in his legendary devastation of Michigan in 1924 in Memorial Stadium.

the game.

"But, coach," said the young reserve. "The man you told me to replace is still breathing."

The Illinois tradition also is Red Grange running for four touchdowns in 12 minutes against Michigan in 1924.

And one still wonders today how even the recollections of that day could have enhanced the deed.

Old-timers still like to tell about a Michigan fan, caught in the middle of the Illini cheering section that day, pulling a handful of money out of his pocket after Grange's fourth touchdown and bellowing to the Illinois fans surrounding him, "I've got $50 I want to bet on Man O' War in the fifth race today."

Those stunning performances of Grange gave rise to an unprecedented burst of enthusiasm among the Illinois fans. And it was reflected in the birth of a symbol of that spirit, Chief Illiniwek, who has been a key figure in the Illini tradition ever since.

Hugh Dvorak, then the director of the school's marching

15

band, first had the idea of a symbolic Illini Indian doing a victory dance, a historic reminder of the proud tribe from which the state's name was taken.

The dance was first performed at the Illinois-Pennsylvania game in 1926 by Lester G. Leutwiler, and four years later, when Webber Borchers served as the symbolic Illini chief, an authentic Indian costume was obtained.

Borchers said, "In the summer of 1930 I went to the Pine Ridge Reservation in South Dakota. I hitch-hiked out, called on an Indian agent and explained my mission. He and an old Indian trader called in an older Sioux Indian woman. She and two younger women made the suit."

The term *Illini*, in Indian tongue, means "brave men," and Zuppke had many players who deserved the accolade when he was head coach. Some of those brave men were so brave, in fact, that even Zuppke's imagination as a coach was tested.

Old-timers remember All-American guard Leroy Wietz with a smile.

"Wietz was a great lineman, but whenever he saw a loose ball bounding around, he was bound and determined to fall on it," recalls Doug Mills, one of his teammates in the late 1920s.

"As the safety on defense in those days, I can remember many times letting a punt go that I didn't think I could handle, only to see Wietz rush back and try to fall on it.

"The only problem was that Wietz didn't have very good eyesight, and nine times out of 10 when Wietz went for a loose ball, he'd only land on a part of it, and it would squirt away from him.

"Zup decided that we had to do something about that, so he assigned someone from our own team to block Wietz any time there was a loose ball. I'm not sure he ever caught on to why he was always running into one of his own teammates every time there was a loose ball."

A great help to Zuppke throughout his career was his team trainer, Matt Bullock, who had his own way of breaking in new reporters from the student newspaper.

Bullock would point to a player and say, "Son, do you know who that is?"

"No," the aspiring young writer would admit.

"Well," said Bullock, fighting back a grin. "That's Joe

16

A modern Chief Illiniwek...a symbol of the Illini tradition.

Nucleus, and Zup is going to build this team around him."

"It's amazing," an old-timer remembers, "how often Joe Nucleus' name appeared in at least one preseason story."

And Zuppke had enough guys named Nucleus to win 131 games in the 29 years he coached at Illinois.

The Ray Eliot years provided a rich legacy to the Illinois tradition, too.

Eliot produced three Big Ten championship teams, two Rose Bowl victories, and enough wins over Northwestern that Eliot never had to do what he once jokingly threatened.

During Eliot's tenure at Illinois, the traditional trophy of the Illinois-Northwestern game, the Sweet Sioux Tomahawk, was exchanged in a ceremony involving the rival coaches at the first basketball game of the year.

On one of those occasions, Eliot handed over the tomahawk to his winning rival, coach Bob Voigts, with a speech of flowery praise for Voigts and the Wildcats.

The ceremony had ended, but to Eliot's surprise the microphone in front of him was not turned off when he turned to Voigts and said with a chuckle, "What I ought to do is bury this in that bald head of yours." The crowd roared.

Eliot not only produced All-Americans of the stature of Alex Agase, Buddy Young, and J. C. Caroline, along with a half-dozen more; he also produced a singing tackle who starred on Broadway.

Pete Palmer, who later went on to play Lil Abner on stage and screen, scored his first big hit as an entertainer by singing the national anthem at an Illinois football game in full uniform, helmet in hand.

Palmer, a reserve on Illinois' Rose Bowl team in 1951, remembers something which happened once when he stopped in front of a mirror to comb his hair before going on the field.

Veteran Burt Ingwersen, an Illini assistant coach under Eliot at the time, walked by, noticed Palmer in front of the mirror, and shook his head in disbelief.

"I still remember his comment," Palmer recalled. "He looked at me and said, 'What the hell is football coming to?' He apologized to me later because he didn't know I was going to be singing the national anthem that day."

Eliot's players still remember what he told them when

Pete Palmer...Illinois singing tackle.

they first arrived on the campus.

Eliot would point to the library and say, "That's where you study."

And he would point to Memorial Stadium and say, "That's where you play."

And then he would add, "If you don't study, you don't play."

Players did a lot of both at Illinois under Eliot, who looked over them all like a mother hen with her chicks.

Sometimes Eliot's protection of them went beyond the bounds of reason, as longtime sportscaster Larry Stewart remembers.

"Ray had a fetish about always wanting to keep his players away from the bright lights of the city when we were playing on the road," said Stewart.

"But he topped all his previous performances once when he took the team to play at Seattle. We got on the bus and went right through downtown Seattle until we were in the middle of an absolute wilderness.

"And, believe it or not, we spent that Friday night in a logging camp...an honest-to-goodness logging camp. And you know what Ray did? He made a bed check that night. Those players couldn't have gone anywhere if they wanted to."

One of the most memorable teams in Illinois history emerged in 1963 out of the ashes of a 15-game losing streak under Pete Elliott.

The Illinois tradition was enlarged by the performances of members of that team like sophomore Jim Grabowski and junior Dick Butkus.

Grabowski was one of a group of brash sophomores who brought new life to Illinois football. One, quarterback Fred Custardo, was so brash he once looked over at his backfield coach, Buck McPhail, and yelled, "Hey, Buck."

"I'll never forget the way he (Buck) walked over to Fred, grabbed him by the jersey and looked straight into his eyes and drawled, 'Do you think...you know me well enough...to call me Buck?'" Grabowski remembers now with a smile.

Custardo, a fun-loving, happy young man, is dead now, the victim of an accident off the playing field; it is one of life's strange ironies that it was Custardo's mother who once ran onto the field (it made a famous picture carried in newspapers around the nation) when Custardo was injured playing football.

The Illinois tradition also is a group of players who would not quit when there is still a second left on the clock, as Bob Blackman's 1974 team refused to do, in the face of all kinds of adversity.

The Illinois tradition, above all else, is a cheering crowd, and on a day not long ago, Illinois Chancellor Jack Peltason thought and said, "I really believe that athletics help cement people to a university. I have no doubt that sport is one of the most common grounds of this society. It is the most class-less and the most race-less. It is an area in which many of our students and alumni find great enjoyment."

The Illinois tradition is all these things—and more.

This is the story of how that tradition was born, was built, and will be remembered.

The fine old wine is ready.

And, in the mind's eye, you can sip it, if you will.

A Player In A Derby Hat

A fan, wearing his Sunday best including a derby hat, played in Illinois' first football victory ever. It was 1890, the year football began on the University of Illinois campus. The embryo Illini team squared off with Illinois Wesleyan, and late in the game, when the Illinois players were tired and bedraggled, there were no fresh reserves left. But Robert Humphrey Forbes, an agricultural engineering student, came out of the crowd to answer the call. He ran onto the field, loosened his tie, and helped Illinois defeat Wesleyan 12-6 on Thanksgiving Day.

Just a year before, in 1889, a young man named Scott Williams had entered the university and asked an upperclassman whom he should see to become a member of the school's football team. The older student looked at Williams with a somewhat puzzled expression and replied, "There ain't no such animal." And there was not.

There was an intercollegiate baseball team at Illinois in 1889, but football was virtually unknown to most of the 519 students on the Urbana campus.

And what little kickball that was played on a pickup level on the open greens could hardly be regarded as football—the way it was beginning to evolve in the East from its rugby and soccer-style beginnings at Harvard, Yale, and Columbia.

The University of Illinois in those early days was an institution struggling for an identity of its own, fighting for legislative funding under President Selim Hobart Peabody. It had been allowed to change its name from Illinois Industrial University in 1885, but it still had just a handful of students by today's standards and a faculty that numbered just 39. Tuition was a pittance compared to today's costs, and the alumni association's constitution of that time provided for dues of $.50 a year and a salary of $25 a year for the secretary-treasurer, "if such a sum should be available after all the bills have been paid."

In his hometown Williams had picked up some rudimentary knowledge of the rugbylike game from a young Harvard alumnus, who had come to Illinois State Normal University High School to teach. It was a roustabout sort of physical activity, and Williams, in particular, enjoyed it. He was disappointed when he came to the university and found that it had no team.

But during the fall of his first year, Williams noticed a card on the bulletin board outside of the university chapel that notified anyone who wanted to play "football" to report to the campus that afternoon.

Happy to find that there was at least some interest in the game on the Illinois campus, Williams hurried over to the appointed area.

What he found was "about a dozen fellows chasing a sort of portable bath tub inflated by lung power, kicking it in any direction whenever they got a chance.

"I watched them until they sat down to rest, then I approached them and bashfully said I would like to play football when they were ready to start the game," Williams recalled in a 1923 interview. "They replied that the game was over, and I could play some other day.

"That made me sore, and I gave that outfit a lecture on football, trying to circle the big tub with my arms and show them how the ball was carried, passed and kicked, also explaining the scrimmage and the points in scoring. The boys lined up, and we played a few minutes in a funny kind of a way, but they liked it and agreed to come out again some other time."

The word began to spread around the campus that there was a brash young man who knew all about the new way to play football.

"Then the row started," Williams told O. S. Storm of the *Sterling* (Illinois) *Gazette* in the 1923 reminiscence. "They had heard it was a 'brutal Indian game,' and they were against it.

First Football Team At Illinois, 1890—Front row, left to right: Arthur Pillsbury, W.F. Slater. Second row: Fred Clarke, Ed Clarke, A.W. Bush, Scott Williams, H.C. Arms. Third row: Philip

Almost the entire population of Champaign-Urbana held the same opinion.

"The upper-classman who pinned the notice on the bulletin board was bawled out good and plenty, and I was told that it wasn't healthy for preps to butt in and start any rough stuff."

*Steele, Roy Wright, A.W. Gates, George A. Huff, Walter F. Shat-
tuck, Ralph W. Hart, H.L. Bowen, W.A. Furber.*

But Williams was not dissuaded from his desire to see a
bona fide football game played on the Illinois campus.

"The next year much of the antagonism had disappeared,"
Williams recalled, "although little interest took its place. A
bunch of us got together, and I strained my oratorical powers in

an impassioned plea for the Athletic Association to permit us to play in the university's name at the Illinois Oratorical Association meeting in Bloomington, athletics having by that time been hung on as a side issue of the oratorical meets."

Williams promised that the players would buy their own uniforms and even pay their own railroad fare for the 50-mile trip to Bloomington to play against Illinois Wesleyan.

"Amidst considerable joshing, we were granted the coveted privilege which we sought," Williams remembered.

The first intercollegiate football team representing Illinois took the field on October 2, 1890, with Scott Williams as its coach, its captain, and its quarterback. On that day he became the father of what has since become one of the most tradition-rich college football histories in the nation.

Illinois Wesleyan won the game 16-0, but the outcome was less important to Williams and his teammates than the battle they had won against those who had opposed putting an inter-collegiate team on the field.

Not long afterward, the president of Purdue University appeared on the Illinois campus to speak.

"He said our university beat his in some ways, but if we would bring our football team over to Lafayette, they would beat the everlasting daylights out of us," Williams recalled.

"The big athletes of the upper classes sat up and took notice. They came to me and asked me about it. They said if we had to play football, as much as they hated to do so, we had to win, and many of them offered their services to me."

One of those athletes who stepped forward that day out of his sense of duty was George Huff, who later would serve Illinois with great distinction as its athletic director.

"G. Huff played for a long time from sheer loyalty, when he would rather have been sawing wood for both exercise and fun," Williams recalled. "But he fell for it, as they all do sooner or later.

"Some fine things have happened in the history of Illinois athletics, but I know of nothing finer than the loyalty that made the prominent athletes of their day submit to the orders of a freshman captain and punish themselves physically and mentally by playing a game that they then despised.

"We accepted Purdue's challenge, and on the way over,

26

being all but overwhelmed with the responsibility that rested upon me as captain, manager and coach, I begged the husky upperclassmen not to kill any of those Indiana boys. They didn't. On the way back I would probably have begged and pleaded with them not to kill me if I hadn't had a sneaking sort of wish that they would put me out of my misery before I had to face the university crowd again. Purdue beat us 62-0.

"If anyone thinks that Illinois loyalty is a development of later days, let them look at the picture of that broken and beaten team playing even then an all-but-despised game, feeling keenly the disgrace they felt they had brought upon the school they loved. Then look at the team as they got off of the cars, meeting instead of curses and imprecations, the cheers of a bunch of students down to welcome them home. They were grabbed and slapped on the back, and heavy hearts beat high again when told with oaths of emphasis that 'You had the nerve to tackle them at their own game. Never mind the score, we'll even that up later. We're proud of you, and we'll stay by you till the cows come home.'"

The student newspaper, the *Illini*, reported that loss to Purdue as follows: "The boys found on arriving in Lafayette that the Purdue eleven had been training under a coacher from Indianapolis for some time and could show our boys more tricks in five minutes than our boys ever knew about football. They had a faculty for appropriating the ball to their own use and only allowed their opponents to gain possession of it about a dozen times during the game. This accounts for the zero on our side of the score. However, our boys learned a great deal more about football than they would have if they had not gone, so they have that for consolation."

Just five days later, on Thanksgiving, the first inter-collegiate football game was played in Urbana at the Champaign County Fairgrounds. It was a rematch with Illinois Wesleyan, which had agreed after its earlier win to visit the Illinois campus later in the fall. Admission charge for the game was "25 cents for gentlemen, with ladies admitted free."

Williams' team proved that it had, to be sure, learned some things from playing against the more experienced Purdue team. Illinois won the rematch, with Robert Humphrey Forbes' help, and finally broke into the scoring column after two consecutive shutouts.

The first touchdown in Illinois football history was scored by halfback William Frederick Slater. In fact, he scored both touchdowns in the game, one in each half.

The *Illini* reported: "Nearly three hundred people gathered to view the game. Our boys had been practicing the tricks which they had learned at Lafayette and were prepared to show the Wesleyan boys a few things. They worked the 'V' often and always to advantage. Our boys worked up rather near the Wesleyan goal; made a rush, and they all went down, but in some way Fred Clarke got out of the heap and made a touchdown. The umpire, however, said that one of our men was offside, and hence the down did not go.

"They lined up again, after some protestations, and almost immediately Slater got the ball, dodged the crowd and made a touchdown....In the second half, the U. of I. worked the ball down about 10 yards from the goal, made a 'V' to rush the ball through, which was broken, and all went down except Slater, who found a four-inch hole between somebody's legs, slipped through and made a touchdown."

That first Illinois team was made up of Herbert Bowen, left end; Ralph Hart and Walter Shattuck, left guards; George Huff, center; Andrew Gates, right guard; James Steele, right tackle; Fred Clarke, right end; Scott Williams, quarterback; Arthur Pillsbury, William F. Slater, and Royal Wright, halfbacks; Ed Clarke and Albert Higgins, fullbacks—and, of course, Robert Humphrey Forbes, who will be remembered for his sartorial splendor, if not his play, the year football began at Illinois.

The Early Days
At Illinois

Football was a swashbuckling, inventive game at Illinois and elsewhere in the pioneer days of the Gay Nineties.

Scott Williams recalled on one occasion: "The style of play at the start resembled basketball in its open formation. Linemen stood an easy distance apart, the ends playing in with the line. There was no interference. The center rolled the ball back with his foot, the quarterback tossed it to a halfback some five or ten yards behind the line, and the half started out on an unknown course with high hopes and the determination to do the best he could.

"Before the first season ended we had caught up on several years advancement made by other teams. We were playing closer together, had some sort of interference, had cut the 'snap back' at center, and were tackling at the knees instead of riding opponents around the waist or neck. We even had acquired the double pass behind the line."

Illinois players soon began trying the V-trick, a popular formation used mainly for returning kickoffs, in which 10 men formed a V-shaped wall of interference and rumbled downfield with the ballcarrier in the middle. It was a forerunner of the flying wedge.

After the humble beginning of the football program at Illinois in 1890, the next year brought not only a growing interest but considerable success.

Robert Lackey, who was captain of the Purdue team which had beaten the fledgling Illinois team in 1890, was asked to come to Illinois to coach. He agreed, and Scott Williams remained on the squad as a player.

Illinois joined with Knox, Eureka, and Illinois Wesleyan to form the Illinois Intercollegiate Football League, with Illinois winning all three of those games and two others. Illinois was beaten 8-0 in its opening game of 1891 by Lake Forest, but that game later was forfeited to Illinois when it was learned that Lake Forest had used ineligible players. This gave Illinois a perfect 6-0, unbeaten record in its second year in the sport.

An article in the October 6, 1891, student newspaper, the *Illini*, explained:

> The day after the Lake Forest game a letter was received from the President of Lake Forest that two players on their team had not been in College for over a year. Five points were awarded to Illinois on forfeit of the Lake Forest game. Knox immediately claimed five points for the game it was to have played with Lake Forest, and somehow or other, their claim was allowed....The committee also decided that Knox had to play Champaign a game of football. The next day (October 2) when our boys appeared for the game, the gates of the park were closed. The reason given was "that the owners had been informed that for the past three days and a half betting had been practiced within the enclosures of that park." Queer though it may seem, not half of the Knox football team came out to the park after dinner, and yet they should have had no knowledge of the park being closed. If their team had put in its appearance, we might have adjourned to the fair grounds or some neighboring pastures and played the game anyway. As they didn't, nothing was left for us to do but come home. The points for the entire contest stood Knox 31 (including the Lake Forest game which they didn't play), Illinois 30.

After its success in 1891, Illinois went into intercollegiate football in a big way in 1892—so big that the team went on a 10-day touring road trip and played six games in eight days. If nothing else, it still stands as a monument to the strength and conditioning of players in those early days of the game.

30

The tour started in St. Louis on Friday, October 22, with Illinois beating Washington University of St. Louis 22-0. The following day the team was in Omaha and whipped Doane College 20-0. The following Monday, October 24, Illinois was beaten by Nebraska 6-0 in Lincoln but bounced back on Wednesday to down Baker University in Baldwin, Kansas, 28-12. On Thursday Illinois took its battle-weary players to Lawrence, Kansas, and was beaten by Kansas 26-4, before winding up the barnstorming with a 48-0 triumph over the Kansas City Athletic Club in Kansas City.

"I played in five of the six games," Williams recalled in 1923. "We won four out of the six. It was magnificent, but it was not football, and no such endurance test would be tolerated nowdays."

Illinois' traveling squad for that trip was a total of 18 players.

The season of 1892 also was marked by the appearance of another new coach, E. K. Hall, who had made his fame as an athlete at Dartmouth.

Boss Hall, as he was known, led the 1892 Illinois team through a 13-game schedule to a record of 9-3-2, including a 12-6 loss to Purdue (which returned to the schedule). Also making their first appearances on the schedule that year were Northwestern and the University of Chicago.

It was not uncommon for the coaches themselves to see some action in the games, and such was the case in the Illinois-Purdue game that season. According to remembrances, Illinois was driving toward the goal when Purdue coach Ben Donnelly jumped into the game to replace one of his tiring charges. Hall, not to be outdone, substituted himself into the game at a position opposite Donnelly, and the two of them stood there glaring at each other as the ball was snapped.

Illinois played Chicago twice in 1892. Chicago was leading 10-4 in the first game when officials called the game on account of darkness. Illinois, however, protested that score as the outcome, and officials ruled that the 4-4 tie at halftime would stand as the final score. The nullified touchdown which Chicago had scored had been made by none other than Amos Alonzo Stagg, who had taken over as coach after leaving Yale. Illinois beat Chicago 28-14 the next time the two teams met on the

This was the way the action looked from the sidelines in the Illinois— Purdue game in 1894.

Illinois home field in the final game of the season.

Hall remained at Illinois for one more year and in 1893 guided the team to a 3-2-3 record. The most notable aspect of the season was the fact that Illinois finally reached parity with Purdue in a 26-26 tie in the next-to-last game of the season. Even though the year was not a roaring success, it did see the emergence of some of the finest talent Illinois put on the field in those early years. That team included an outstanding tackle, Arthur Pixley, and Robert Hotchkiss, who would later gain fame as a halfback.

Williams continued to play for Illinois until 1893 when he left to study at Cornell.

"Until I left in 1893, I played in most of the games each

season though I had no regular position," Williams told O. S. Storm in 1923. "I was assistant coach all of that time, my chief duty being to take some player the coach was anxious to develop and play against him until I had taught him to play his position better than I could. I played every position except center and guard in a university game before I was through.

"After three years, a fairly satisfactory Illinois athletic association was going strong....A word of appreciation of the great kindness and courtesy of Walter Camp of Yale should never be forgotten. From the goodness of his heart, he answered all letters of inquiry sent him by players and officials from schools all over the country. The printed rules were vague and easily misunderstood, and we wrote him several times to get the

33

straight of things."

Illinois had another new coach in 1894. Louis D. Vail, who had played at Pennsylvania, took over for Hall. Illinois' school colors had been Dartmouth green the two years before, in honor of Hall, but were officially changed to orange and blue in 1894. They have been the same ever since.

All kinds of strange things were happening in 1894. For one thing spectators were allowed on the field so they could get a closer look at the play, and the *Illini* reporter of the day lamented, "Some means ought to be provided for keeping the crowd off the field as it is certainly a disgrace to have them...in the way of the players."

One dispute followed another that year as game officiating came under public criticism for the first time.

Consider this excerpt from an article in the *Illini* about the game with Chicago which ended in forfeit: "Hotchkiss (Illinois) carried the ball 90 yards for a touchdown. Captain Allen (Chicago) yelled time, but the referee would not give it. (Robert) Gaut kicked goal, and the score stood 12 to 10 in favor of Illinois. The umpire asked Chicago to play ball, and they refused. Vail (the Illinois coach) offered to retire from the game. Captain Allen refused to talk to him and called his men from the field, refusing to play. The umpire waited the time limit allowed for a team to resume play and then gave Illinois the game 6-0. As to the propriety of Mr. Vail playing, [it can be pointed out that] Mr. Stagg for two successive years played with the team. Even this year he has participated in one game."

Three days later Illinois met the Indianapolis Light Artillery team, and the officials again came under fire.

The *Illini* reported: "Time and again the visitors were held to four downs, but instead of giving the (Illinois) Varsity the ball, it was given to I. L. A. to try again. Time and again did they fumble the ball, and some one of the home team (Illinois) fell on it, only to have the satisfaction and temper, as well, rudely shattered by having the ball being taken from them and returned to I. L. A.

"With the score: Illinois 14, I. L. A. 12, the linesman called 'time,' but the referee thought the wheels in his cranium kept better time than the stop watch and ordered the play to go on...I. L. A. tried a touchdown, fumbling the ball, and when the players got up, the gathering twilight revealed Scott and Chester holding the ball. The referee announced, 'Artillery touchdown.'"

It was the Illinois fans who exploded like artillery fire, but the 18-14 defeat stood.

The Return Of "G" Huff

Illinois needed a new football coach in 1895, and this time they picked a local boy. His name: George Huff.

He was born on a farm near Champaign and entered the University of Illinois when he was only 15 years old. He played on its first football team three years later even though baseball was always his favorite sport, but he learned to like football once exposed to it. In 1893 he went to Dartmouth with a plan to study medicine and played football there for two more years.

Little did anyone know when Huff returned to Illinois as its football coach in 1895 that he would eventually be the architect of the modern Illini sports program. He would hold the post of athletic director from 1901 until his death in 1936, and under his leadership the entire Illinois athletic program would flourish.

But Huff's chief concern in 1895 was simply to produce a good football team, and he did that. In fact, both teams he coached had identical 4-2-1 records.

In 1897, however, Huff decided to devote his time to coaching the sport he loved best—baseball—and Illinois was once again looking for a new man to head its football program.

The mid-1890s were a notable time at Illinois because it was on January 11, 1895, at a meeting in the Palmer House hotel in Chicago, that President Andrew Sloan Draper of Illinois gathered with his illustrious counterparts from Michigan, Northwestern, Minnesota, Wisconsin, and Purdue (whose president, James W. Sharp, had urged the meeting). It was at that meeting that they formed the Intercollegiate Conference of Faculty Representatives. It would become popularly known as the Western Athletic Conference and, finally, the Big Ten.

The rules they eventually set down firmly established a basis for intercollegiate competition, including football, and brought some structure and sensibility to an athletic era which virtually had none of either.

In 1897 Illinois again looked to the East for a football coach and secured the services of Fred Smith, who had been an outstanding halfback for Princeton.

Illinois compiled a 6-2 record under Smith and finally was able to achieve a long-awaited victory over Purdue—and by a whopping 32-4 margin on Illinois Field.

The big game of that season was with A. A. Stagg's Chicago team led by fullback Clarence Herschberger, who would eventually be the first Midwest player to break the Eastern dominance on the postseason All-American teams selected by Walter Camp. Illinois, however, had its own star fullback in 1897—a rousing runner named Arthur Johnson. The game turned into a battle royal, with both Herschberger and Johnson carried from the field with broken collar bones before the game ended. Chicago was the winner by an 18-12 score.

It also was in 1897 that Illinois participated in the first night and first indoor football game ever played—on November 20 under the electric lights of the old Chicago Coliseum. There was tanbark on the field instead of turf, and the opponent was the Carlisle Indians. A 100-yard run by Illinois halfback Arthur Hall was wiped out by an official's decision that he had stepped on the out-of-bounds line, and the Indian team won the game 23-6 after trailing at halftime.

About 10,000 people reportedly attended the game for which the Illini and Indians each received $4,000 after expenses were paid.

Two special trains carried 700 Illinois rooters to Chicago. The *Chicago Tribune* reported:

A gathering of all the tribes of palefaces from the big camps of all the universities and from the scattered families that dwell in the thick woods of the common reservations saw their warriors massacred by the redskins last

George Huff served as Illinois football coach for two years and was the architect of the modern Illini sports program as athletic director until he died in 1936.

night in the big council tepee in Woodlawn.

Nearly 10,000 singers of the war songs gathered in response to the signal fires that have been burning for a whole moon on the high bluffs of the Illini and saw the warriors of the red men battle to a victory which was translated into the whiteman's tongue as 23-6. They came with their squaws and even with their papooses, and the braves smoked the pipe of peace and the cigarette of battle while the two war bands of their young men battled before them.

Smith remained as Illinois coach for one more year, and his second team was a disappointment. Illinois' first meeting ever with Michigan resulted in a 12-5 defeat, and the first game against Notre Dame brought a 5-0 setback. The team finished the year with a 4-5 record. In 1899 Smith was succeeded by another former Princeton player, Neilson Poe, but Illinois fortunes went further downhill—so far downhill that, as a result of the 3-5-1 record, the athletic association decided not to award the players "I" letters as penance for the poor showing.

Illinois improved to 7-3-2 in 1900 with Fred Smith back as coach, but most of the victories were achieved against lightweight opposition, and the only Western Conference member Illinois defeated was Purdue, by a 17-5 margin. Illinois played scoreless ties with Northwestern and Indiana and was beaten by Minnesota 23-0, Wisconsin 27-0, and Michigan 12-0.

Edgar Holt, another Princeton man who had been Smith's assistant in 1900, took over as head coach in 1901 and held the position for two seasons, when Illinois posted creditable 8-2 and 10-2-1 records.

Chicago returned to the Illini schedule in 1901 and was beaten by a one-sided 24-0 margin in a game that brought fame to Jake Stahl, who later would lead the Boston Red Sox to victory in baseball's World Series as its manager. According to historical accounts of the game, Stahl was "continually drawn back from his guard position to carry the ball, and he smashed his way through the Maroons like a battering ram."

Historians regard that team as the best Illinois had produced at that point in time. Captain of the team was Justa Lindgren, who would gain honor that season as a player, but greater honor would come his way at Illinois in the future, as both coach and as a total academic man.

By the season of 1902 Illinois was playing seven teams in the Western Conference—beating Purdue 29-5, Indiana 47-0, Northwestern 17-0, and Iowa 80-0; losing to Chicago 6-0 and Minnesota 17-5; and playing a scoreless tie with Ohio State.

Illinois football appeared on the upswing, but that surge hit a stumbling block in 1903 when George Woodruff was head coach. Woodruff, who had coached Pennsylvania to considerable success, saw his team win what were regarded as seven warm-up games and roll past Purdue 24-0, but Illinois lost its last six games to Chicago, Northwestern, Indiana, Minnesota, Iowa, and Nebraska and was held without a point in the last four. That put Woodruff on a train headed back to the East.

The late-season disaster brought a new coaching philosophy to Illinois, and the school decided to have four alumni—Arthur Hall, Clyde Mathews, Fred Lowenthal, and Justa Lindgren—act as co-equal coaches. The 1904 team was much improved (9-2-1) under the leadership of its former players. Lowenthal acted as head coach in 1905, Lindgren in 1906, and Hall took over in 1907.

For the first time, under Hall, Illinois would have a coach who would lead the team for more than two years, and this helped to provide a continuity in the program that it badly needed at the time.

Michigan and Chicago teams had moved far ahead of Illinois in the early 1900s with programs led by men who had established themselves at their respective schools, Stagg at Chicago and the legendary Fielding H. Yost at Michigan. The Michigan teams from the period 1901 through 1905 were so explosive offensively that they became known as the "Point-A-Minute Machine." In 1901, Yost's first season, Michigan scored 550 points while holding the opposition scoreless. Michigan would be unbeaten in 55 straight games before losing to Chicago and Stagg in 1905.

Football, however, now was under fire in a mounting wave of criticism of its many injuries, and, had not President Theodore Roosevelt intervened and forced some changes in the most dangerous aspects of the game as it was being played, college football might have died.

Illinois made a drastic cutback in the number of games it played in 1907 (Hall's first year as head coach) amidst the rising tide of concern. That year Illinois lost to Chicago by a one-sided 42-6 margin and lost to Iowa, while defeating Wisconsin, Purdue, and Indiana.

The clamor for a more open game that would reduce the number of injuries gave birth to the legalization of the forward pass.

Unlike some of his colleagues in the coaching profession, Arthur Hall moved quickly to full use of the new offensive weapon.

He took a willowy 130-pound youngster, Pomery Sinnock, and developed him into a full-fledged passing quarterback. The 1907 and 1908 teams were built around his talents, and, in the final game of the 1908 season against Northwestern, Sinnock completed 25 forward passes in a 64-8 rout.

Two years later, after a 5-2 record in 1909, Hall guided Illinois to its first Western Conference championship. The team not only was unbeaten and untied, but unscored on.

Illinois opened the 1910 season with victories over Millikin 13-0 and Drake 29-0, and the next weekend (on October 15) a tradition was born. The first football homecoming celebration held in the nation began on the U. of I. campus. The opponent was Chicago and Stagg.

Credit for conceiving the idea of a homecoming celebration connected with a football game goes to a pair of enterprising undergraduates, W. Elmer Ekblaw and C.F. "Dab" Williams.

"We wanted to do something constructive for Illinois," Williams once wrote. "We considered this, that, and the other thing, but got nowhere in particular fast. At long last the idea of a super reunion began to evolve in our minds."

Finally, the two called on President Edmund James and Dean Thomas Arkle Clark, who pledged their full support, and the first football homecoming celebration became a reality.

The hero of the 1910 team and the star of that first homecoming game was a square-jawed quarterback and place-kicking artist named Otto Seiler.

But Illinois fans were deeply concerned about their chances when it was learned early in the week that Seiler was ill and hospitalized. Seiler was a determined young man. That Sat-

urday morning he arose from his hospital bed, was discharged, and was suited up in the afternoon.

His 38-yard, dropkick field goal broke up a dogged defensive duel and gave Illinois a 3-0 victory over a team which had won six straight games between the two schools. The homecoming celebration went on until the wee hours of the morning, and the name on everyone's lips was Otto Seiler.

On two other occasions during the spectacular season, Seiler's kicks produced 3-0 Illinois victories—against Indiana and Syracuse. Illinois also whipped Northwestern 27-0 and Purdue 11-0. Minnesota had a strong team that season as well but had played only two conference opponents, and Illinois was regarded as the Western champion.

42

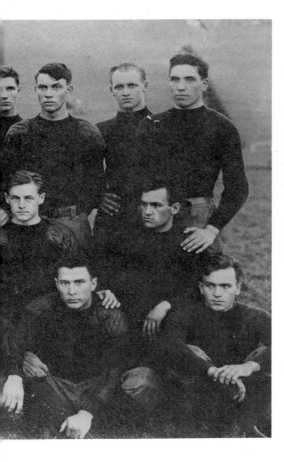

Some members of the famed 1910 Illinois team that was unbeaten, untied, and unscored on pose for a cameraman.

In later days Seiler would say: "There may have been better lines in the history of American football, but I doubt it. I feel like I am in a position to judge the character of that line because I did the kicking most of the time, and I could have sat down and enjoyed a cup of tea and then kicked the ball. No one would have been in the way or had a chance to block that kick."

In addition to Seiler, letter winners on that famed team were Glenn Butzer (captain), C. B. Oliver, Otto Springs, Charles Belting, John Twist, Chester Davis, Thomas Lyons, Charles Wham, Harold Lanum, John Merriman, Louis Bernstein, Chester Dillon, William Woolston, and Chester Roberts.

Seiler returned in 1911, but many of the veteran linemen

Otto Seiler was America's first football homecoming hero.

were missing, and Illinois had to settle for a 4-2-1 record. That season, however, was marked by a stirring Illinois upset bid that fell short. Minnesota had already sewn up the Western title when it arrived at Illinois for the season-ending game on November 15. Heavily favored Minnesota finally emerged with an 11-0 victory after being held scoreless until late in the third quarter. Even in defeat it was a fine hour for Illinois.

The 1912 season produced a 3-3-1 record, and, after only one victory in the Western Conference and a 6-0 defeat at the hands of Northwestern in the final game of the season, Illinois fans were hungry for a coach who could lead the team to the kind of national prominence that Wisconsin, Michigan, and Minnesota were then enjoying.

Huff, as athletic director, was charged with finding Illinois that kind of coach. The man he chose would surprise many of the Illinois alumni, who were expecting a big-name college coach from another school. Instead, Huff looked to a young high school coach who was doing quite well at Oak Park. And those who tittered at Huff's selection would learn to respect his judgment.

The man Huff hired was Bob Zuppke.

The Little Dutchman

They called him the "Little Dutchman"—this man with a roundish, choir-boy face and blond hair that looked like the tassle of freshly shucked corn from a Central Illinois farm.

He was born in Germany, but his family emigrated to the United States when he was two years old. They settled among the good burghers of Milwaukee, and he attended grade school and high school there.

It was there that Bob Zuppke got his first taste of football, and it would stay with him the rest of his life. From West Division High in Milwaukee, Zuppke's next stops were Wisconsin State Normal in Whitewater and then the University of Wisconsin in Madison.

Zuppke was a member of the Wisconsin football squad in 1903 and 1904 but never won a varsity letter in the sport, although he did get his "W" in 1905 as a member of the school's basketball team.

Oddly enough, Zuppke turned down the first coaching job he was ever offered—a chance to coach and teach at a high school in Madison.

He was developing a strong interest in painting, and he decided he would try to further his study of art in New York. Assorted commercial art jobs kept him in and out of employment, and finally he turned to coaching. His first post was at Muskegon, Michigan, and he had considerable success there from 1906 through 1909.

Recalling that first interview for the coaching job at

Bob Zuppke: the man and the legend.

Muskegon, Zuppke once told a friend: "I remember buying a straw hat for a dollar—quite an item in those days—for my appearance before the school board. I wasn't too sure I really wanted the job because a lawyer in Muskegon had been coaching the team during his spare time and openly resented a successor.

"In my first game I remember the opposition made a quick touchdown to take the lead, and I saw the lawyer with a smug smile on his face. We finally won by a good score, though, and I never heard any more from him."

In 1910 Zuppke accepted the head football coaching job at Oak Park High School in Illinois.

Zuppke did not fare badly as coach at Oak Park either, once past his first game. Oak Park lost Zuppke's debut but lost only once more in three years. Zuppke began to establish himself as one of the most inventive minds football has ever known. He was one of the first coaches in the nation to teach the spiral snap from center, and his teams used a short end-over-end forward pass well ahead of the time when passing became the major talk of the college game, with Gus Dorias throwing to Knute Rockne at Notre Dame in 1913.

Zuppke's Oak Park teams were regarded as the schoolboy national champions in both 1911 and 1912, and all kinds of colleges were looking to him as a possible future coach.

Illinois landed him.

"The reputation of George Huff was largely the factor that influenced me to come to Illinois," Zuppke once said.

"I felt that if he was anything like the kind of man everyone said he was, I would get a square deal as a coach.

"I found that his reputation was more than justified. He was a great man to work for. 'G' always gave credit when it was deserved. As he was an understanding man, he knew when there was credit to recognize. There was not an ounce of envy in his whole system. He was fair, generous, and charitable.

"Many people prate about the golden rule. 'G' put it into practice."

Zuppke's first contract, still on file in the archives of the Illinois Athletic Association, called for him to be paid $2,750 per year. He turned out to be worth every penny of it.

Zuppke also had the good fortune at Illinois to inherit as

an assistant Justa Lindgren, who spent most of his time in charge of the linemen while Zuppke worked with the backs. They were partners throughout Zuppke's career.

"He was my balance wheel," Zuppke once said of Lindgren. "When he saw what I was doing was right, he'd offer no comment. If he didn't agree with some new idea I had, he'd say so. Then I'd think it over and say, 'Maybe you're right.' We'd study it out together, and if we agreed it was no good, we'd drop the matter."

Twenty-three players reported for Zuppke's first Illinois team in 1913.

"We took to him right away," recalls Perry Graves, who was among those players and now is 85 years old. "Every one of us respected him. He had a way of talking to you and making you feel you could do whatever he asked."

Before his death, Ralph "Slooey" Chapman, another of these original Zuppke players, also had a personal remembrance of those early days.

"Zup's slogan was to shoot at the moon," Chapman told a reporter. "A man gets a lot of inspiration from a fellow like Zup. Zup stirred us up mentally. I liked to play football for the fun of it but play to win. The competitive spirit was strong in me."

Harold Pogue, who would become a star halfback for Zuppke, recalled the opening practice of the 1913 season before his death in 1969.

Zup, according to Pogue, stepped before the squad and said, "It's what you deliver yourself, boys, that counts. When a ball is snapped, remember that you're part of a machine and that the success of our team will depend on each individual, giving us everything he has in his heart and body. This is a team game, and where we go to a large extent depends on what you are willing to give and contribute to the team effort.

"You must carry out your assignments. You must stretch yourself for every inch of yourself if we are to be a winner."

Oddly, Harold Pogue's name was not on a list of candidates freshman coach Ralph Jones gave to Zuppke when he arrived on the campus. Jones had cut him from the squad at the end of his freshman year, along with all other players weighing less than 150 pounds. Pogue weighed 142 at the time. But old-timers say that Zuppke noticed Pogue running in an intramural track meet, liked his speed, and invited him to report in the fall. Pogue was surprised when one of Zuppke's managers came to his Alpha Tau Omega fraternity house with a personal message from Zuppke, because Pogue himself had not thought he had done very well in that freshman season. Gladly, however, he obliged.

Pogue not only was fast, but he had a piston-driven choppy stride that made him difficult to tackle when an opponent did get within range. He became known as "the runner with disappearing legs."

Pogue did not have good eyesight—when he was off the field he wore thick glasses—which was a particular handicap when he handled long punts or kicks.

When asked once to recall his greatest thrill in football for a 1932 series in the *Chicago Tribune*, he told Stewart Owen it came on a punt return in a game against Chicago in 1913.

"My greatest thrill came not so much as a result of the play as of my mental state," Pogue was quoted. "Most of the Chicago players were veterans, fellows I had read about while a freshman, and even while I was in high school.

"I was considerable of a greenhorn, having come from a small high school (in Sullivan) and not having played on the freshman-varsity at Illinois. As if that were not sufficient handicap, it was reported before we went out on the field that the largest crowd that had ever been seen in the central West up to that time was in the stands.

"Consequently, when I ran out on the field, my knees were wobbling so that I could hardly stand up.

"Illinois kicked off. Chicago tried two or three plays without making any material gain and then punted. Nels Norgren, at that time the greatest punter in the West, was doing the kicking. I, of course, had heard of him, and I stood in such awe of his kicking that, as safetyman, I was playing way back at the other end of the field, almost too far away from the ball to reach me in two punts, even with Norgren punting.

"It was a beautiful kick, but I realized at once I was entirely too far back to catch it. Starting forward on a dead run, I caught the ball, however, on the first bounce, and that was the last I remembered until I realized that I had run nearly the length of the field and had made a touchdown in the first minute of play.

"I was probably the most surprised as well as the most thrilled person on the field. I have always had my suspicions that the only reason I got through the Chicago team was that I was just too scared to permit anyone to touch me.

"We had a 7 to 0 lead through the first half, but in the second half Chicago made four touchdowns and won 28 to 7."

That loss to Chicago at Stagg Field was the first of the season for Illinois after starting the year with four wins over Kentucky, Missouri, Northwestern, and Indiana. The Illini would play a scoreless tie the following weekend with Purdue and fall to powerful Minnesota 19-9 in the season finale.

The Illini finished Zuppke's first year with a 4-2-1 record, 2-2-1 in the conference, but the little Dutchman had laid the foundation for greatness the following season.

Unbeaten
National Champions

"We didn't get a rating before the season started, but that didn't bother any of us," says Perry Graves. "It just made us enjoy it all that much more."

With Graves and captain Ralph "Slooey" Chapman anchoring the line and Harold Pogue and Bart Macomber running wild in the backfield, Coach Bob Zuppke had a team in 1914 that was far and away better than anyone—most of all, the experts—had expected.

But the man who put it all together for Illinois in 1914 was a cool, clear-headed field leader of a quarterback named George "Potsy" Clark, who Graves likes to remember now as "a real brainy boy."

He was, in Zuppke's own opinion, the best quarterback he ever had, and Clark would later distinguish himself as a coach. He had a clear, calculating mind for the game even then.

This Illinois team, however, was a terror on defense as well as offense, and it was as deceiving as was Graves' own playing style at end.

"After every play Perry looked like he was gasping for air," an old-timer remembers, "and the other team, figuring he was dead on his feet, would send a play against him, only to find out how wrong they really were."

Illinois shut out the first four opponents it faced; included were one-sided wins over Indiana 51-0, Ohio State 37-0, and Northwestern 33-0. Minnesota finally broke the scoring ice but lost 21-6.

The victory over Minnesota confirmed beyond anyone's doubts that Illinois was a bona fide Western Conference title contender.

Sid Casner wrote in the 1914 homecoming game program:

With the fifth annual homecoming, combined with the Chicago-Illinois game rapidly approaching, the Twin Cities are seething with intense excitement. Never before in the history of Illinois athletics has such a fervent football spirit pervaded the campus. Players, coaches, rooters, faculty, and townspeople—all alike—are enkindled with a superabundance of enthusiasm in the fortunes of the eleven. A general feeling of confidence in coaches Zuppke and Lindgren prevails; a feeling that this is Illinois' year in Western football.

And this sentiment is justified. At the opening of official practice last September, instead of an awkward, inexperienced squad, over 40 well-knit warriors presented themselves to coach Zuppke. In this group were 15 "I" men, all of whom had been under conference fire. In addition there were a number of former yearlings who possessed blue ribbons as a stamp of Coach Jones' approval. These men had the benefit of the first regular spring practice, and had an opportunity to familiarize themselves with Zuppke's methods.

On the victory over Minnesota he wrote: "For three quarters both teams fought up and down the gridiron, neither being successful in crossing the tantalizing goal line. But the onslaught of Captain Chapman's huskies were not to be denied. During the final session they hurled themselves upon the Gophers with an irresistible impetuosity which brooked no obstacles, and in an exceedingly short time, put the game on the rollers, so to speak. The initial barrier had been surmounted. The Alps are yet to be climbed."

"The Alps" were Chicago and Amos Alonzo Stagg.

Against Ohio State, Pogue had scored three touchdowns, and Macomber drop-kicked three field goals. Neither Pogue nor Clark played the following weekend against Northwestern, but Illinois won handily anyway. Pogue was back again to spark the

52

victory over the Gophers, scoring the first Illinois touchdown by intercepting a pass and running it back all the way.

A crowd of 24,000, an unusually high turnout for those days, was on hand for the invasion of Stagg's Maroons.

Chicago led at halftime 7-0 and showed signs of being the winner, accounts of the game indicate, but Illinois completely dominated the second half. Macomber passed for one touchdown, and Clark made a short run for the second, before

Illinois' first All-American, Ralph "Slooey" Chapman, was greeted by 3,000 fans when he came home from World War I.

Zuppke's First Championship Team, 1914—Front row, left to right: Orlie Rue, Alex Wagner, J.W. Watson, Captain R.D. Chapman, Eugene Schobinger, L.F. Armstrong. Second row: P.H. Graves, George Clark, H.A. Pogue, Coach Bob Zuppke, J.W.

54

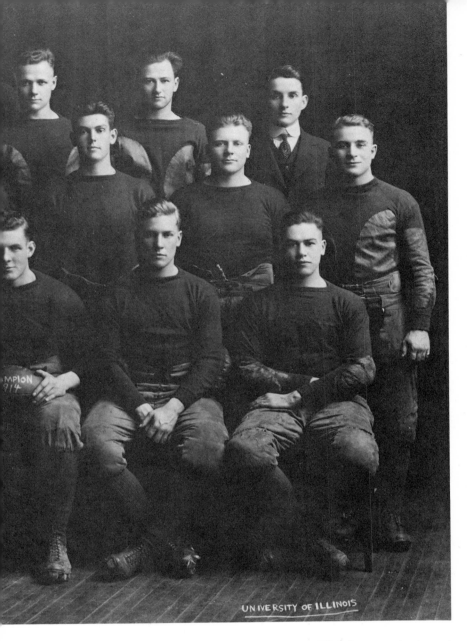

Nelson, Frank Stewart, F.B. Macomber. Third row: Assistant Coach Justa Lindgren, M.R. Petty, O. Madsen, Trainer Glimstedt, C.K. Squier, S.R. Derby, Manager A.B. Rayburn.

exploding for a 90-yard kickoff runback for another. The 21-7 final score sent the Illini crowd into a frenzy.

The Alps had been scaled, and the next weekend the mere Badgers of Wisconsin would be battered 24-9 in what may have been the best game of the year for Pogue and Clark.

Clark broke away for a 70-yard punt return in the first two minutes of the game, and just a few minutes later Pogue escaped for a 65-yard run from scrimmage. In the second half Pogue returned a punt for a score from more than 60 yards away.

The win sewed up Illinois' first undisputed Western Conference title. And Illinois would eventually share the mythical national championship with Army.

Other members of the team included George "Cap" Squier, S. R. Derby, Olva Madsen, Lennox Armstrong, J. W. Watson, Frank Stewart, Manley R. Petty, Jesse Nelson, Frank Pethybridge, Orlie Rue, and Ernie Schobinger.

Both Armstrong and Macomber had played for Zuppke earlier at Oak Park, making the title especially gratifying because of that relationship.

Many of the same players were back in 1915. Pogue was injured a major portion of the season, but Illinois would again be unbeaten although tied twice. The championship was shared with Minnesota on the basis of the 6-6 tie between the two teams.

It was in that Minnesota game that Clark earned his badge for courage.

Mike Tobin, the first sports information director at Illinois, recalled the game on one occasion. He wrote:

(Clark's) qualities of brain, speed and gameness all united against Minnesota. The championship was at stake. Potsy's jaw had been broken, but that didn't phase him. The docs said he could play if he wore a mask and had his teeth wired together. Nice job to call signals without your lips moving, but Potsy did it somehow.

Minnesota scored first, but missed goal. Later Illinois' chance came. Potsy passed to Macomber. No good. Quick as a flash, Potsy reversed the play. Macomber passed to him, and he dodged the Gopher secondary and raced across the goal. That tied Illinois with Minnesota for the championship.

Despite the disappointment of the tie, it had been another highly successful year for Illinois, and Zuppke and the fans loved it. And they did not easily forget.

Four years later Chapman returned to Champaign-Urbana on a nine o'clock train from Chicago after serving in World War I. He had served as a lieutenant in the infantry, and an enemy plane swooped down and riddled him with bullets. He was hospitalized for more than a year, undergoing operation after operation. Finally, he was healed.

According to Tobin, there were 3,000 fans at the Illinois Central platform to greet him the night he came "home."

There were the traditional nine "rahs," and then the crowd yelled: "Chapman, Chapman, Chapman!"

GRAVES

Time Out: Perry Graves

He is Illinois' oldest living All-American football player. In fact, he was one of the first Illini ever accorded the honor, along with Ralph "Slooey" Chapman, both of them named to different All-American squads in 1914.

He was a starting end on Bob Zuppke's first Big Ten championship team of that year, a team which shared the mythical national championship with Army. He is 85 years old, and his name is Perry Graves.

He drove the 100 miles from his home in Robinson to attend the 60-year reunion of his graduating class of 1915 on the U. of I. campus on a bright spring day in 1975.

"My family doesn't like me driving this far by myself," said Graves, with a roguish sort of twinkle in his eye, "but my doctor told me to go ahead and do it if I wanted to, so I did."

Graves always has liked to travel, and he has decided that his advancing age should not hold him back. A man who has visited 23 different countries is not one to shirk from a 200-mile trip, even as an octogenarian.

His wife, Champaign native Marvel White, died in 1965, and he lives alone in retirement, while his sons manage the lumberyard business he started in Robinson in 1925.

He welcomed the opportunity on this weekend to reminisce with old classmates.

"I grew up in Rockford and played high school football there. We had some great teams there, but my family was poor, and I couldn't go to college right after I graduated in 1909.

Perry Graves earned All-American honors as an end in 1914.

"I worked for two years in Rockford at a factory to earn enough money to start out for college. I decided I'd go to Pittsburgh because I wanted to be an engineer, and they had a good school for that where you could study two terms and work a term. I stayed there a year and decided I really didn't like the East. People weren't friendly there like they were in the Midwest, so I'd decided I'd come back home and go to school at Illinois."

Graves played football as a freshman reserve at Pitt and recalls one game in particular when he went against the Carlisle Indian team led by the legendary Jim Thorpe.

In 1912 he went out for football at Illinois.

"They took one look at a bunch of us and cut us off the junior varsity squad," Graves remembers. "I guess maybe they didn't think I was big enough to play. A good friend of mine who was an I-Man talked to them about me, though, and they took me back. I ended up being the captain of the junior varsity team that year." As a junior in 1913, Graves played on the first team Zuppke coached at Illinois.

Graves was only a few pounds over 140 in those days. He was one of only 23 players who reported for Zuppke's first varsity team in 1913. Others included Chapman, quarterback Potsy Clark, halfback Harold Pogue, and fullback Bart Macomber, all of whom would be key men the following year in the perfect 7-0 season of 1914.

"It was the Chicago game of 1913 that made up Zup's mind to play me as an end. Clark was hurt, and they were trying to make a quarterback out of me, but I was hitting all those Chicago players so hard that Zup told me to go to end the next week," Graves remembers.

"I liked playing end because I was fast and could get downfield quick on the punts. Macomber was a great punter. He'd tell me right where he was going to punt it, and I could expect the ball to be right there."

Graves, whom Zuppke once described as "a dynamo," remembers squaring off on the opposite side of the line with a Minnesota tackle who outweighed him "by a 100 pounds."

But size was not everything in those days.

"Speed meant a lot," Graves recalled. "Matt Bullock, the Illinois trainer, used to say that I was the fastest man at getting

60

a jump downfield he'd ever seen. I guess I was the fastest man on the team. Zup had us line up once at one end of the field and run to the other, and I beat everybody. Clark and Pogue were really fast, too. Pogue was a great runner. He had a way of kicking his feet high, and that made him a tough man to tackle."

Graves remembers Zuppke as a master strategist, but more as a firm taskmaster.

"We used to scrimmage every day of the week except Friday, and then we'd play on Saturday," Graves said with a smile. "Zup used to practice right up until it was dark. I remember many a night when I had to go back to the fraternity house and get my dinner out of the stove after everybody else had eaten.

"Zup was tough, and he really worked you. I remember once one of our players, Cap Squier, sitting in the locker room and saying he'd quit, but he wouldn't dare make Zup mad.

"Zup never swore, but he had names he called people when he'd get mad at them. I remember once he looked at one player and said, 'you yellow rabbit.' He used to call me 'Rat.' He had different names he used on different people."

Graves not only played football for Illinois, he owned his own concession stand at the game, an exercise in business he doubtlessly was happy to have later on.

"I guess it was G. Huff who gave me the concession privilege," said Graves. "I'd buy stuff like peanuts, popcorn, and chewing gum, and then I'd get me a couple of young fellows to sell it at the games. I'd also sell candy at the fraternity houses, and I'd have the concession at the baseball games, too.

"I was playing third base on the baseball team and operating the concession stand at the same time. When I missed a couple of ground balls—I guess I was looking up into the stands to see how the salesmen were doing—'G' came charging out and yelled, 'Graves, get your mind on the game, or you're going to be out of business!'"

An Upset King
Takes The Throne

"HOLD ON TIGHT WHEN YOU READ THIS!"

That was the headline in the November 4, 1916, *Chicago Herald*.

This particular headline appeared above an article from Minneapolis which described one of the most famous football upsets of all time, the 14-9 surprise by Illinois of Minnesota's "wonder team." Not even the most optimistic Illini fan gave Illinois much more chance of victory than a snowball surviving July.

Ring Lardner, then writing the "Wake of the News" column for the *Chicago Tribune*'s sports section, put tongue in cheek and suggested in print before the game that perhaps Zuppke would be wise not to continue the trip to Minneapolis but instead stay in Chicago and go to the theater.

After all, Minnesota had many of the same players back from the 1915 team which shared the conference title with Illinois, while the Illini had lost Harold Pogue, Potsy Clark, and others.

The Gophers had rolled over North Dakota 47-7, South Dakota 81-0, and Iowa 67-0. The famed Walter Camp had decided to come in from the East in anticipation of declaring Minnesota the national champion, it was assumed, at season's end. Minnesota officials, so the story goes, had constructed a special press box in honor of the arrival of the "father" of Eastern football.

The 1916 Illinois team was lightly regarded at the start of

the season and showed no signs of being underrated when it lost to Colgate 15-3 and Ohio State 7-6 between wins over Kansas and Purdue.

Throughout the week of pregame practice, legend has it, Zuppke built up the Gophers to his own players as if they were a team of superhumans, a team that no foe could expect to beat—least of all this less-than-mighty group of Illini.

"If they laugh at us," Zuppke supposedly told the squad, "we'll just laugh, too."

Zuppke did not take Lardner's advice, and the Illini went off to Minneapolis anyway. But Zuppke continued to act as if he felt the Illini had no chance whatsoever of coming close to this Minnesota team.

And the night before the game he did a startling thing. He suspended the team's training rules for that evening.

"If you guys are going to the slaughter and get murdered tomorrow," said Zuppke, "we will break training and have a good time tonight by having food, drink, and we will also go to a show."

The Illini did not return to their hotel rooms until 12:30 a.m.

Illinois, however, was the first on the field that crisp November day because Zuppke's watch was running well ahead of time, and when the invincible Gophers trotted out and began working out, every Illini eye swiveled in its socket.

"Hey, Lindy," Ed "Dutch" Sternaman, the Illini quarterback, yelled at line coach Justa Lindgren. "They don't look so big."

That remark touched off Zuppke's psychological time bomb that he had been wiring all week.

"Yea," said another. "They don't look like anything that couldn't be handled."

And on it went until Zuppke had them all before him in the locker room again just before the opening kickoff.

The record of everything Zuppke said in those last few minutes just before his team took the field for the kickoff is made hazy by time, but on one sentence he spoke that day, there is little conjecture.

"I am Louis the Fourteenth," said Zuppke, with a wide smile. "And, after us, the deluge."

The tension broken, Zuppke laid down a well-considered battle plan.

"Minnesota is a very superstitious team," Zuppke said, striding in the dungeon-like locker room as he talked. "They have a formula they always follow on the first three plays. First, Sprafka will carry the ball; next, Wyman; and then Long. On the first three plays tackle these men in that order."

"But what if someone else has the ball?" a voice asked.

"Then," said Zuppke, "I'll run out on the field and tackle that man myself."

Zuppke then unveiled the offensive strategy. Illinois would use a spread formation with wide intervals between each lineman, a move designed to disorganize the Minnesota defenders.

The Illini kicked off, and on the first three plays Sprafka, Wyman, and Long carried the ball—just as Zuppke had predicted—and they were stopped almost in their tracks each time by a swarming Illinois defense.

The first time Illinois had the ball the spread formation was unveiled, and halfback Bart Macomber (the team captain) passed to Sternaman for a 25-yard gain on the first play. Illinois moved for two more first downs to the Gophers' five-yard line. A penalty moved it closer, and Macomber slashed across for the touchdown from a yard away and then kicked the extra point.

The next time Minnesota had possession the Gophers went to the air themselves, but Illinois end Ren Kraft intercepted the pass thrown by Minnesota's Pudge Wyman and ran it back 50 yards for another Illinois touchdown. Macomber's kick made it 14-0.

"Not once in the half did the home team cross the Illini 40 yard line," an account of the game testifies. "Four successful forward passes out of five attempts were big factors in the Zupmen's advantage."

Macomber came off the field at halftime with a rip in his uniform.

"I missed Zup's halftime talk because I was fixing Macomber's pants," trainer Matt Bullock once said. "I was sew-

Bart Macomber sparked Bob Zuppke's Illinois team to "miracle victory" over Minnesota's wonder team.

MACOMBER

ing them up on the shower-room floor. But I'll wager he didn't have to tell those kids much. That 14-point lead told them all they wanted to know. They had the start to one of the greatest upsets in history, and you can bet they weren't going to let it slip out of their hands in the second half."

What Zuppke said, according to Macomber's recollection, was that "Minnesota was not through but would come back strong. He also told me to stall and keep Minnesota bottled up down in their own territory."

Minnesota came back to score in the third quarter, with Sprafka going in from the five yard line. Brilliant punting by Macomber and a now-inspired Illini defense held the Gophers at bay the rest of the day, however.

"That fourth quarter was the hardest, closest fought football I ever saw, neither team giving more than the other," Bullock remembered before his death. "It was a great thrill, my greatest, and I'll never forget it."

The waning minutes of the game were nightmarish to Macomber, who once described the game before his death to Chuck Flynn, former sports information director and the assistant to the U. of I. president.

"I never ached more than in that last quarter," Macomber told Flynn. "I knew if Minnesota got the ball, it was just too bad as we had played the entire game with our original 11 men, and Minnesota was sending in new and bigger material all during the period."

But those 11 Illini iron men hung on against 33 of the finest that Minnesota coach Dr. Henry Williams could muster.

Others who played the full 60 minutes that day, in addition to Macomber, Sternaman, and Kraft, were Swede Rundquist, Otis Petty, Harry Schlaudeman, Frank Stewart, Ross Petty, Paul Christensen, Bill Anderson, and Bob Knop.

The loss cost Minnesota the conference title, with Ohio State winning. Walter Camp named Macomber to his All-American team. And Zuppke had pulled off his first big college football upset. But it would hardly be his last.

66

Time Out: George Halas

With a career in football that spans over 60 years as a player, coach or owner, George Halas of the Chicago Bears has known more than his share of magic moments during his long association with the game.

One of his fondest memories is of the famed Illinois upset of mighty Minnesota in 1916. Halas, a star end for the Illini and coach Bob Zuppke in those days, remembers it well—even though he wasn't able to play that day because of an injury.

"My leg had been broken prior to the game and I was walking on crutches, but Zup had taken me to Minnesota for the game anyway and it was a great thrill just to watch an upset like that one," he said.

"I knew how well, of course, that Zup prepared a team for a game like that one, but to see it all unfolding just the way he'd planned it...well, you almost couldn't believe it.

"I still can recall the feeling of exhilaration we all had when that game ended. And I can remember how I threw my crutches up in the air and ran out on the field when it finally was over."

Halas took a more active role in many other Illini football victories in that era.

One of his most amusing recollections is of a game against Wisconsin in 1917.

"I was returning kickoffs that day and I remember one coming in my direction," Halas recalls. "I took the ball and started running with it and all of a sudden I looked down and it was completely deflated. That stunned me and I slowed down to a walk. I didn't know what else to do so I just ran over and handed it to the official and he didn't know what to do about it either.

"If I'd have had a little more moxie, I would have kept right on going. I'm not sure any of the other players could have seen that I was carrying that deflated football and I might have run all the way for a touchdown."

"That's one of the funniest things ever to happen to me as a player, though. I never saw it happen before or since in any game."

Halas played basketball and baseball as well as football at Illinois.

"Ralph Jones, the basketball coach, asked me to come out my junior year," said Halas. "I wasn't much of a scorer in basketball. The opponents never paid much attention to my shooting. My job was to get the ball off the board. But I did score the winning basket against Wisconsin—they were our big rival in those days—that season and that was a thrill.

Halas was good enough as a baseball player to sign a contract with the New York Yankees, but he had trouble hitting "the big league curve ball." Not long afterward, the nation was at war and Halas joined the Navy. At Great Lakes, Halas returned to football and played on the service team that was invited to play in the 1919 Rose Bowl game.

A year later, A. E. Staley, a starch maker in Decatur, Illinois, offered Halas the job as athletic director at his plant. That meant Halas would coach the company's semi-pro football and baseball teams.

There were only a handful of good semi-pro football teams in those days and, under Halas, the Staleys quickly became one of them. For most players, their careers ended once college was over.

A remark Zuppke once made gave Halas the idea that there might be a future for pro football.

"It was at our football banquet in 1917," Halas remembers. "Zup got up and spoke to us and I remember him saying, 'Just when you get to know something about football, I lose you.'"

On September 17 of 1920, Halas and 10 other men sat on

the running boards of autos in a showroom in Canton and founded the American Professional Football Association, the forerunner of the modern NFL.

"Most of those teams practiced only a couple evenings each week," said Halas, "but one of the agreements I had with Mr. Staley was that we'd have two hours each day to practice football."

That Staley team soon afterward moved to Chicago, of course, and with Halas as the principal owner, became the Chicago Bears.

But the influence of Zuppke and Illinois Athletic Director George Huff remained strong.

"After we'd taken Red Grange out of school to play for us in 1925, Zup and Mr. Huff said they wanted to talk to me," Halas recalls. "I went over to see them and they stressed to me they didn't think it was proper for the pro teams to take players until they were finished with school. At the next league meeting in February, I proposed that no player could sign with an NFL team until his class graduated. That rule still stands and I think it's a good one. We've always had a good relationship with the colleges because of it.

"Playing for Zuppke was a privilege. I knew all about him when he was at Oak Park and I was growing up in Chicago. My brother Walter played for him at Illinois before I did."

Halas has seen the dramatic development of football in terms of fan interest on both the college and pro level in his 80-plus years and even now he admits it's all been slightly stunning.

"I knew we had a good game even back in the old days," he said. "But never in my wildest dreams did I think it would be anything like it is today."

Back-To-Back Championships

On a bright fall day in 1962 Burt Ingwersen and Ralph Fletcher sat down with Bert Bertine, sports editor of the *Champaign-Urbana Courier*, to discuss their playing days at Illinois in the late teens of this century.

Before the 1960s ended, all three had died—Fletcher and Bertine in 1967 and Ingwersen in 1969.

Bertine, an Illinois graduate and a man whose sportswriting career in Champaign-Urbana spanned 32 years, was not only a highly admired citizen in his community but a pure pro when it came to informing his readers.

Illinois players and coaches respected and liked him. He had a way of opening them up, and Bertine's readers always benefited from it, as they did on that day in 1962 when he returned to his office and batted out a story of two old-timers reminiscing.

"Ralph was a halfback, and he got all the headlines because his brother, Bob, a wingback, and I cleared the path for him all the time," Ingwersen joked to Bertine.

According to Bertine's story Fletcher shot back a verbal arrow himself and said, "Take off your shirt, Burt, and show them those old cleat marks. You guys were so slow, I always was running up your backs."

The fact, of course, was that they were both stars, along with halfback Larry "Laurie" Walquist, All-American center John Depler, and All-American end Chuck Carney of Bob Zuppke-coached teams that won Western Conference championships in both 1918 and 1919. The 1919 team shared the mythical national crown with Harvard and Notre Dame.

Oddly enough both Fletcher and Ingwersen started their football careers in opposition to parental wishes.

"I lived in Fulton which had a high school but no athletic program," said Ingwersen. "Believe me it was tough to persuade my dad to send me to high school across the river in Clinton, Iowa, which had all sports, especially when it cost him $5.50 a month for my tuition. He was against football, but after he'd seen me play in a game he rarely missed one."

Fletcher also looked back to precollege days and said: "Even though I had an older brother named Glenn who played quarterback at Purdue, my father was against football. I had never even seen a game until I played in one.

"We moved from Aurora from the farm when I started high school. That was in 1913. I went out for the team and played as a freshman. Bob and I drove Dad to that first game, and because he didn't know how to drive he had to stay and watch it. He was an immediate convert."

Both Ingwersen and Fletcher were experienced, talented players by the time Zuppke got his hands on them.

"I came to Illinois chiefly because Bart Macomber, an All-American in 1915, wrote me a letter asking me to come," said Ingwersen. "He knew a friend of mine who told him about me."

Ingwersen played center for Illinois in 1917, a 5-2-1 year overall but a season in which the Illini were just 2-2-1 in the conference and tied for fifth. Ingwersen moved to tackle in 1918, the year Fletcher joined the team as a sophomore halfback.

Those were World War I years, of course, and all members of the football team also were members of the Student Army Training Corps.

"We had to drill every night outside the Armory after football practice," Ingwersen recalled. "When we'd go to a game we'd have to wear our uniforms, and we'd march between train stations, or from the train to our hotel or dormitory."

That 1918 team was 5-2 over all, losing a pair of 7-0 games with Great Lakes and Municipal Pier service teams stocked with inducted former college stars but beating all four league opponents and never allowing a touchdown in conference play. Iowa

Burt Ingwersen was star tackle on Illinois' back-to-back championship teams in 1918 and 1919.

was beaten 19-0, Wisconsin 22-0, Ohio State 13-0, and Chicago 29-0.

Many of the players who had been called in World War I returned to campuses in 1919, and Illinois faced more formidable opposition from within its conference.

But Illinois also was helped by the war's end; Zuppke regained several good players.

"The alumni were really enthused because of this," Fletcher said in his recollection with Bertine. "They talked Zup into the idea he had so many good players his first two teams were of equal strength.

"Platooning was unheard of in that era. The substitution rules, for one thing, permitted little leeway. For another, few coaches had that much material. Varsity players were expected to go 60 minutes or close to it."

But Zuppke, perhaps for the only time in his coaching career, thought maybe the "Green Street coaches," as the rabid alumni followers were known in those days, might have something.

"At any rate we opened against Purdue, and in the third quarter we had a 14-0 lead and appeared to have the game well in command," said Ingwersen.

"Zup took us all out as a team, a shocking thing then. You have to remember that we couldn't go back in under the substitution rules, and once you were taken out after the half, that was it.

"We were already in the locker room taking our showers when we heard this big roar and learned Purdue had scored. The

This 1919 Illini team scored a stunning upset victory over Ohio State in the season finale to clinch the conference championship.

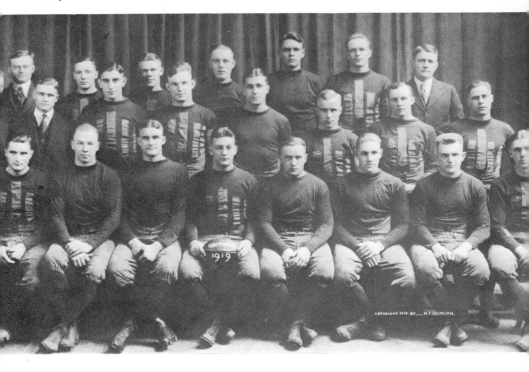

73

Chuck Carney, an Illini All-American in 1920, led Illini come-back against Ohio State in 1919 title game.

game ended with Purdue on our five yard line bidding for the tying touchdown.

"Boy, was Zup mad! He swore in the dressing room that he'd never listen to the alumni again."

And, to anyone's knowledge, Zuppke never once violated that oath.

The next game was against Iowa, a power in those days, which had been handed its lone college defeat in 1918 by Illinois. And the Hawkeyes of 1919, with the famed Duke Slater and Glenn and Aubrey Devine, were beaten again by a narrow 9-7 margin.

It was in the 1919 Illinois-Iowa game that Zuppke went to referee Walter Eckersall and told him that the Illini were going to use an onside kick and for him to be sure to watch for it. Walquist kicked the flat ball from the 45 yard line, sped down-field as the Iowa safetyman stood idly by, grabbed the loose ball, and went into the end zone for a touchdown.

Illinois was upset once in 1919, by Wisconsin 14-10, but beat the other four league teams it faced later in the year—

Chicago 10-0, Minnesota 10-6, Michigan 29-7, and Ohio State 9-7—to finish 6-1, with all its games that season played against conference opposition.

That season-ending game against Dr. John Wilce's Buckeyes still is regarded as one of the biggest victories in Illini football history.

Ohio State came into the game unbeaten, led by one of its all-time great backs, Chic Harley. Harley had been the star of unbeaten Ohio State teams in both 1916 and 1917 that had won undisputed conference titles. Harley, however, had gone off to war in 1918, and the Buckeyes had fallen to 3-3 for the season without him.

But with Harley back in 1919, the Buckeyes were again on the march and were regarded as at least a two-touchdown favorite over Illinois in the finale in Columbus.

That game turned into a tenacious defensive battle, with Ohio State leading 7-6 with just under two minutes left.

"It was an awfully rough game, I remember that," recalls Chuck Carney. "A lot of players from both teams were laid out."

With the Illini trailing by one point, Zuppke and the Illini faced a do-or-die situation when they took possession deep in their own territory. Zuppke called for an all-out passing attack, with Walquist throwing.

"I remember Zup looked to Walquist and said, 'No matter what signals they call, take the ball and throw it to Carney.' That's what he did, and I must have caught five or six," said Carney, who now resides in Manchester, Massachusetts.

But by then the last few seconds of the game were ticking away with the Illini on the Ohio State 20 yard line. There appeared to be only time enough for one play.

Carney, who would earn All-American honors the following year (1920) and eventually be inducted into the college football Hall of Fame, still remembers the frenzy on the Illinois sidelines at that moment of intense, mind-bending pressure.

"Ralph Fletcher, our regular kicker, was hurt," said Carney. "Dick Reichle also was on that team, and he'd done some kicking, but he also was hurt that day. Zuppke started looking for someone who could try to kick, and I remember Bob Fletcher running up to him and saying, 'I'll kick it.'"

75

Bobby Fletcher kicked winning field goal that stunned Ohio State and Chic Harley in 1919.

And he did. The curly-haired sophomore sent the dropkick sailing through the goal posts 25 yards away with just seconds left, to win the game 9-7 and clinch another championship for Illinois.

"I found out later," said Carney, "that Bobby had never even tried a field goal kick before that one. I remember how Harley broke down when he saw the ball go through."

It marked the only time in Harley's fantastic three-year career at Ohio State that he tasted defeat.

"After the game was over, I remember we went back to the athletic club where we were staying to wait to take the train back home," said Carney. "An alumnus walked up to Bobby Fletcher and said he'd give him a sizable amount of money—as I recall it was over a thousand dollars—for the shoe he'd kicked the field goal with, but Bobby wouldn't sell it to him.

"I looked at the guy and said, 'Hey, I'd sell you my whole suit for that much,'" Carney said and laughed.

Putting The "Fight" In The Illini

The legend of just when Illinois football teams became known as the "Fighting Illini" instead of simply "Illini" is subject to some conjecture.

"In sports cartoons in the early 1900's the Illini Indian was represented as battling with the Michigan Wolverine, etc.," the late Illini sports information director Mike Tobin once wrote.

But Tobin's belief was that the first writer to make emphatic use of the description "Fighting Illini" was Harvey Woodruff of the *Chicago Tribune*, who was so moved by an Illini performance in 1921 that the entire lead paragraph of his game report was used to reiterate the term.

Illinois was winless in four conference games heading into the season finale against a powerful Ohio State team that needed only a win to at least share the conference title.

Ohio State had beaten a good 5-2 Illini team led by Chuck Carney, center John Depler, and fullback Jack Crangle, 7-0 in 1920, costing the Illini a conference championship.

But the Illini would have their revenge. The 1921 game was played in Columbus, and the Buckeye fans were frenzied for homecoming after OSU had rolled relentlessly over Michigan, Minnesota, Chicago, and Purdue, shutting out all four league rivals in a spectacular show of strength.

Illinois, meanwhile, generally was regarded as the weakest team in the league. The Illini not only had been beaten by Iowa, Wisconsin, Michigan, and Chicago, but had managed a total of only eight points—two field goals and a safety—in all four games, while giving up 51.

So what did Zuppke do in the face of such clear indications of an Ohio State runaway? He publicly predicted an Illinois victory. The brash bluff by Zuppke brought guffaws from Champaign to Columbus.

Zuppke added to the incredulous bravado of the week the night before the game. When he assembled the squad for practice in Columbus, one of his assistants asked him what he wanted the reserves to do.

"Take them over into a corner," Zuppke blustered. "We'll only be using 11 men tomorrow."

And Zup did just that. He used only 11 men and, in fact, left two of his top players on the bench for the entire game.

He decided before the game that Carney, who had been accorded All-American recognition the previous season, and Dick Reichle were not ready. Zup instead started a pair of youngsters, Johnny Sabo and Dave Wilson, at the two ends.

Zuppke had another ace up his sleeve. As he frequently did when he could feel a big upset in the offing, he added a trick play to his team's game plan. This time it was a formation Zuppke called "the telescopic shift."

The wily Dutchman flanked four linemen far to the right, leaving his center in the normal position sandwiched between the two remaining linemen. He sent Laurie Walquist, his star halfback and top pass receiver, into a flanked position behind the four-man spread forward wall. For all purposes it was a set version of the modern screen pass from a single-wing-styled formation. Frequently that day when the Illini lined up in the formation, it was simply a decoy, but it added to the psychological mood that Zuppke had been building all week.

It was not so much what Illinois did offensively that day as what the Illini did defensively.

Ohio State boasted one of the nation's most respected passing attacks of that season, nourished the previous season by the Buckeye coach Dr. John W. Wilce. But the target-splitting attack of Sonny Workman throwing to Truck Myers never got into gear on this mid-November Saturday.

Many years later in recalling the game Zuppke revealed his defensive strategy to a reporter. "I told Vee Green, one of our guards who dropped back on defense against passes, to cover anything that worked twice. Green did that and knocked down some of their favorite plays. Then I had Johnny Sabo dropping back, too, and once he ran back 25 yards from the line of scrimmage to intercept an Ohio pass."

Ohio State threatened several times early in the game, but interceptions or third-down failures by inches stymied the Buckeyes. On one particular goalward thrust Ohio State drove to the Illini 11 yard line only to have linebacker-fullback Crangle stop the Buckeye ballcarrier at the line of scrimmage on a crucial fourth-and-one play.

There were not many breaks in the hard-fought game, but Illinois got one in the second quarter and made the most of it. Don Peden attempted a pass to Wilson after the Illini moved the ball to the Bucks' 17 yard line. Wilson held on to the throw momentarily, but then it suddenly escaped from his grasp and bounced off the chest of OSU's Myers. The sure-handed Walquist, however, picked it off in a dead run and rambled into the end zone untouched, for the only touchdown of the game. Sabo kicked the extra point to make it 7-0.

After that, the incredible 11 Illini Iron Men seemed to gain a new burst of energy for the second half. Time after time they turned back Ohio State scoring threats as Wilce ran a total of 33 players into the game trying to wear down the battle-weary Illini. But on this day it could not be done.

Sabo, Green, Peden, Wilson, Walquist, Crangle, Milt Olander, Al Mohr, Otto Vogel, Clarence Drayer, and Joe Sternaman would not allow it, battle-weary though they were when the clock ticked away those last delirious seconds.

The campus newspaper, the *Illini*, reported that students who had crammed into the Old Gym annex to receive the play-by-play of the game by telegraph went wild when the final score was posted. They staged a snake dance that poured through the campus and finally tied up traffic in downtown Champaign.

According to newspaper reports, more than 3,000 fans were out of bed—if they ever made it there—before dawn to welcome the team home at the railroad station.

Zuppke, smiling and bright-eyed, stepped down from the platform and said: "I told the team that by beating Ohio they could create an imperishable, undying tradition; that their achievement in coming out of the slough of despondency would always live in Illinois annals."

Somehow, in the dizzying drama at Ohio State that weekend, the tradition of the "Fighting Illini" upset had been confirmed—and possibly christened.

A Cow Pasture
"Bowl" Game

One of the most legendary football games ever played in the Midwest occurred on a frost-bitten Sunday in November of 1921. The college season had ended, but early-day semipro teams in Illinois were still playing. Two of the best of that breed—teams from Taylorville and Carlinville—were to meet on November 27 on a field carved out of a cow pasture near Taylorville.

Rumor spread through Taylorville a few days before the game, however, that Carlinville had more than the normal hometown confidence that its team would win the game. Carlinville fans, so the legend goes, were looking for "all takers" and willing to bet big sums of money on their favorites.

Suspicions in Taylorville reached full flame, so the story goes, when a traveling salesman revealed, "You'll be playing the whole Notre Dame team Sunday."

According to old-timers' recollections, the first thought of the Taylorville contingent was simply to go ahead and play the game with the team it had but refuse to put down any bets on the game. Taylorville, after all, had a strong team led by quarterback Charlie Dressen, who would later become a long-time major league baseball manager.

But the decision was made by Taylorville to bring in some "ringers" of their own. A telephone call was made to one of two young men from Taylorville who had been members of Bob Zuppke's 1921 Illinois team.

"About 10 of us got calls to come to Taylorville to play in

the game," 75-year-old Harry Gamage recalled on a day in 1975 in his home in Wakonda, South Dakota. Gamage had played his freshman year at Western Illinois at Macomb but moved to Illinois as a sophomore.

"'Dope' Simpson and Vern Mullen, two Taylorville boys who played end at Illinois, took charge and got us all down there," remembered Gamage.

"We were met at the train, the old inter-urban, as I recall, and I was immediately taken to the home of some person there, and I didn't see any of the other players until we got down to the hotel on Sunday morning.

"I remember Jack Crangle had his face all taped up, but everybody must have known it was him. You could tell Jack by his walk. Laurie Walquist was there, and so was Joe Sternaman. I played center in the game, although I normally played guard. Mullen and Simpson played the ends. We had a full Illinois line, as I recall, except for one tackle, and Ross Petty, who had played for us the year before in 1920, was in there."

Gamage remembers that there were nine Notre Dame players on the Carlinville team.

"They had Chet Wynne...Roger Kiley...Harry Mear, who later coached at Georgia and Mississippi...Eddie Anderson, who coached at Iowa...and some others," said Gamage.

According to one account of the famed game, Carlinville's Notre Dame "ringers" went into the game immediately, producing a lineup that included three Irish All-Americans—Wynne, Kiley, and Anderson.

Dick Simpson, a Taylorville newspaperman who played in the game, once recalled in an article he wrote many years later that Carlinville "had all the best of the going in the first half."

But a blocked punt gave Taylorville the ball on the one yard line, and Dressen eventually scored for Taylorville on a "quarterback spinner." The half ended with Taylorville the surprising leader at 7-0, and none of the Illini imports, other than hometown boys Roy Simpson and Mullen, had played in the game.

The decision was made at halftime to insert the Illinois lineup into the game. Sternaman lined up at quarterback, Crangle at fullback, and Walquist (the Illini captain in 1921) at one halfback.

"The second half was a different story," Dick Simpson wrote in his reminiscence. "Notre Dame (Carlinville) had a lot more trouble gaining with Crangle and the Illinois regular backs backing up the line."

Sternaman connected on three successful dropkicks for field goals in the second half, and the game ended with Taylorville and the Illini imports winning 16-0.

There are all kinds of stories about the huge amounts of money that changed hands in bets that day. Estimates have been made that anywhere from $30,000 to $100,000 in wagers were riding on the outcome.

"When the game ended a Virden merchant who had mortgaged his home and his business to bet $1,600 on Taylorville, rushed on to the field and, with tears streaming down his face, threw his arms around Coach (Grover) Hoover, and said, 'You saved my home for me,'" Dick Simpson wrote.

But it would be a costly game for the college players involved. All the Illinois players would, two months later, lose any college eligibility they had remaining, and most of the Notre Dame players also would be declared ineligible.

Wisconsin questioned the eligibility of Walquist when he showed up to play basketball for the Illini against the Badgers that same winter. The investigation that followed confirmed that the players had taken part in an unauthorized game.

"After having lost most of the games in 1921, Zup had to come right back in 1922 and play without all us fellows," said Gamage. "But Mr. Huff and Zup were good to me, even though we'd pulled this so-called stunt of going to Taylorville.

"We shouldn't have done it. Of course, in those days, kids were hard up. They were washing dishes and this and that to make money, and if we could slip out and make $15 or $20 playing football on a Sunday, we'd do it. Many times a few guys would go over to Danville, say, and play on some town teams.

"But there was a rule in the conference that if you played on any team other than your own team during the school year, you're automatically ineligible. But some of us didn't know about that rule, and that's what hurt us so bad.

"I always regretted I'd done it, but Mr. Huff still was good to me. He got me a high school coaching in Fairmont, West Virginia, and a few years later, in the fall of '24, he gave me $1500 to come back and help coach the freshman team at Illinois."

Gamage went on to become head coach at Kentucky, where his teams were 35-25-5. He would wind up his coaching career with great success at the University of South Dakota. He was inducted into the Helms Athletic Foundation's College Hall of Fame as a coach in 1963.

Two other Illini "ringers," Walquist and Joe Sternaman, continued their football careers on the pro level with the Chicago Bears.

But the Taylorville-Carlinville game had made its mark. It brought strict adherence to college eligibility codes and set the stage for appointment of a full-time Western Conference commissioner to assure that the rules were followed.

And even today old-timers still talk about the time Illinois and Notre Dame played a cow pasture bowl game, disguised as Taylorville and Carlinville, in 1921.

"Something Greater, Somehow"

The popularity of college football was beginning to mushroom in the early 1920s. Visionary athletic directors like Illinois' George Huff saw a new era on the horizon—the days when 60,000, 70,000 persons and even more would storm a stadium on a Saturday afternoon to see their favorite team play.

For the final game of the 1920 season against Ohio State, some 20,000 fans had poured into Illinois Field to see the Illini go against the Buckeyes. The little field with wooden bleachers on University Avenue in Urbana could seat only 17,000. Huff believed that 40,000 or more tickets could have been sold for that game if there had been seating available.

It was on that day, the story goes, that the man whom his friends had affectionately called "G" Huff dreamed a grand dream—a dream of a stadium that would rival any in the country in size and splendor.

He thought of Harvard's horseshoe and the Yale Bowl and said, "I am thinking of something like these, but something greater, somehow."

Perhaps it was President David Kinley who described Huff's dream best when he said, "We want our stadium to bring a touch of Greek glory to the prairie."

In the spring of 1921, with the support of President Kinley, Huff was ready to announce his plans for a fund drive to build a new Illinois stadium. He made it known that a new stadium was as much necessity as showcase.

Getting quality competition costs money, Huff said, and

Bob Zuppke and Athletic Director George Huff watch as work begins on Memorial Stadium. Horse-drawn carts carry dirt away from the area.

he added: "A guarantee of $15,000 is the limit that can stand behind a game on Illinois Field. (Some) schools are already demanding $45,000 guarantees. This means that Illinois will be left off the schedule of teams which can get higher guarantees, if nothing is done to relieve the situation."

Huff decided that the new stadium would be a memorial to the Illinois heroes who died in World War I, and he first took his plan to the students of the University of Illinois.

An April 24, 1921, newspaper account describes that day as follows: "The gym annex looked like the Chicago Coliseum during the Republican convention. It was packed with men and girls, seated in orderly rows, with county, state, and country standards lifted high. President David Kinley spoke first at the

Memorial Stadium in 1924 and in the current era.

auditorium, then at the gym annex. He gave dignity to the stadium idea which sobered the vast assemblages. When G. Huff rose to speak, the din of cheering lasted very long."

"I want to see a great stadium at the University of Illinois," Huff told the audience. "I believe you will get it. I believe there is a great spirit at this university. The stadium will be many things—a memorial to Illini who have died in the war, a recreational field, and an imposing place for our varsity game.

But it will also be an unprecedented expression of Illinois spirit."

Bob Zuppke was the final speaker and, according to accounts of the meeting, pandemonium broke out once the dynamic Zuppke asked, "And who will make the first pledge?"

Ten minutes later Zuppke announced a total of $700,000 in pledges from the student body alone. And even more important, they pledged their support to help raise additional funds for the drive.

Frederic A. Russell, the unofficial community leader, and W. Elmer Ekblaw, the official campaign manager, joined with Huff and Zuppke to keep the stadium drive in high gear. They made visits to Illini clubs throughout the nation.

In one of his memorable speeches to one of them Zuppke said: "The Memorial should be an honor court; since 183 Illini were killed in the war, there should be 183 columns in the honor court. People should enter the honor court first and then the Stadium."

The fund drive was widely supported.

Avery Brundage, an ex-Illini trackman who was just beginning to build a huge fortune and would eventually become the powerful chairman of the International Olympic Committee, donated $1,000 and said, "As a monument to past and an inspiration to present and future teams, I am glad to contribute to the building of the most imposing stadium in the country."

"I am buying $10,000 worth of happiness," said Robert F. Carr, class of 1893 and president of Dearborn Drug and Chemical Company of Chicago.

But all of the contributions were not that large. In fact 26,000 people from throughout the nation contributed to the project. On September 11, 1922, Athletic Director Huff broke ground on the 56-acre tract of land, and by the middle of the following December foundations had been completed.

Slowly, painstakingly, the stadium began to take shape, with contractors fighting the problems of delayed steel shipments and an inadequate work force. But the Huff dream would become a reality.

When it was finished, these words written by Huff's aide, Mike Tobin, would be carved in the stone:

May this stadium ever be a temple of sportsmanship, inspiring the athletes of the University of Illinois and those who cheer them as they play, always to uphold the spirit and tradition of Illinois athletics: "To play manfully and courageously to the last, no matter what the odds—to play fairly within the spirit and the letter of the rules—to win without boasting and lose without excuses."

May these ideals of manliness, courage and true sportsmanship find expression not only with the stadium, but throughout the life of The University. Above all, may the stadium always be the symbol of a great united University, drawing closer together in common bond and spirit all the men and women of Illinois.

Memorial Stadium stands today, 50 years after its dedication, as a monument and showcase, just as Huff and President Kinley had wanted it to be.

It is interesting, of course, looking back, that Illinois moved toward building this gigantic new stadium at the time it did.

Huff not only had a vision of the stunning growth of college football in 1920, but the Illini soon would have a player whose performances would be fitting for a stadium of such quality.

He would excite the fans as no other college football player ever had. From throughout the nation they would jam Memorial Stadium to see him run. Sportswriter Grantland Rice would nickname him "The Galloping Ghost."

He was, of course, Red Grange.

A Man Named Grange

No football hero ever had a more humble, inauspicious beginning to his college career than Harold "Red" Grange. He arrived on the Illinois campus in the fall of 1922 with a few, modest personal belongings packed in what he once described as a "battered old steamer trunk."

Grange went to Illinois planning on competing in what he considered his "best two sports"—baseball and track—but not long after he moved in at the Zeta Psi fraternity house all the pledges were lined up and asked what activities they were going to participate in. Grange told of his plans for baseball and track, but he stopped there.

"But, didn't you play football in high school?" somebody asked.

"Yes," said Grange. "I played for four years, but I don't think I'm good enough to play football for Illinois."

"You're going out for football," came the crisp reply.

It was decided—or was it?

A few days later Grange reported for the first day of freshman practice, took one look at the size of the other players there to try out, and promptly left.

He was not the most popular guy in the fraternity house that night when he returned and told his friends that he had walked off.

"Some guy hit me with a paddle, and I knocked a hole in the plaster of the ceiling I jumped so high," Grange once recalled.

The next day he was back out on the practice field. Most of the uniforms had been given out by then, and when he reported for his equipment he was given the unusually high number of 77. The equipment boy who passed out that jersey to Grange that day could have had no way of knowing he was passing out a number that would one day become one of the most famous in all of sports.

"The first night they lined us all up and told us to run," Grange remembered. "They must have eliminated half of the 150 or so who turned out after that, and I felt better when they kept me around. When you're out there from a small town, you don't have much confidence in yourself, but after you see how bad some of the other players are, you get a little confidence."

Anyone would have thought Grange might have gained some confidence from his high school career. At Wheaton High School, Grange had carried the ball 1,260 times in 36 games, gained 10,800 yards, and scored 180 touchdowns.

He was born June 13, 1903, in Forksville, Pennsylvania, the son of a lumber camp foreman, Lyle Grange. The death of his mother when he was five years old led to the family's move to Wheaton, where three of Grange's uncles were living at the time. Red's father eventually landed a job as Wheaton's one-man police force, and young Harold, once he reached high school age, would take part-time employment delivering ice from a horse-drawn wagon.

Grange was a natural athlete in his schoolboy years. He ran the 100-yard dash in 9.81 seconds, broad jumped 23 feet, and high jumped six feet.

But there was no long line of college recruiters at Grange's door then as there would be today for an athlete of half his physical potential. When he had competed in the state high school track meet in Champaign the spring of his senior year, he had met Illini coach Bob Zuppke, and Zuppke had indicated he would be interested in seeing Grange at Illinois. But there was no recruiting, no super sales pitch. It was more of something like, "Well, Harold, if you come to Illinois next fall, we'd be interested in seeing you." That was Zuppke.

An alumnus from Michigan did visit Grange in Wheaton

Red Grange: The Iceman Cometh to Illinois.

and encourage him strongly to go there, but there were no scholarships in those days, and Grange did not think he could afford the out-of-state tuition at Michigan. A boyhood friend, George Dawson, older than Grange, was already playing football at Illinois and encouraged Grange to join him there. Grange followed Dawson to Illinois and into the Zeta Psi fraternity house. Grange still has warm memories of those fraternity brothers who saw to it that he went out for football. Their confidence in his football ability soon was fully justified.

Grange made the starting backfield at left halfback on the freshman team coached by Burt Ingwersen, joining Moon Baker at quarterback, Earl Britton at fullback, and Paul Cook at right half.

"I've always said the best team I ever played on at Illinois was that freshman team of 1922," Grange once said. "The first time we played against the varsity we'd been practicing together for two days, and they'd been practicing for two weeks and they only beat us 21-19, and Moon Baker missed two drop kicks that could have won it for us. We beat them, though, before we were through."

Two members of that freshman team, in addition to Grange, went on to earn All-American honors, but both at other schools. Baker transferred to Northwestern and earned all-star honors there, while tackle Frank Wickhorst went on to become an All-American at Navy.

But even the transfer of those two stars in embryo did not drastically drain away from the strength of the Illinois freshman football class of 1922. That same year the varsity finished with a 2-5 record, but help was on the way.

The next year five of those freshmen would break into the 11-man starting lineup as sophomores. And the most spectacular of them all would be Grange.

It was obvious in the fall of 1923 when Grange returned to the Illinois campus that Zuppke had big things in mind for his new halfback.

Grange had come back more mature physically than when he had left in the spring. He had been working on the ice wagon back in Wheaton "from six in the morning to seven o'clock at night six days a week," as Grange himself recalls. He had made $37.50 per week and was happy to get that much. The money would be used to pay the expenses of his second year in college.

Zuppke quickly installed Grange in the 11-man first unit. On October 3, 1923, an article in the *Courier* of Champaign-Urbana reported: "The composition of the Illinois backfield is fairly certain with Harold Grange and Wallie McIlwain at half-back, Earl Britton or Walter Crawford at fullback, and Harry Hall at quarterback. Grange is expected to make a good account of himself. He has shown up well in all of the scrimmages." The reporter also noted prophetically, "Grange's specialty is open field running."

The next day, when The Wonder Store of Champaign ran an advertisement for union suits for sale at a price of $1.49, the newspaper's sports section reported, as the season opener drew near: "The debut of Zuppke's new back will be anxiously awaited. Grange has trotted through the freshmen ever since practice opened."

That debut was well worth the wait for Illinois fans.

Grange's first varsity game was played on October 6, 1923, at Illinois Field, against a Nebraska team which was regarded as one of the best in the nation after beating Notre Dame the previous season.

Illinois won the opener 24-7 from a team that would again beat Notre Dame later in the year (this time a Notre Dame with the storied "Four Horsemen").

Grange was brilliant. He scored all three Illini touchdowns, including one on a crowd-electrifying, 60-yard punt return from his safety position. Britton kicked three extra points and a field goal.

The Illini went on to win their next seven games against Butler 21-7, Iowa 9-6, Northwestern 29-0, Chicago 7-0, Wisconsin 10-0, Mississippi A&M 27-0, and Ohio State 9-0.

"The high spot of the season was the opening of the new Stadium," an article in the 1925 University of Illinois *Bulletin* says. "Before 60,000 people Illinois defeated Chicago in a brilliant exhibition. Grange scored Illinois' only touchdown, and the Illini won, handing Chicago its only loss of the season."

That game was played in a downpour.

"I think it was the worst rainstorm I've ever seen," Grange would say many years later. "The next day when I went out to practice, there must have been 3,000 ladies' slippers still stuck in the mud around the stadium." But the wet conditions did not deter Grange. He gained 173 yards in 17 carries.

The victory over Ohio State in the season finale in Columbus left Michigan and Illinois tied for the conference championship, each unbeaten.

Grange finished the season as the leading scorer in the Big Ten with 12 touchdowns and 72 points. Grange, team captain and tackle Jim McMillen, and end Frank Rokusek were all named to the all-conference team.

Grange was named to the All-America team selected by Walter Camp, who wrote: "...Grange of Illinois is the star backfield man of the Middle West Conference, and that means he is traveling in high class. Grange has been the terror of Zuppke's opponents at all times, and when needed in critical moments he has made good with the needed runs."

The sophomore star, who only a year before had entered in near-obscurity, was now a national name. But the new fame did not change Grange's easygoing personality.

Fred H. Turner, Dean of Students Emeritus at Illinois, recalls the Grange of those days as "shy, reticent, and modest."

Wendell Trenchard of DeLand, Illinois, a fraternity brother, said, "He was reserved and quiet and never let his success go to his head."

One of his teammates, center Gil Roberts, says, "He always gave full credit to his blockers. And we didn't care if he got the credit. We figured that if we all carried out our assignments, Red would do his job."

Twelve Minutes
For Eternity

Throughout the summer of 1924, even when the major league baseball pennant races were winding down to a World Series between young Bucky Harris' Washington Senators and John McGraw's New York Giants, college football fans in the Midwest were talking about the approaching battle between Illinois and Michigan, the two unbeaten teams of 1923.

Illinois had picked this game for the formal dedication of its new Memorial Stadium.

The psychological warfare leading up to the game had carried on throughout the summer. Illinois coach Bob Zuppke had bombarded his players all summer with mail which emphasized how lightly the Michigan team was taking this Illini team, how confident the Wolverines were of victory.

But there were two games before the much-ballyhooed meeting with Michigan, and Illinois, looking ahead to that game, almost was upset in its season opener with Nebraska. The Illini squeaked by 9-6, thanks to a field goal by Earl Britton. Butler was no problem in the second game, with Illinois winning 10-0, and all of a sudden the long-awaited meeting was at hand.

From Friday morning, October 17, on, Champaign-Urbana had been turned into a wonderland of open-mouthed anticipation.

Champaign Police Chief A. V. Keller had asked for assistance from the Chicago Police Department to handle the influx of football-happy visitors. Thirty-five patrolmen, nightsticks

A winning combination: Red Grange and Bob Zuppke.

swinging at their side, had been dispatched for special duty in the gaily decorated college town.

"A procession of taxis bringing fans from Chicago has begun pouring in," an article in the October 17, 1924, *Champaign-Urbana Courier* reported. "There was an incessant stream of machines coming into town today."

And the fans kept coming, carried into the Twin Cities in Willys-Knight Coach Sedans which sold for $1,625 and Hup Mobile Club Sedans which, tinsel-trimmed, were priced at $1,825. A few of the more affluent motored snobbishly into the city in Nash Advanced Four-Door Sedans which wore price tags of $2,320 in the showrooms.

The *Courier* also reported that on Friday, "Flags fluttered from every masthead, and bunting draped every lightpost...fraternity and sorority houses all seemed to bloom over-night, all of them competing to outdo the other in exotic display of color and enthusiasm."

Harry L. Farrell, the noted sportswriter for United Press in New York, had made his way west of the Hudson for the monumental meeting of the football giants, and he wrote in his early-week report to his readers: "Out here in the West, where men are men and football teams are made of them, nobody wants to discuss anything but the battle impending between Michigan and Illinois. More than 70,000 spectators are expected, and double that number of seats could have been sold if there were places for that number. There is more real enthusiasm around here than there has been in New Haven or Boston for the Harvard-Yale games."

Zuppke conducted all his practices the week of the Michigan game in the tightest of secrecy, and there were late reports that the Illini might be suffering some injuries.

The night before the game Farrell wrote, "Distressing rumors have spread that many of the Zuppkemen have colds, sore feet, and even torn fingernails."

There was some justification for the concerns among Illini fans. Wallie McIlwain, who was one of Grange's best blockers, was ill with a stomach disorder, but by the time game day arrived he was fully recovered and ready to play.

The morning of Saturday, October 18, 1924, arrived with the sun a glowing round ball in the azure, Indian-summer sky. It was unseasonably warm, and when Zuppke took his team back into the locker room after their opening warm-up, he told his team to remove their leg stockings.

"Every one of us looked at Zuppke in consternation," center Gil Roberts now recalls. "One of our big linemen, Dick Hall, who was a big moose, but no raving beauty, said, 'Coach, our legs will get cut up.'"

Zup shot back quickly in his clipped, staccato speech, saying, "Well, you're no bloomin' chorus girls. Take 'em off."

The players obeyed.

Grange remembers that Zuppke was pacing the floor, his mind immersed in deep thought, when he looked down and appeared to pick up a coin off the locker room floor.

"Yost planted this dime," said Zuppke, referring to his bitter rival, Fielding H. "Hurry-Up" Yost, the longtime Michigan coach who was also athletic director.

"I picked up a dime off the locker room floor the last time

99

we played at Michigan, and we lost," Zuppke said.

Grange recalls that Zuppke walked over to the window, threw it open, and "sailed the dime out" with great theatrics.

Soon afterward the Illini were back on the field, their bare legs shining in the bright sunlight, which had soared the temperature into the low 80s.

Yost and his coach, George Little, rubbed their eyes, not certain of what was happening. They immediately went over to the Illinois players, however, and began checking to see if any lubricant had been applied to the Illinois' players' legs. They found none, but Zuppke had already won the psychological war.

The first 12 minutes of that Michigan game have become one of sport's most memorable legends, one of football's best known litanies in individual greatness.

In the first 12 minutes of the game Grange scored four touchdowns against a team which had allowed only four in the previous two seasons.

The play-by-play of the dramatic beginning of the game was recorded for history as follows in the *Chicago Tribune*:

> Steger kicked off to Grange, who got the ball on his own five-yard line and started around to his left. He then cut into the right to dodge a tackler and got loose with a clear field for a 95-yard run from the kickoff for a touchdown. Britton kicked the goal for the extra point, and the score was 7-0 in favor of the Illini in about one minute of play.
>
> Steger kicked off to Grange again, but this time he was brought down on his own 20-yard line. McIlwain made a couple of yards, and then Britton punted high to Michigan on the Illinois 36-yard line. Steger then executed a neat pass to Miller for nine yards, and Miller added two on a plunge for a first down on the Illinois 24-yard line. Steger made two through the middle of the line and then tried another pass, but it was grounded. Another plunge gained only a yard, and then a fake place kick was tried. But it was fumbled, and it was Illinois' ball on its own 33-yard line.
>
> McIlwain made a yard through the right side of the

line, and then the ball was given to Grange again, and once more he circled and dodged through the whole Michigan team for a 67-yard run for a touchdown. Britton again added a point by placekick, and the count was 14-0.

Steger kicked off over the goal line, and Illinois put the ball in play on its 20-yard line. Hall failed to gain, and Michigan was penalized five yards. McIlwain made a yard, and Grange made five, then Britton punted to Michigan's 20-yard line. Steger made two yards, and Rockwell punted to the Illinois 44-yard line. McIlwain failed to gain, so the ball was given to Grange again. He got loose and ran 56 yards for a touchdown. Britton failed to add a point with the kick, and the score was 20-0.

Steger kicked off over the goal line, and Illinois put the ball in play on the 20-yard line. Britton punted to Rockwell, who fumbled. Illinois recovered the ball on Michigan's 44-yard line. Grange was handed the ball and ran 44 yards for a touchdown. Britton added a point with a placekick, and the score was 27-0.

Steger kicked off to McIlwain, who returned to the Illinois 25-yard line. Grange was then taken out of the game, and Gallivan took his place. The rest of the quarter consisted of a few exchanges of punts, and when time was called, Michigan had the ball on its own 40-yard line. Score: ILLINOIS 27, MICHIGAN 0.

When Grange reached the bench after the stunning fourth touchdown, he told trainer Matt Bullock he was too tired to go on. Zuppke sent his understudy, Ray Gallivan, in to replace him.

Grange returned to the game in the third quarter and scored another touchdown on a 12-yard run. He passed for still another score. The final score was Illinois 39, Michigan 14.

Fans who were among the thousands of delirious onlookers that day have vivid memories of that performance.

"It seemed like everytime you looked out on the field that day, Grange was scoring a touchdown," remembers Gordon Bilderback of Champaign. "I couldn't believe it. It all happened so fast."

"I had to rub my eyes to believe it," the late Jerry Sholem,

a longtime Champaign-Urbana merchant and Illini fan, recalled not long before his death. "It was so thrilling, so sensational, it couldn't happen again in a thousand years."

"It stunned me, stunned the crowd, and especially stunned Michigan," said the late Raymond E. Dunn of Urbana. "His performance left everyone spellbound."

"I've never seen anything to approach that performance," said the late Harold M. Osborn, an Illini track star who competed in two Olympiads.

"Four girls fell over backward out of the temporary bleachers which had been set up on the south end of the stadium after Grange scored his final touchdown," Sholem also recalled. "Fortunately, they weren't sitting that high off the ground."

The most amazing thing about Grange, according to his friend C. E. Bowen, was "that he did everything he did weighing only 175 pounds."

Fifty years later when Grange thought back on that game, he commented: "I don't think I ever played in any other game where every man did exactly what he was supposed to do. In

Dedication game action (October 18, 1924): Red Grange starts for goal line against Michigan.

that first quarter, if a man was supposed to block the end, he blocked the end. If he was supposed to hit the tackle, he hit the tackle. I don't think any college team in the nation could have licked us on that day. Maybe on the Friday before or the Sunday afterward, they might have beat our brains in, but not on that one Saturday.

"Zup had worked on that game from the start of the summer. He started telling us all kinds of things Yost had been saying about us all summer. It wasn't until a long time afterward that I found out that Yost had been in Europe the whole summer. He had gotten us so riled up about Yost that we just couldn't lose. Everything was right for the game. Zup's brother only attended one game a year, and he'd never seen Illinois lose. He was there wearing the orange and blue tie which he kept in a safety deposit box except the one time a year when he wore it to an Illinois football game.

"I was surprised when they kicked the opening kickoff to me. It wasn't that I thought I was a big shot or anything, but we generally tried to kick it to a guard or tackle or someone like that. I guess Steger wanted to test me right out. I remember very well starting down the middle with the opening kickoff, and then we had a pileup around the 35 yard line. I ran into a lot of traffic, and all of a sudden I was in the clear. It seemed to be that way the rest of the first quarter.

"I just felt like I was a cog in a good machine. I always felt that way."

A 15-Game
Winning Streak

The Illinois-Michigan game of 1924 was the highlight of the season, but a 15-game Illinois winning streak came to an end later in the year in a 21-21 tie with Amos Alonzo Stagg's University of Chicago team. A week after the Chicago game, the Illini would be beaten 20-7 in Minneapolis by Minnesota in one of the major upsets of the Red Grange era at Illinois.

Grange looks back on that 1924 game against Chicago as "the toughest game I ever played in."

Some of the sport's most noted historians believe that Grange may have turned in his greatest all-around performance that afternoon. He ran for three touchdowns and had a fourth long run called back by a penalty. He accounted for 300 yards on runs and returns. And in the final minutes of the game he collapsed on the turf of Stagg Field in Chicago from sheer exhaustion as he waited for a play at defensive safety.

"Stagg had three fullbacks, and he kept interchanging them," Grange remembers. "They'd five and six-yard you to death. That's the way the best one of them got his name. They called Austin McCarty, 'Five Yards' McCarty. Stagg could run you down with those trap plays."

The score was tied 21-21 in the fourth quarter of the game, but an interception by Illinois' Chuck Kassel broke up a Chicago scoring threat and gave the Illini new life. The Illini took over on their own 10 yard line, and Grange promptly swept left end for 51 yards but the play was called back on a holding penalty. Instead of being on Chicago's 39 yard line with more than two minutes left, the Illini were pushed back deep into their own territory and the game ended in the tie.

The emotional drain of the Michigan game and the physical beating of the Chicago game took their toll on Grange and the Illini, and a week later Illinois was shocked by Minnesota as the Gophers dedicated their new stadium.

In a performance almost as notable as the one Grange had accomplished against Michigan, Minnesota's Clarence Schutte ran for all three Gopher scores. Grange was held to one from 10 yards away in the first quarter. Grange suffered an injured shoulder in the third quarter and went to the sidelines. Quarterback Harry Hall also was injured earlier.

According to accounts of the game Grange was returning a pass interception when he was knocked out of bounds by Herman Ascher's rolling block. But Grange did not think he was fully downed or out of bounds and stumbled to his feet and made a move as if to run again. Minnesota center Con Cooper hit Grange again—hard enough that Zuppke complained vehemently about unsportsmanlike conduct. According to the story Zuppke was upset enough about the incident that the Illini and Minnesota did not meet again for 17 years until Zuppke finally relented in 1941.

The loss to Minnesota cost the Illini the Big Ten championship, Chicago winning the title with the unusual record of three wins, no losses, and three ties. The Illini finished second with a 3-1-1 league record and 6-1-1 for the season, but the loss to Minnesota was a bitter pill for Zuppke to swallow. It was Minnesota's only Big Ten victory that season.

According to Charles Johnson, retired sports editor of the *Minneapolis Star* and *Tribune*, there was a tradition at Minnesota at the time that visiting teams would be postgame dinner guests of the Gophers and attend the theater together.

But Zuppke would have none of that tradition in 1924. "We are going nowhere," bellowed Zuppke.

Some of Illinois' top players from the 1924 team were missing in 1925 due to graduation, and quarterback Harry Hall's status was uncertain because of a collarbone injury he sustained in the upset loss to Minnesota. Standout players like Frank Rokusek, Gil Roberts, Heinie Schultz, and Wallie McIlwain had graduated.

Earl Britton was one of the returnees, but Zuppke felt impelled to move Britton into the line for a while to add experience there.

The game that this young Illini team began pointing for from the start of the season was against the University of Pennsylvania. But by the time Illinois reached the game against Penn it had won only once in four games and had barely beaten Butler 16-13. The Illini lost close ones to Nebraska 14-10 and Iowa 12-0 before Michigan nipped Illinois and Grange 3-0 in Ann Arbor. The Michigan loss was a particularly disappointing one for Grange because the Illini had gone scoreless just a year after his phenomenal game against the Wolverines in Champaign. For this game Zuppke also had named Grange as the "quarterback."

It meant that it would be Grange calling the signals. But it was the opposing quarterback, Benny Friedman, who starred. He kicked a 25-yard field goal in the second quarter to win it and was credited with an outstanding defensive performance, particularly in guarding against the loping runs of Grange.

One week later, however, the game Zuppke had been waiting for was at hand. The scene was Franklin Field in Philadelphia. Illinois was 1-3, Penn was 5-0 and had just beaten Chicago 7-0 the weekend before. The Illini were a decided underdog, but three trainloads of Illinois fans made the trip anyway.

The day arrived cold and rainy. The field was a quagmire. Penn fans had no doubt that if Grange could ever be stopped, he could be destroyed on a field of such slippery footing. They were wrong.

Before the game was five minutes old Grange had scored, romping 55 yards around end with his feet spewing water into the air as he ran. Soon afterward he was off again, this time gathering in a Penn punt and escaping for 55 yards to set up Britton's three-yard touchdown plunge. The Quakers scored two points when Britton was downed for a safety in his own end zone after his punt attempt was blocked, but the Illini went to their locker room at halftime with an 18-2 lead after Grange scored once late in the second quarter on a 12-yard ramble. Grange scored once again in the second half, and the stunned crowd of 65,000 walked out of the rain-swept stadium still rubbing their eyes in disbelief over the 24-2 Illinois ambush of the

East's top team. Grange finished with 363 yards gained in 36 carries, a performance that left the gaggle of Eastern sportswriters agog. Britton and halfback Pug Daugherity also had been brilliant.

Some tell the story about how Laurence Stallings, author of *What Price Glory?*, had been sent to the game to do a color story. He was so shocked by Grange's performance that day that he reportedly struggled for an hour at the typewriter, groping to find words to describe Grange's feats, and, finally—crestfallen—he tore up what he had written and exclaimed, "I can't write it. It's too big."

The cocky little bantam rooster of a writer, Damon Runyon, had no such hesitation, however. He wrote: "This man Red Grange of Illinois is three or four men and a horse rolled into one...He is Jack Dempsey, Babe Ruth, Al Jolson, Paavo Nurmi, and Man O' War. Put them all together, and they spell Grange."

Buoyed by the win over Penn, the Illini won their last three games of the season over Chicago 13-6, Wabash 27-13, and Ohio State 14-9, to finish 5-3 for the season. Grange was named to the All-American team for the third straight year.

A day later Grange and his new "manager," Champaign theater owner C.C. "Cash and Carry" Pyle met with George Halas in the Morrison Hotel and signed a contract to play for the Chicago Bears. Grange's college athletic career was over.

During his three-year career at Illinois Grange gained 3,637 yards running and 643 by passing. In those three years he played in 20 games. In only three of them did he gain less than 100 yards on the ground, including kick and punt returns. In only five games did he fail to score. But the statistics do not come close to telling the story of the magic of Grange's play.

Maybe Grantland Rice did in his often-quoted verse:
> There are two shapes now moving,
> Two ghosts that drift and glide,
> And which of them to tackle
> Each rival must decide.
> They shift with special swiftness,
> Across the swarded range.
> And one of them's a shadow,
> And one of them is Grange.

Red Grange and his famed "77" after his final college game.

Time Out: Red Grange

Red Grange's years of life have almost caught up with the famous No. 77 that he wore. But there is still some spring left in his once-swift step; his wit is still sharp and his mind vibrant with recollection, Even his hair is still tinged with the auburn that gave him his nickname.

There is an old proverb which says that "after the game, the king and pawn go into the same box," but there is still something somehow mystical that separates Grange from the others.

He is a living legend. And 50 years to the day after that legend was born (on October 18, 1924, when he ran for four touchdowns in 12 minutes against Michigan), he said, "I always felt it was my privilege to play football for Illinois."

The greatness of Grange was only exceeded by his modesty.

"I remember the first time I met Babe Ruth," said Grange. "We were playing in New York after I'd joined the Chicago Bears, and he came up to my room at the Astor Hotel to say hello. He told me, 'Kid, don't believe everything they write or say about you, and don't pick up too many checks.' I've gone along with his advice pretty well.

"Now that I'm older, though, I accept it when people say anything nice about me because I haven't heard much good said about anyone in the last few years."

Grange, however, learned even at the zenith of his football career not to expect his name to be a household word with everyone. He enjoys telling about the time he and Chicago Bears owner George Halas were invited to the White House to meet the president. Calvin Coolidge was the nation's chief executive at the time.

"Mr. President," said an aide. "I'd like to introduce you to Mr. Grange and Mr. Halas of the Chicago Bears."

"Wonderful," said Silent Cal. "I always did like animal acts."

It is one of Grange's favorite stories—perhaps again an indicator of the measure of the man.

Grange is still a smooth spinner of yarn, a talent doubtlessly nurtured by his experience as a television commentator after his playing days were over.

He is now "semi-retired," by his own definition, which means, according to Grange, "that if I get up in the morning and don't feel like doing anything, I don't." He lives in a rambling white home on Indian Acres Estates in Florida with his wife and two dogs. A well-kept golf course and a fishing boat on a lake are nearby. It is the kind of life you would expect a football legend to live at 70-odd years. Comfortable. Quiet. Even serene. And tanned by the warmth of the sun from the cloudless, blue skies.

Perhaps, he has had his fill of traveling because he does not often stray from that solitude now.

He remembers the days when he played eight games in eight different cities in 11 days in a barnstorming tour with the Bears not long after he left the Illinois campus.

"I think the game is much better today than it was when I played, because of the rule changes," he says in wistful remembrance. "In my day you had to be five yards behind the line of scrimmage to pass the ball, and once you got in closer than that their whole line was up to meet you.

"There was no such thing as bringing the ball into the hash marks when you got close to the sidelines, but I think I played in the game that brought that rule change about. It was the 1930s, and I was with the Bears. We were playing Portsmouth, which would eventually be the Detroit franchise, for the championship. But it had been very cold and snowy in Chicago, and I remember Halas decided that we'd have to play it in the indoor stadium in Chicago on Madison Street.

111

"They'd had a circus in there the week before, and they'd put about a foot of dirt...and some other stuff, too...on the floor. The field they set up was only 80 yards long; everytime we got inside the 20-yard line, they'd penalize us back to make up for the extra 20 yards. You never knew for sure half the time where you were.

"But the sidelines were within a foot of the wall, and they made a special rule that anytime the ball went close to the sidelines, they'd bring it back toward the center of the field. It was a third of the width of the field, as I recall. Anyway, it worked so well that the next year Halas proposed the rule for the National Football League, and it was approved.

"There were tough substitution rules in my day, too. If you came out of a game in one quarter, you couldn't go back in until the next quarter."

Grange recalls once when Bob Zuppke told his Illinois players before the game began, "The only man who comes out of this game today is a dead man."

Grange admits he wonders now why there were not more injuries with the equipment he and his teammates wore in those days.

"When you don't know any better, I suppose you don't think about it," said Grange. "And we had the best equipment there was. I guess 50 years from now they'll look back at the equipment players are wearing today and laugh at it. Our equipment weighed about three times as much as the present stuff. I look back at those old helmets, and I wonder how any of us came out without being groggy for the rest of our lives. Maybe we all are.

"Those old helmets were just leather and a sling for your head. The equipment in those days was just leather, felt and wool. That was your padding. Today they have the plastics and foam rubber. They're a lot lighter. You can move in them. They're pliable.

"Being able to handle the equipment was a big thing in those days. I remember once at Illinois, Doug Fessenden, who had won the 440 in the Big Ten in something like 43 seconds,

Red Grange in Memorial Stadium in 1974.

112

decided he was going to come out for football. Put a track suit on him, and he could beat any of us. But once they put a football suit on him, we had plenty of guys who could run away from him.

"I always felt I could run 100 yards as fast in a football suit as I could in a track suit. It helped some fellows and hurt others. I suppose it had something to do with the gait you had. I never thought trackmen made good football players because they always seemed to run out in front of themselves. The greatest backs I ever came in contact with were guys who spread their legs more and seemed to be in better balance."

How could the teams of the Red Grange era do against the players of today?

"They're much bigger than we were, of course," said Grange. "But I don't know if they're any faster. I really don't think so, as I remember the backfield we had at Illinois.

"Earl Britton won the Illinois Intercollegiate Meet in the 440 for two straight years. I ran the 100 in 9.8 in high school, although I never ran track in college. Wallie McIlwain was a sprinter in high school, and he could run under 10 flat. And our quarterback, Harry Hall, also had been a trackman. Britton and McIlwain were two of the greatest blockers who ever lived, and they could keep up with anyone.

"The players today might overpower us with their size, but I don't think they would out-gut us. They'd know they'd been in a football game.

"But another question you'd have to ask is: whose game are we going to play. Theirs? Or ours? Are they going to go in and play offense or defense, or are they going to go in and play both ways the way we used to? I'd like to see one of those gimpy-legged National Professional League quarterbacks playing defense. Hell, you'd score 100 points on them."

Grange is frequently asked which player he personally considers the best of all time, and he keeps coming up with the same answer: Bronko Nagurski, his onetime teammate on the Chicago Bears and an all-time great at the University of Minnesota.

"I've always contended that Bronk was the greatest football player I ever saw," said Grange in all sincerity. "There may have been better football players, but I've never come in

114

contact with them.

"A lot of people ask me how great Bronk really was and how he'd compare with the modern player. Well, the only way I can make any comparisons is like this: on offense he was equal to Larry Csonka and probably better because he was faster and just as big; and on defense, he probably was equal to Dick Butkus and Ray Nitschke in their prime. Put those two together, and you've got one helluva football player and a great guy to go with it.

"I've watched Bronk a hundred times go back to the huddle and pat the guys on the back who blocked for him. Bronk liked contact. A lot of football players like football but don't like contact. And there are a lot of guys who like contact that aren't football players. The only thing Bronk couldn't do was pass. He kept throwing me that end-over-end pass."

Grange admits that he may be somewhat prejudiced when it comes to talking about former teammates, the way coaches are prone to add to the accomplishments of the men who played for them.

"You know Ernest Hemingway played tackle for Zup at Oak Park High School, and Zup used to go to Cuba to visit him. Zup always used to tell me what a great tackle Hemingway was," Grange says with a smile. "One night, after I'd finished playing football, I sat down with Zup and had a couple of drinks with him, and I asked him again about Hemingway. I asked him if he was really that good. 'Naw, Red,' he said, 'he wasn't worth a damn as a tackle.' But he was quite a writer, I'll say that."

Zuppke, of course, holds a special niche in Grange's gallery of memorabilia.

"Zup had a great knack for handling kids," said Grange, looking back. "He could get 400 per cent out of any one of them. He was a step ahead of his time. I think the old-time coaches are the guys who really gave us football. Most of the ways you can run a football were worked out 50...75 years ago by some pretty smart guys.

"There are only so many holes you can run through. There are only 11 men. And there are only so many ways you can do it. Halas used to tell me he'd go back in a playbook that was 25 years old and get something, and people would say, 'Look at

115

that. There's something new.' Some day I expect to see the spinner come back. I asked Zup once in 1930 when they came out with the so-called new T-formation if he'd ever seen anything like it. 'Naw, Red,' he told me, 'not since Oak Park High School in 1913.'"

Grange has equally fond memories for C. C. "Cash and Carry" Pyle, the cornfield bon vivant who negotiated his contract with the Bears after his last game with Illinois.

"Charlie came to me one day and said, 'Red, how would you like to earn $100,000?' I told him, 'Charlie, I think you've got the wrong guy. I don't do anything like that.' But he told me he thought he could get me that kind of money for playing football, and darned if he didn't," Grange said with a laugh.

"Charlie was one of the world's great characters. He had a string of theaters, including the Virginia in Champaign, when I met him. He was the kind of guy who put on events at the six-day bicycle races just to hear his name over the loudspeaker.

"He was quite a promoter, quite a guy. He was 42 years old when I met him. He was a great dresser. He had a little moustache and always wore a derby and spats and carried a cane. He was married five times to three women, which should tell you a little bit about the kind of guy Charlie was. At that time Charlie lived in an apartment, and his wife lived in a house. He told her she could expect a call anytime he was coming over for a visit, and he expected the same courtesy from her.

"A lot of people thought Charlie cheated me later on, but any mistakes I made in any business ventures were of my own doing. I would have hated to have lived and not met Charlie Pyle."

Many people who have known the good fortune would have hated to have lived and not met Red Grange.

Two Losses-In Three Years

Unlike the professional game where fame can be more enduring, college football heroes are born, flash across the horizon, and are gone upon completion of eligibility.

In 1926 Bob Zuppke could only reflect on the feats of Red Grange. Some coaches might have buried their heads in the sand, but Zup's reaction was hardly ostrichlike. Instead he fashioned a solid team which compiled a 6-2 record, and a year later, in 1927, the Illini were unbeaten, won the conference title, and in some circles were regarded as national champions. Illinois was awarded the Rissman Trophy, a forerunner of the modern Knute Rockne award, one of the symbols of the country's No. 1 team at that time.

The Illini won back-to-back conference titles in 1927 and 1928, and, during the three-year span from 1927 through 1929, Illinois lost only two games, although there were two ties during the period.

The 1927 team was 7-0-1 overall, the lone pockmark a 12-12 nonconference tie with Iowa State. The 1928 team was 7-1, losing to Michigan 3-0 but still winning the league crown outright. And even though the Illini finished second to Purdue in the conference standings in 1929, they still were a creditable 6-1-1 for the season.

Illinois may not have had Grange in the last four years of the Roaring Twenties, but the fans sang anyway—to the tune of

117

Illinois' kicking star of the 1920s, Forrest "Frosty" Peters.
26 victories, four losses, and two ties.

The highlight of the 1926 season was another win over
Penn.

"As one of Zup's freshman coaches that year, one of my
duties was to scout Pennsylvania," Harry Gamage recalled.

"Pennsylvania was known that season for its 'hidden ball' attack. The fullback would take the ball, spin to the tailback and start backing to the line of scrimmage, and the wingbacks would come around and take it. From the time that back started spinning you never did see the ball. They all wore a leather elbow pad which looked just like part of a football, and was the same color as the pigskin. The backs would fake with their elbow up, and it looked like everyone was carrying the ball.

"I took the freshman team and taught them this hidden ball offense and ran all over the varsity in one practice. Zup raised holy hell to his varsity and started changing them all around. Finally, the last night of practice, he changed them to a 6-3-2 defense. Nobody had seen many of those at that time. But it did a lot better job of stopping us, and that's what he decided to use."

Gamage remembers that Zuppke was still muttering when

Frosty Peters' kick sails through the uprights to give Illinois a 3-0 victory over mighty Penn in 1926.

he came off the practice field that night, though, and threatened to use a white football in the game if Penn went on the field with the pigskin-appearing elbow pads.

Penn wore the pads, and Zup used no white football, but the Illini beat the Eastern power for the second straight year, this time 3-0 on Frosty Peters' dropkick.

In many ways the 1927 team was clearly one of Zuppke's favorites. It did not have Red, but it did have a Grange. Red's younger brother, Garland, was a starting end on the squad. While Red was a dazzling talent, Garland was simply a good, solid football player, and he was typical of the players on the 1927 Illini. Zuppke liked to refer to them as "the team of average men."

Virtually every man on the 1927 team started out as an unknown from the standpoint of national recognition, but by the time the season ended, two of the linemen, center Bob Reitsch and guard Russ Crane, would earn All-American laurels. The lightweight line also included Bill McClure, Ernie "Peanuts" Schultz, Lou Gordon, and future star Albert "Butch" Nowack (the only man in the starting unit who weighed over 200 pounds). The backfield also was pony-sized. Fred "Fritz" Humbert was the biggest man at a mere 166 pounds. Blair French and Doug Mills were just 148 pounds, and most of the others were not much heavier.

The Midwest sporting press was not terribly awed by the Illini team Zuppke prepared to put on the field in 1927. The scribes rated Illinois as the fifth best team in the West, picking Minnesota No. 1 and Ohio State No. 2.

Illinois won the opener from Bradley 19-0 and the next week prepared to take on Butler. There was more than passing concern about Illinois' chances in the second game, however, when it was learned that the Sigma Pi fraternity on the campus had been quarantined because of a scarlet fever epidemic. Humbert, Schultz, Eddie Winsper, Harry Richman, and Howard Ullman, among others who were members of the house, would not be allowed to play, but the fears were unwarranted. Illinois rolled past Butler 58-0. The next week Zuppke's team was tied by Iowa State 12-12.

It was a good thing that the quarantine was lifted in time for the conference opener with Northwestern. The Illini barely

Captain Butch Nowack, carrying the ball, leads Illinois onto the practice field in 1928.

managed a 7-6 win. Michigan and a tough Iowa team fell by identical 14-0 scores on consecutive weekends. By then Illinois was starting to be recognized as a potential title contender, and John Whitaker, the sports editor of the *Courier* at the time, wrote: "It may come to pass that the experts who assigned the Indians to sixth and seventh place in the blue book will visit the press quarters next Saturday afternoon so that they may type off retractions before the conference race has been decided and alibis are too late."

Illinois rolled over Chicago 15-6, and that left only the season-ending game against Ohio State for a clear title. The Buckeyes fell 13-0, Illinois wore the mantle of champion, and there was more than one Midwestern sportswriter with a touch of egg left on his face.

But while Illinois' championship of 1927 startled the Midwest, there was nothing surprising about the title in 1928.

Not long after the 1927 campaign ended, and Nowack was elected captain for the next year, the dance-hall bouncer from

Pana stood up at a banquet in the presence of his teammates and told them: "I want every man back early next fall. We want another championship."

Nowack, who played 233 minutes out of a possible 300 in five Big Ten games in 1927, would lead Illinois to that title in 1928.

Before that campaign began, however, Dixon Stewart of United Press issued a warning in his preseason article on Illinois.

He wrote:

Bob Zuppke's Illinois team will enter the 1928 Western Conference race with an entire team of members from "the starless squad" which won the 1927 championship.

The Illini chieftain faces a harder task than he did last year when he took a squad of unknowns and led them to the title. Last year the Illini attracted little attention until the season was well under way, and few rivals "pointed" for them. This year, with Illinois fighting to retain the championship, every one of the five conference opponents will be "keyed" to trip the champions.

On paper Illinois should be the strongest team in the conference. Fifteen of the 28 players who won varsity letters in 1927 being back in the fold. In addition, Frosty Peters, dropkicking star of 1926, will be trying for a berth after a year's absence.

Zuppke points out that fight, as well as playing ability, had a lot to do with the championship achievement of last season and that such aggressive players as Reitsch, Muegge, and Schulz will not be easily replaced.

French, Stewart, and D'Ambrosio, who bore the brunt of the backfield burden last season, graduated, but Zuppke has Stuessy, Mills, Timm and Humbert in case he desires to put an entire team of veterans in action.

Despite this kind of preseason pressure, Illinois again won the title.

Doug Mills, who was a regular in 1927, 1928, and 1929 and the man who eventually became head basketball coach as well as athletic director at Illinois, has fond memories of that era.

"Those teams all had great unity," Mills recalled on a peaceful spring day in 1975. "I think that was a mark of most good teams, though.

"We had fine players for our captains all three years. Bob Reitsch, in 1927, was a real battler. He was very fair of skin and blond, and I can remember when he came out of a game he was always black-and-blue. The bruises really showed up on him. They called him 'Fighting Bob.' He wasn't real big for a lineman, but he had a lot of fight in him.

"Butch Nowack was a great character, but he was one of those guys you couldn't help but love. Butch loved to chew tobacco, and when he'd get down on the line he'd squirt that tobacco juice all over the hands of the other team's lineman who had lined up across from him. They'd complain to the officials, and we got some unsportsmanlike conduct penalties because of it, but Butch loved to irritate the opponents.

Doug Mills as a player in 1927, '28, and '29 and later as the Illini athletic director.

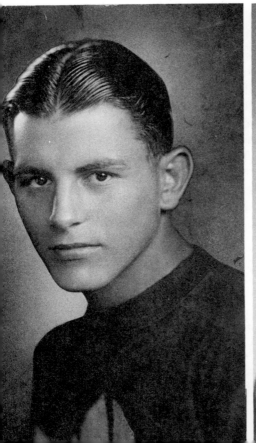

"But he was a great team man. I can remember many a time when I was at the bottom of a pileup, and I'd look up there, and there was Butch picking people up and throwing them off to get at the bottom of the pile and help me up. He protected the guys who played with him.

"Russ Crane was our captain in 1929, and he was another fine lineman who led by example."

The era of the late twenties was not marked by many of the fancy plays that made Zuppke famous.

"The team was so sound that I guess Zup didn't think we needed anything like that," said Mills. "All three of those teams could block and run, and we didn't have to pass much. We did a lot of running out of the double wing."

Mills believes that he might have run the first naked reverse by accident in the 1929 game against Iowa, however.

"It was the dedication game for their new stadium," Mills remembers now, "and the game was played in a snowstorm. Iowa had scored early in the game (Bill Glasgow escaped for a 78-yard touchdown run) to give Burt Ingwersen's team the lead. It was a little bit dry then, but 10 minutes later the field was a quagmire of snow and mud.

"Anyway, we were still scoreless when the third quarter got started, and I went to the fullback spot, and Jud Timm moved over to wingback. On one particular play I was supposed to get the ball, fake to the fullback who was playing wingback, and hand off to the other halfback. The guards pulled, just as they were supposed to, and went to the left, but the wingback didn't come around to take the ball. All of a sudden I was stuck with it. I saw the right end cut in, so I just put the ball under my arm and took off. I could have run 100 yards. There wasn't anybody within 30 yards of me.

"The funny thing was after the game. The reporters asked Zup about that play, and he said, 'We've been working on that play all year. We've just been waiting for the right spot to use it.' I happened to be coming out of the shower and heard him telling a reporter from Des Moines about it. He even had me believing that we'd practiced it all year after hearing him talk to all those reporters."

Zuppke showed no signs of mellowing from his strict code of hard practice work in the late 1920s either, Mills reflected.

"No, Zup was always a great one for scrimmage and contact," said Mills. "If you didn't hit during the week, you weren't going to be playing on Saturday. If you had anything left, you were in shape to play. But I never saw Zup abuse a player, though. If you had an injury, he'd pull you out of contact and protect you.

"Zup had a way of getting to you if he wanted to get you going. I remember one time when he got after a big tackle by the name of Lloyd Burdick. We were getting ready for a game with Chicago, and Zup liked nothing better than to beat Amos Alonzo Stagg. He kept telling Burdick that he was going to have to get tougher if we were going to beat Chicago.

Leroy Wietz was an All-American lineman for Illinois in 1928.

"'If you keep playing like this, Burdick, you'll go through life this way,' Zup told him. 'You'll marry some little gal, and she's going to hen-peck you, and then you're going to die and go to heaven and have to play for Stagg.' Zup broke the tension with that remark, and Burdick played well the rest of the week."

Mills remembers one time in particular when Zuppke was giving him a rough time. It was in 1929 when Mills had been moved to quarterback due to an injury to Peters:

"The last thing I wanted to do was play quarterback because I know how tough Zup always was on his quarterbacks. He was really on me, and I was ready to quit that night when I came off the field. I reminded Zup that night that I didn't ask to play quarterback. 'All right, Mills,' he said. 'Let me give you a ride home.' I really didn't know what was going to happen to me once he got me in that electric car he drove in those days, but he talked to me like a father. He said he'd asked me to play quarterback because I was the only man on the team he felt could do it. He had a way of getting to you in a fatherly way when that's what he wanted to do."

Mills got the feeling that night that Zuppke, his coaching personality submerged, really liked him as a person.

Mills would have more proof several years later when Zuppke brought him back to Illinois as one of his assistant coaches, setting the stage for the day when Illinois' entire athletic program would be under Mills' direction.

126

Time Out: Bob Reitsch

It has been almost 50 years since Bob Reitsch earned All-American honors at Illinois as a center and team captain in 1927. But he still remembers those days as though they were a fortnight ago.

Most of all, he remembers his coach, Bob Zuppke.

"You couldn't help but feel the man's leadership, drive, and zeal to put the best possible team on the field," Reitsch recalled recently in his vacation home in Borrego Springs, California.

"I remember the thing he used to say the most, 'You represent The Fighting Illini...give the best you have.'"

Reitsch remembers that Zuppke "was a great one for giving people different names."

"He used to call me 'Reach' because he thought it was more musical," Reitsch says with a laugh. "He called (Arthur) D'Ambrosio 'The Bullfighter.' I remember once he saw Bubbles Mitterwallner walking to practice, and he walked right through a big puddle, and Zup said, 'There's the "Deep Sea Beast."'" There was another fellow he called 'Step And A Half' and another he called 'Two Nickels.' I think he did it to relax you... to make you feel like you were one of his family."

The thing at which Zuppke was best, according to Reitsch, was "his great ability to recognize talent and then put it together and mold it into a team."

Reitsch remembers getting word in January of 1927 that Zuppke wanted to see him at Huff Gymnasium.

Bob Reitsch in 1927.

"Well, I went out there, and Zup was walking up and down in the hall," said Reitsch. "He kept on pacing and talking, and I remember he said to me, 'We're going to have a real football team next year, but nobody knows it yet. We have a lot of juicy freshmen. I want you to make sure everyone is out for spring practice.' And what a spring practice we had. Zuppke and his assistants really worked us hard.

"We had a lot of guys in 1927 who really wanted to play the game. I remember one fellow named Blair French from Murphysboro. He was so small that they didn't have a uniform to fit him when he came in as a freshman. But he wanted to play so badly, he rounded up the uniform he wore in high school and wore it to practice at Illinois until they could get him one that fit. He wasn't big, but he could really block. He gave me the hardest block I ever had when I was playing at Illinois. That's the kind of fellows we had that season.

"And Zuppke's prediction about the 1927 season came true. We won the Big Ten championship."

Zuppke had his own way of getting a point across to his players, Reitsch remembers. Once, in Reitsch's junior year in 1926, the team was feeling the absence of Red Grange's leadership following his departure after the 1925 season.

"All of us smart linemen were trying to tell the backs what play we thought would work and so forth," Reitsch says and laughs. "Zuppke started telling us a story about how the Mexican armies fought among themselves because they didn't have enough to eat.

"Anyway, Zuppke brought out a pouch and told each of us linemen to take a bite of what was in it. It was spinach! And then Zup said, 'Now I want you linemen to keep your mouths shut and let the quarterbacks call the plays.'"

The game that Reitsch remembers the most was the Grange-engineered upset of mighty Pennsylvania in 1925, Reitsch's sophomore season and his first year as a regular in the line.

Reitsch remembers: "We left Illinois on a Thursday and arrived in Philadelphia on a Friday noon. It had been raining and snowing all the time. I remember us going out to the Penn Stadium, and there were nothing but lakes all over it, so they took us over to a country club. It was a beautiful place near

Philadelphia, and we worked out there.

"Zuppke finally let the rest of the squad go, but he told Grange, (Earl) Britton, and myself to stay and practice punting and kicking. Britton, in the meantime, had rolled up a great big snowball, and just as he threw the snowball at Matt Bullock, our trainer, Zuppke walked up. 'What are you doing here?' Zup roared. 'Why are you doing this sort of stuff when we're playing Pennsylvania tomorrow? Let's get serious, Illinois.'

"That evening was something else, too. We hadn't even any more than sat down to eat when the waiters were bringing in big platters of buttered toast. The butter was just dripping off of it.

"Zuppke stood up and said, 'What is that?' He told us that was what Chicago had eaten last week before they were beaten by Penn.

"'They turned out to be a bunch of sow-bellies,' Zuppke said. 'Take it right back now and bring us dry toast because we're going to beat Pennsylvania tomorrow.'

"I remember the next morning. There was this group of black cars coming up the road to pick us up to take us to the game. I remember Zup saying, 'Those look like funeral directors' cars. Where are the cabs?'

"We couldn't find any cabs, and we had to ride to the stadium in those black cars, even though Zuppke didn't like it one bit."

Reitsch also has memories of that immortal upset of Penn.

He recalls: "Zup gave us a fired-up talk before the game, and just about the time we were ready to go out on the field the Penn coach came by our dressing room and said that the Illinois band still hadn't arrived yet and that they'd like to hold up the game until they got there. I remember Zup said, 'But my team is ready to play now.' The Penn coach said okay, they'd go ahead. And soon afterward we could hear the Illinois band coming up, off in the distance. Now we were really ready. We could hardly wait to get out there.

"Zup told us before we went on the field that Grange was not to have the ball for the first five minutes. We worked the ball back and forth until we got it in just the right position, and Grange ran left end for the touchdown.

"When that happened, we got fired up like we'd never been fired up before. It sure was a lot of fun riding back to

130

Champaign on the train, and what a treat it was to see about 5,000 people waiting to meet us at the station that Sunday evening."

And on a day in midwinter of 1975 in Borrego Springs, a thousand miles from Memorial Stadium, the Illini Marching Band played a fight song again...on the phonograph.

Daring Young Men
On A Flying Trapeze

"The 'Flying Trapeze' was a method of play, a philosophy, more than it was one particular maneuver," said Jack Beynon, thinking back.

It was 1934, and the nation was saddled with the Great Depression. Illinois' football fortunes had crashed along with the stock market in the early 1930s.

The Illini fell to 2-6-1 in 1931 and were winless in seven conference games. Fortunes improved slightly in 1932 with a 5-4 overall mark, although the Illini still had a losing record in the league at 2-4.

But in 1934 Illinois would have a football team that would uplift the mental spirit of those whose lives were burdened with constantly gloomy news from Wall Street.

The revival actually began in 1933 when Illinois posted a 5-3 record and 3-2 mark in the league, a season when the Illini lost a pair of 7-6 games to Michigan and Ohio State.

It would reach full flower the following year with a team that probably played the most dazzling, devil-may-care football of any team in Bob Zuppke's long career as head coach—and, perhaps, in Illini football history.

They would become known as the daring young men on Zuppke's "Flying Trapeze."

"There was the one play that was named the 'Flying Trapeze,' but just about everything we did that year was based on the principle of laterals, reverses, and so forth that all went together in the 'Flying Trapeze,'" recalled Beynon, the star

132

quarterback of the day and the man who directed it on the field.

It was an outgrowth of the old Zuppke, Oak Park, flea-flicker play that revolved around a pass to an end, who would flip the ball laterally to a halfback swinging wide around end.

"The play was based on the idea of multiple handling of the ball, and I think it was Zuppke who gave it the name, saying something about its success relating to the opponents' spending all their time watching the men on the flying trapeze," said Beynon, now a judge in the 17th Circuit Court in Rockford. "Zup had three basketball players in the backfield—Les Lindberg, Frank Froschauer, and myself—and we all could handle the ball."

It was in the third game of the 1934 season, after opening wins over Bradley and Washington of St. Louis, that the play achieved national fame. The Buckeyes of Ohio State were the rivals, and the Illini were rated an underdog.

The "Flying Trapeze" play produced the winning touchdown for Illinois in a heart-thumping 14-13 victory.

Illinois put the ball in play on the Buckeye 36 yard line, and the Illini circus began:

—Fullback John Theodore took the ball on a direct snap from center Elvin Sayre and faked a plunge into the line.

—Just before he reached the line of scrimmage, Theodore tossed a short lateral to co-captain Chuck Bennis, a guard who had suddenly emerged from the line after throwing a quick block.

—Bennis dropped back and fired another lateral to Lindberg, who quickly ran to the right, then whirled and shot a 25-yard cross field lateral to Beynon, a superb passer.

—Beynon, who had gone into the Ohio State secondary as if he were a possible receiver, had backtracked to the Illini side of the line of scrimmage and took the lateral from Lindberg.

—Beynon looped a rainbow pass into the waiting hands of Gene Dykstra, all alone in the end zone, for a 36-yard touchdown catch.

"The play carried perfect timing, deception, and execution," said Bennie Oosterbaan, who was the Michigan assistant coach who scouted the game for the Wolverines that day.

A variation of that Flying Trapeze play would haunt

133

Bob Zuppke (center) poses with the co-captains of his famed "Flying Trapeze" team: Chuck Bennis, left, and quarterback Jack Beynon. They brought life to Illini fans burdened by the gloomy news on Wall Street.

Michigan the following weekend.

Theodore took the snap, lateraled to Lindberg, who, in turn, passed the ball to halfback Crain Portman. Instead of lateraling to Beynon, Portman only bluffed one and ran over left end, picking up 27 yards to the Michigan 14 yard line.

Theodore eventually scored on the drive, ramming goalward from the one foot line for a score that was hotly protested by the Michigan captain Gerald Ford, who questioned that Theodore had actually crossed the line. The Michigan captain of that year is the same Gerald Ford who became President Ford. But Ford's political persuasiveness fell on deaf ears that day, and the Illini touchdown stood. The extra point that followed produced a 7-6 Illini victory.

Two weeks later against Northwestern the Illini would continue all the apparent razzle-dazzle in the backfield, but Theodore would keep the ball and ramble at will up the middle while the shocked Wildcats stood around and waited for the circus to start. The Illini emerged with a 14-3 win.

"We used the 'Flying Trapeze' method so much in practice that we really didn't think too much about it," said Beynon. "As I recall, the week before the Ohio State game Ted Husing had come into town to announce the game for one of the networks, and Zup told me to go out for dinner with him and tell him anything he wanted to know about our offense.

"Nobody thought we had a chance to beat Ohio State, and I think Husing was taking us as lightly as everyone else. I remember him asking me, 'Got any complicated plays?'

"'Well, we toss the ball around a little bit, but nothing too complicated,' I told him.

"But I guess that Flying Trapeze play in that game really surprised him. People tell me he never did get it described just exactly right and finally just said, 'Well, Illinois definitely scored.' I remember he came back later in the year, and Zup told me to go out for dinner with him again. This time, as soon as we sat down at the table, he said, 'Okay, Beynon, draw me a diagram of every play where more than two people touch the ball.'

"I always felt another interesting thing we did in the 1934 season was try a free kick after a fair catch. I remember the first time I did it, I walked over to the ref and said I wanted the free kick. The ref said there was no such thing. Bill Knight was the umpire, and he said, 'I think he's right. You'd better check the rule book.' And I was right, and we used the free kick once in a while that year."

Zuppke had considerable confidence in the mental capacity of the 1934 team and, for that reason, had a highly diverse offense.

"In 1934 Zup devised a system that allowed everyone to do basically the same thing, no matter what formation we were in," said Beynon. "We'd be in the single wing one week, the double wing the next, the short punt the week after, and the Notre Dame box the next, and he devised it in such a way that the only people it confused were the people who scouted us. It

135

wasn't complex to us because we numbered the plays the same way, regardless of the formation, and it was just a matter of being in a different spot when we set up. It provided us with complete flexibility."

By the time the Illini arrived for their seventh game of the season they boasted a perfect 6-0 record. But that team had one glaring weakness—a lack of depth—and it was exposed against Wisconsin.

"Yes," Beynon remembers, "we were thin. We played both ways, and all of us played just about the entire game. There were 300 minutes to be played in our five league games, and I think I played in 297.

"By the time we got to Wisconsin we were mentally and physically exhausted. I remember Zup and I used to talk over the game plan the Friday before we played on Saturday, and we stopped in Freeport to stay the night on the way to Madison. I remember that night Zup came to my room, and he started talking.

"He said he felt we were really beat up physically, and he didn't know whether he could get us up the next day. I said I knew we'd just had the worst week of practice we'd ever had and that we were all tired and bruised. When he left that night, I still didn't know what he would do.

"I found out the next day in the locker room that he'd decided to take a gamble. Everyone was dressed, and Zup still hadn't come in. Everyone's knuckles were turning white. And then, just before we were to go on the field, somebody threw the door open, and there was Zup standing outside laughing and joking. He stuck his head in the door and said, 'Well, if you guys can't beat this team, there's nothing I can say to help you.' I'd never seen him more relaxed. Unfortunately, that's the way we played. We were too relaxed, and we really didn't get going until too late in the game."

Wisconsin beat the Illini 7-3 on a second quarter touchdown. Lindberg dropped back as if to punt, then looked to pass. He was hit by three Badgers just as his arm jerked forward, and the ball popped into the arms of Wisconsin defender Al Mahnke who ran 22 yards untouched for the game's only score.

The Illini rapped Chicago 6-0 in the final game of the year to finish with a 7-1 record, but the loss to Wisconsin cost the

Illini a share of the championship. Minnesota claimed the title with a 5-0 mark, with Ohio State finishing percentage points above the Illini for second place. Minnesota had a 5-1 league mark compared to Illinois' 4-1 Big Ten finish.

But in those days things could have been a lot worse. You could have been in the soup line. Any job at all was a good one.

Chuck Galbreath, a tackle on that team, remembers digging dandelions out of the sod at Memorial Stadium for three hours one day just to earn a dollar.

According to Galbreath, the stadium grounds keeper, Ben Crackel "came around and raised the devil because we weren't picking them fast enough—all we had was a knife and a bucket."

But even though the Illini fell short of the title, it had been a fun year for Zuppke, his players, and the Illini fans.

The two cocaptains, Bennis and Beynon, had made their mark, especially with Zuppke.

"Bennis was bow-legged, and I was knock-kneed," Beynon says and laughs now. "Zup always said that we were the only captains he ever had who ran out on the field with our bodies spelling 'Ox.'"

Time Out: John Theodore

John Theodore, the friendly postmaster of Urbana for many years, likes to kid about his recent "presidential pardon."

Not long after Gerald Ford assumed the presidency Theodore wrote him a letter recalling the game his Illinois team played against Ford's Michigan team in 1934.

Illinois won the game 7-6 on a touchdown that officials ruled Theodore had scored from the three yard line. Michigan players, including Ford, heatedly protested the official's call, complaining that Theodore had not quite made it across the goal line, but the referee's decision stood.

"I had always felt guilty about the game because I knew at the time that I hadn't really scored," said Theodore. "One night I had some friends in after a football game, and I told them I played against Ford and I mentioned that particular game. They suggested that I write him a letter, and I said, 'You know what, I think I will.' And I did, and I admitted to him that I hadn't really scored on that touchdown that won the game for us.

"I got a nice letter a month or so later from the president, and he said, 'If you have felt "guilty about the incident" in the past, I don't think you need to in the future.' I guess that could be interpreted as a pardon, couldn't it?"

Theodore has some other flavorful memories of that play in the 1934 Michigan game.

He recalls: "We had a first and ten at the three yard line, but by fourth down we were still a couple of feet away. I took the snap, and I could tell I was a least a foot short, and we had a

John Theodore...
remembrances of
"Flying Trapeze" days.

tackle named (Chuck) Galbreath who was over the line and he kept yelling for me to fumble the ball to him. Just about that time they signaled a touchdown."

When the players unpiled, Galbreath had the ball, but the TD was credited to Theodore.

"I remember some of the fellows on our bench coming up to me and saying: '...But you didn't score, did you?' Zuppke didn't ask me about it, but I remember the next week at practice him telling me that when I got down on the goal line, I was going to have to run harder than I did against Michigan. Zup must have known," said Theodore.

Theodore still treasures his own personal memories of Zuppke, the way he does his personal letter from the president. "I learned some valuable lessons from Zuppke. A lot of people thought he was pretty hard-nosed. He could make you mad, but he was a very kind and considerate person, too. I remember one of the fellows on our team really hated him because he felt Zup never gave him a chance. Later, though, Zuppke wrote one of the nicest letters of recommendation anyone could have asked for the young man when he wanted to go to officer's training school. The other thing I remember most about him was that he didn't take excuses for anything. I think it made you try and work a lot harder that way than if you were playing for someone who was a lot more lenient."

Theodore, as the Illini fullback in 1934 and 1935, was a key figure in "The Flying Trapeze."

"Maybe some of those fancy plays wouldn't work nowdays," smiles Theodore, "but they sure worked well at the time. I remember we had one simple play where the ball came to the fullback, and then the fullback turned with his back to the line. Then he'd either hand off or keep it himself. Once I was very slow in completing the play. I thought Zup would really jump on me, but he said, 'It looks like we might be able to make that a play. We'll hold it for a three-count delay and then complete it.' Can you imagine doing that with the kinds of line rushes they have nowadays. The next thing you'd hear would be someone say, 'The funeral arrangements are incomplete.'"

Theodore takes special pride in the fact that the 1934 team beat Ohio State as well as Michigan on consecutive Saturdays. He came very close, however, to not even seeing the Ohio State game that year—much less playing in it.

"Before the Ohio State game that year they gave all the players passes to get into the game," Theodore recalls. "Zup told me the night before that I was going to start my first game, and I was really excited...so excited that I'd forgotten to bring my pass to the game the next day. I went to the gate anyway, and I knew the man who was there and he was going to let me in without the pass. But George Huff happened to be right behind me, and he told the man on the gate I wasn't going in without a pass. The team manager came along and saw what the situation was and said, 'I'll run down and get a note from Zuppke.' But G. Huff said no, 'He's going to have to go home and get his pass.' Fortunately for me it was Boy Scout Day, and they let the scouts in free if they were in uniform, so I disguised myself as a scout leader and slipped into the stadium that way.

"I'll always remember G. Huff for how firm he was about rules. To him, a rule was a rule. If it was a rule, you didn't break it. It was a good lesson to learn in life. Even now I'd hesitate about parking in a 'No Parking' zone even if I knew I was only going to be there a minute."

The Illini finished with a 7-1 record in 1934, and Theodore remembers, "The only game we were supposed to win that year was the Wisconsin game, and, as it wound up, that was the only game we lost."

The Illini were only 3-5 the following year, but they did beat Southern California in Los Angeles 19-0. And the trip itself was a big thrill for Theodore.

"We traveled by train in those days, and it seemed like it took us a week to get there. We had one car for our equipment, so we could have a little exercise, and we had our own dining car," Theodore recalls. "I remember Zup told us that we could order anything we wanted to eat on the trip back. I'd never had shrimp before, so that's what I ordered. I took one look at the shrimp and said, 'These are crawdads.' We used to go down by the river when I grew up in Spring Valley and catch them by the tubful. But I ate them and liked them...still do."

Theodore was injured prior to his senior season and did not get to play again for the Illini, but Illinois football was good to him.

He learned lessons from teachers like Zuppke and G. Huff and, 40 years later, in a letter from the president, he learned another: confession—even about a touchdown he did not score—is good for the soul.

Even if the statute of limitations had run out on that football game in 1934, Theodore still likes to show friends his "pardon from the president."

Zuppke's Last Hurrah

Illinois fell back into the football doldrums after its flirtation with greatness in 1934.

A slight resurgence brought a 4-3-1 mark in 1936, but the Illini still were just .500 in the Big Ten at 2-2-1. The 1937 team slipped to 3-3-2, and the 1938 team tumbled to 3-5.

The alumni were growing restless, and after the 1938 season, a move began to seek Zuppke's retirement as coach. George Huff had died in 1936 at the age of 64 and had been replaced as athletic director by Wendell "Weenie" Wilson who had played under Zuppke and coached briefly under him.

In the face of this rising pressure for his resignation at the age of 62, Zuppke was offered a deal. He would be paid $6,000 a year in retirement income until he reached 65 years of age and $4,000 each year afterward.

Grudgingly, Zuppke accepted the offer and prepared his resignation for the board of trustees, which met on November 29, 1938.

One of the members of the board of trustees at that time was Harold Pogue, the same man who had starred for Zuppke on his 1914 national championship team and who had gone on to establish himself as a prominent Decatur businessman, as well as a powerful voice in Democratic politics in the state.

When the subject of Zuppke's resignation came before the board that day, varied recollections indicate that an alarmed Pogue immediately requested a recess. He went to the nearest telephone and quickly reached Zuppke, who was at home in his apartment on West University Avenue in Champaign. Pogue asked Zuppke if this was really what he wanted to do.

No, said Zuppke, he wanted to coach at Illinois until he reached the age of 65.

In his later years and right up until the time of his death in 1969, Pogue declined to shed much light on just what took place behind the closed doors of that board meeting when he returned.

The belief is, however, that Pogue launched into a speech in behalf of Zuppke that would have rivaled any of the little Dutchman's own great locker room oratory.

In any case the board rejected the resignation that Zuppke had offered under pressure. Pogue's motion to that effect carried by what has been reported as an 8 to 1 margin.

The next season Zuppke would give Illinois fans a game that will live forever in Illini history as one of the greatest of all time. This aging, coaching warrior would have his last hurrah, his last big blockbuster of an upset, with an incredible 16-7 triumph over Michigan and Tom Harmon in 1939.

"No one but Bob Zuppke could have done it," wrote John Dietrich in the *Cleveland Plain Dealer*. "No one but Zuppke could reach into the hearts of his players and light the flame of emotion that sends them into a football game as into a crusade. Only a Zuppke could have taken a thrice-beaten Illinois team, its armament looking no more formidable than a tin sword and a pop gun, and with it have felled mighty Michigan."

Harmon, on his way toward eventually capturing the Heisman Trophy, was being boomed by Michigan fans and that state's sporting press as a better runner than Grange. Harmon, they intimated, would do to Illinois what Grange had done to Michigan 24 years before.

Zuppke jumped on their confidence with both feet. The master of football psychology stepped before his squad that week and, according to reports, firmly demanded, "Are you going to let this upstart Harmon show up our own Red Grange?"

This time more than one writer saw a potential Zuppke-designed upset in the making. Steve Snider of United Press echoed the less public feelings of others when he wrote: "Until the Illini began to object to the comparison between Harmon and Grange, this Michigan-Illinois game was just a routine game for Michigan's undefeated Big Ten leaders. The Wolves figured under ordinary circumstances as three touchdowns superior. Regardless of the lack of material, however, Bob Zuppke usually manages to swing an upset a season, and this may be it."

There was a sign early in the game that Zuppke's hope was not hollow. By the time the first quarter ended, Harmon's best blocker, Forest Evashevski (later the coach at Iowa), was injured and had to be carried off the field on a stretcher. During that first quarter Illinois had failed to score but had twice been in field goal range, although both of Mel Brewer's boots had gone awry. Soon after the second quarter began, however, Brewer guided a three pointer through the uprights from the 31 yard line, producing a 3-0 Illini edge. Once the ice was broken, Michigan retaliated on a 41-yard touchdown pass to Harmon from Dave Strong.

At that point it seemed only a matter of time before Michigan would go into its high-scoring act and the Illini would be buried under an avalanche of Wolverine touchdowns.

But Zuppke reached down deep in his arsenal of the unexpected before the first half ended. He picked one of the oldest cons in the football playbook, the "sleeper" pass play. Fullback George Rettinger did not go to the huddle and was nonchalantly picking at the grass on the sidelines when the rest of his teammates went to the huddle.

But once the play went into motion Rettinger was streaking down the sidelines. Jimmy Smith's needle-threading pass caught him at full gait, and Rettinger was on a 48-yard roller coaster into the end zone. The first half ended with Illinois ahead 9-7.

Before the third quarter ended, with Michigan having trouble moving the ball even with Harmon running and passing, the Illini capitalized on a golden opportunity. Fli Anders recovered a Wolverine fumble on the Michigan 34. With Smith and Don Elting leading the charge, Illinois drilled the ball to a fourth down on the Michigan three yard line. A stir swept through the crowd, the feeling welling in the throng in Memorial Stadium that it was now or never for the inspired Illini.

Zuppke, who had stung Michigan with the old "sleeper" play in the first half, went back to more trickery in the crucial situation, using a quick-count play call. When Ralph Ehni got into a set position, he called out "Check." Bob O'Neill, All-American Jim Reeder, Mel Brewer, Wesley Martin, Tom Riggs, and Paul Milosevich all made a move as if to stand up from their line positions, but at just that instant center Bill Lenich whipped the ball back to Smith, who charged headlong past the befuddled Wolverines into the end zone. Rettinger kicked the extra point, and the gutty Illini held on to that 16-7 lead until time ran out.

"I guess that was probably the best game I ever played for Illinois. It and the Ohio State game my last year were the best," recalls Jimmy Smith, who passed for one score and ran for another that day.

Smith, who now owns and operates a hardware store in Anna (in southern Illinois), remembers how, as a sophomore, he held his breath in the first half watching his touchdown pass sail toward Rettinger.

"Harmon came within a foot of intercepting the ball," Smith says now. "I always felt he was playing 'cat' on that play and didn't have it timed just right. It was so close that I'd already started moving in the direction I thought Harmon would be.

"We tore three jerseys off Harmon that day, though, and I don't think anyone could have beaten us the way we played.

"We went out on the field that day determined to prove to ourselves and to Michigan that we could beat them.

"I think we really had dedicated ourselves the night before. We spent the night at the Champaign Country Club, and normally when you'd have that many guys together there'd be some horseplay, but there wasn't any that night.

"Mel Brewer was our captain that year, and his mother had passed away earlier in the week and he'd missed the entire week of practice, but he came back that night to be ready to play the next day.

"That night there was no talking, no horseplay, no nothing. It seemed like a kind of grim determination came over us all. I think this prevailed right up until we stepped on the field."

Chicago Daily News sports editor John Carmichael was at the Army-Notre Dame game in New York that day, but he

145

reported the reaction in the Irish dressing room from coaches Elmer Layden and Joe Boland.

Carmichael wrote: "Boland broke the strained silence, his whisper awe-inspiring. 'Illinois leading?' he asked himself. 'Wouldn't it be something for the old man to put this one over? Boy, oh boy. He's in the weeds, all right, and when he lays for you, he'll beat you 90 percent of the time.' Layden's lips eased out of a straight line, 'One more touchdown, and he's got 'em. Isn't there something grand about a man like him beating his way back like this?'"

To use a favorite expression of the longtime Madison, Wisconsin, sportswriter Roundy Coughlin, "What could have been more fairer?"

When the final gun had sounded, the crowd streamed down onto the field. A photographer took a picture of the panorama with the scoreboard still flashing the final score in the background.

The Illini sports publicity office took that picture and turned it into a Christmas card from the Illinois athletic family for the following holiday. Inside was the message which said: "May your Christmas and New Year be as merry and happy as all Illini were on Nov. 4, 1939."

It was clearly the high point of a 3-4-1 Illinois season and gave Zuppke one last opportunity to thumb his nose at the critics who had come within an eyelash of forcing him into retirement before he was ready.

It was a matter of Zuppke proving firmly—irrevocably—that he was one of the master strategists, tacticians, and psychologists the game has ever known.

But the times were changing more dramatically than ever in the late 1930s. Zuppke, the believer in pure amateurism, was falling further and further behind his rivals in the raw talent which his teams had to offer. Recruiting was becoming the key to the game now, and Zuppke steadfastly refused to involve himself in the wooing of the high school stars.

His 1940 team won only one game in eight, beating Bradley 31-0 in the season opener. The 1941 squad won twice, from Miami of Ohio and Drake, in eight games. In Zuppke's last two seasons the Illini were winless in Big Ten play.

Wilson took a leave of absence as athletic director in 1940

and decided in 1941 not to return to the post, choosing instead to devote full time to his business interests in the Southwest.

Doug Mills was named athletic director in 1941 after a year as acting director. After the 1941 season Zuppke went to him and told him he was ready to step out as coach.

This time Zuppke's resignation was accepted by the board of trustees, and a colorful coaching era went into retirement with him.

Bob Zuppke: the legend still lives.

Bob Zuppke: An Epitaph

The legacy Bob Zuppke left to football is so varied that it is not easy to catalogue.

Fred Young, the retired sports editor of the *Bloomington Pantagraph* and a long-time Big Ten football official, was asked not long ago what he remembers best about the man who died in 1957 at the age of 78.

"His honesty," Young answers quickly. "That was the thing that stood out about Zup as well as George Huff."

Young is 82 years old now, but he still writes a column frequently in the *Pantagraph*. He and Zuppke were great friends through the years, and Young treasures the memories of that relationship now.

"I can remember one time I was working a game at Eureka, and the field had a bad lighting system, and I got my knee torn up," said Young. "I hadn't any more than gotten off the operating table when I got a call from Zup asking me how I was doing."

Young was able to look at Zuppke from two perspectives: as a sportswriter and as an official who worked the games Zuppke's teams played. He saw the same man under each hat: Zuppke was a gentleman.

"I recall once when I worked one of Zup's games with Indiana, and I had a real tough pass interference call and it went against Zup's team," said Young. "The next weekend I had a game at Illinois, and Zup never even mentioned that call when I saw him before the game.

"In fact, I can't remember a time when Zup ever questioned a call I made. In those days, the officials dressed in the same room that the coaches did, and he would have had plenty of chances to complain had he ever wanted to, but I never once heard him attack an official."

A characteristic that Young remembers is that of Zuppke as both a practical joker and the object of more than one prank himself.

"He always liked to kid (Knute) Rockne of Notre Dame whenever he had the chance. Zup and Pop Warner also were great friends," said Young, "and I can remember once Zup telling me about the time he and Pop were sharing a room at a coaching clinic out in the Susquehanna Valley of Pennsylvania. Zup kept telling Pop how his feet were hurting, and Pop kept telling him how everyone's feet always hurt in the Valley because they weren't used to walking up and down the inclines. That night when Zup got back to their room and took off his shoes he was furious. He took his shoes off and found the toes stuffed with paper. Pop had put the paper in there as a joke on Zup."

Zuppke's young assistants also had a favorite trick they liked to play on the old master and his veteran aide, Justa Lindgren. When Zuppke and Lindgren were not watching, one of the young aides would switch the ties in their lockers. Paying no attention, they would put them on, tie them, and be on their way. The next day the ritual would be reversed, and neither would be the wiser.

The electric car that Zuppke drove at one time made him now and then the butt of a joke of his own making. Zuppke would be driving through the campus, stop the car, get out, and begin talking to someone. When the conversation ended, he would walk off on his merry way, leaving the car wherever it had been parked. Zuppke frequently had to retrace his steps several hours later to locate the "abandoned" auto.

"One thing that few people probably remember about Zup was how much he liked to dance," said Young. "He wasn't much for society, but he did enjoy going someplace where he could dance with his first wife, Fanny."

The first Mrs. Zuppke died in 1936. He was married again at the age of 77 to his housekeeper of 23 years, Leona.

One thing Zuppke prided himself on in his later years was his ability to find humor in the game and in himself.

"There were too many sourpusses among the coaches in the early days," he once said. "All they knew was football, all they talked about was football. They were at a loss on any other subject. I believe in having an interest in many things."

That is probably why Zuppke adjusted so well to his coaching retirement. He devoted most of his time then to his painting, something he dabbled in during the off-season throughout his coaching career at Illinois. After his retirement, he wintered in Arizona, summered in Michigan, and was in Champaign most of the spring and fall.

Reminiscing, Young said, "I think his interest in art helped sustain him in his retirement. But he still maintained his interest in football. I stopped by now and then to see him after he'd retired from coaching, and he'd always want to talk about football."

Zuppke never found anything incongruous about a football coach being a landscape artist. On one occasion he expressed his views on the subject.

"Some are surprised that a football coach should be interested in art, yet art and athletics are not apart.

"Fine athletes always have rhythm, balance, coordination and the other feelings that we associate with art, music. Muscular coordination is just as necessary to painters as athletes.

"An athlete is a fine piece of moving composition—a painting is merely immobile composition that may depict movement. They talk about the 'touch' in putting and billiards, why not the 'touch' in handling the brush? A painter must have expressive hands—so must an athlete.

"Athletics and art both require endurance. It takes vigor to paint powerfully over every inch of a canvas. I can't imagine a 'sissy' making a vital painting. Poor paintings lack movement— everything is dead. I'll venture to say most of the great artists had vigor and endurance.

"An athlete probably is the most graceful human being we have and is an inspiration to an artist. Why shouldn't the athlete have art in him? The athlete is symmetrical, with a rhythmic movement—fine paintings have symmetry and—rhythm. If you could tie a brush to the motion of a graceful football player,

151

such as Red Grange, you would get a beautiful, rhythmic design.

"Why are not more athletes artists? Because they are rarely in an environment which encourages them.

"Athletes, painters and musicians must have great qualities of concentration. In golf in a critical moment a putt is lost because the player didn't concentrate enough.

"Nothing is sillier than the 'brawn but not brain' slur sometimes made about athletes. My belief is that there is usually more brain with brawn than without.

"Is there any more beautiful picture than eleven fine specimens of youth, graceful and coordinated, running out on a football field? After all, they present a living picture of everything the artist tries to capture. Beside them, painting is just an imitation of life."

In the later years of his life, Zuppke's paintings drew considerable critical acclaim.

"There are two schools of thought on my painting," he once laughed. "Some stand in front of my water colors and oils and say, 'Great power. Great technique. Great knowledge of color.' Another group stands in front of one of my canvases and murmurs, 'He must have been a great football coach.'"

Without question, he was that.

A New Era Begins:
The Ray Eliot Years

When Ray Eliot was appointed to be Bob Zuppke's successor as Illinois football coach in 1942, the decision was not especially greeted with thundering applause from the school's alumni and fans.

But there was no doubt about it being a popular choice among the Illinois players. Eliot had served for four years as an assistant on Zuppke's staff and had established a strong rapport with the squad.

"This is just what the players wanted," said Jimmy Smith, the team's captain-elect, shortly after Eliot's hiring was announced. "We've been for him 100 percent. He's one of us. From here on, we'll not concede a thing to any team."

Eliot's selection also was a popular one with Zuppke, who was quoted: "He is a very good and logical choice. He is a hard worker, a student of the game, enthusiastic and popular with the boys. He knows the game from all angles, having coached backfields, lines and ends. The board couldn't have made a better choice. Eliot is a fine character. I never lost faith in him during the dark days at Illinois. He was doing his level best."

Others of influence in the Champaign-Urbana community had strongly supported Eliot. One was Frank Robeson, in whose department store Eliot worked as a student. "Ray is one of the most capable boys I ever saw. He's absolutely tops. Unless I miss my guess, he'll make an excellent coach. He has a big viewpoint. He sees the whole picture. He has tremendous energy and intelligence with it. I think he may be one of the

153

best coaches in the country," he said.

But perhaps as strong a force as any man in moving the school's powers toward the selection of Eliot was Zuppke's line coach, Justa Lindgren, a highly respected member of the regular academe as a member of the chemistry department. It was Lindgren who unofficially launched a campaign for Eliot at an Illini Club banquet in Chicago soon after the 1941 season ended and Zuppke announced his plans to step down. "This Eliot fellow," Lindgren told friends, "is one of the greatest young coaches in the country. He is the logical choice to replace Zuppke." Eliot had been Lindgren's protege.

Four days after Zuppke's resignation, a delegation of Illini lettermen headed by end Jim McCarthy and center Ken Cheeley buttonholed Chet Davis, chairman of the athletic committee of the board of trustees, and made it plain how the other players felt about Eliot.

The Eliot bandwagon was rolling, and, at that point, it was obvious that it was picking up steam with each passing day.

"When I was finally hired, it came upon me so quickly it stunned me," Eliot recalled in a recent interview.

Athletic Director Doug Mills, who had recommended Eliot to the athletic board, walked into Eliot's office and said simply, "Congratulations, you're our new football coach!"

Eliot remembers, "I never got my hopes built up too high, although I can assure you that I wanted the job as much as I ever wanted anything. Once it finally happened, I think it took me four days to realize what an awesome thing it was.

"After that, there was the rush of press conferences and so forth, and I jumped right into the job working like the devil."

In his quiet moments, though, he and his wife, Margaret, (known as Maggie) would talk about the mind-bending pace of the new job. And he would admit, in those private, intimate conversations that a man shares only with the person closest to him, that he could almost feel the shadow of Zuppke's success hovering over him.

"If I work hard and give it the best I have, I'll be doing all I can do," he said.

And he would turn off the lights and go to bed. Tomorrow he would earn his $6,000-a-year salary.

Ray Eliot had learned early in life that only a day's work is

Ray Eliot (left) and Captain Jimmy Smith lead Eliot's first Illini team on the field for practice in 1942.

worth a day's pay. He grew up in Brighton, Massachusetts, and it was not an easy life. His father died when he was seven years of age. As soon as he was able, he went to work, first as a grocery store delivery boy. Later he would be employed in a bakery doing odd jobs. Through scrimping and saving by both of them, Eliot's mother was able to afford his eventual enrollment at a prep school in Maine. He played football and baseball there and was named to the state's all-star team in both sports. He decided then that he would be a coach someday.

"At that time the University of Illinois had a wonderful school for athletic coaches, and one of their pamphlets came to the prep school I was attending," Eliot recalls now.

"I think I'd also had a hankering to be a coach, even when I was a youngster. I was so intrigued with the courses Illinois offered, I decided I'd enroll there."

At Illinois he played football for Zuppke with some notable success as a bespectacled lineman—he had serious vision problems from childhood—and soon afterward landed his long-awaited first coaching job.

In 1932 La Rue Van Meter, who had just led little Johnston City to the state high school basketball championship, was named athletic director, football coach, and basketball coach at Illinois College. He hired Eliot as an assistant in football and head baseball coach. But Van Meter did not really relish the idea of coaching football as well as basketball. The next year he turned the head coaching duties in football over to Eliot. During his five years at the small college in Jacksonville, Eliot would also coach the school's swimming team four of those years.

"I'm the only coach ever to win the conference championship in swimming three times in four years with a team that didn't even have a pool," he likes to say. There was, in fact, no facility at the school, but the team trained at the nearby Jacksonville School for the Deaf, which had one.

Eliot also was establishing a reputation as a fine young football coach. In four years his teams compiled a 26-8-1 record, but it was a learning experience. He sat at the foot of pioneer coaches like William McAndrew of Southern Illinois and A. J. Robertson of Bradley, and he added their ideas on coaching to the ones he already absorbed from Zuppke.

Eliot quickly established himself as a strategist in his own right at Jacksonville. While he was there, he popularized the screen pass, remembering a game he had seen as a boy between Harvard and Yale when it was used. Robertson, seeing it used by Illinois College, incorporated it into his offense at Bradley.

But soon the University of Illinois would be looking for a line coach to assist Lindgren. Athletic Director George Huff invited Eliot to apply for the job. He was quickly hired.

"I enjoyed myself immensely in Jacksonville," Eliot recalls. "I could have stayed there forever, but when the opportunity came to come back to the university, it was something I felt I had to do. I took a cut in salary, but that didn't matter. I knew I was going to be coaching at Illinois, and that was all that mattered."

It did not bother Eliot, either, that after a game with Bradley, Zuppke was so impressed with Bradley's version of the screen pass that he put it in Illinois' offensive repertoire and, as a tribute to Robertson, called it "the Peoria pass."

Eliot did not have the bravado to tell Zup that he was the one who had given the play to the Bradley coach—diagrammed it for him, in fact—two years earlier while he was at Illinois College.

Assistant coaches under Zuppke in those days, especially the young ones, were to be seen working, not heard blustering. Zuppke wanted workhorses, not peacocks, and Eliot did his best to meet those expectations.

Eliot challenged Zuppke only once during their employer-employee relationship.

Zuppke did not believe in the use of game films, while Eliot had great confidence in them. They clashed on that point. Zuppke finally relented, giving permission for Eliot to take some of his linemen into a darkened cavern below the stadium and show them in black-and-white where they had erred in the previous game.

It was further evidence that Zuppke, great coach that he was at the height of his career, was not keeping pace with the game as it was beginning to evolve.

Even then, without knowing it, Eliot was establishing himself as a "coach of the future." That future was just around the corner.

157

"It's Not The Size
Of The Body..."

It did not take Ray Eliot long to put his personal imprint on Illinois football. His first team in 1942 fit perfectly Eliot's own mold as a player—it was small but spirited.

And the player who best typified that team was a young, swarthy-complected Assyrian named Alex Agase.

Agase, only 159 pounds when he came to Illinois, had won only one letter as a player in high school.

"I'll never forget how insecure he was when he came to us," Eliot remembers. "He told me he really didn't think he was big enough to play in the Big Ten."

Eliot would have none of it.

"Young man," Eliot told Agase, "it's not the size of the body that counts. It's the size of your heart."

It was not very long thereafter that Agase proved that his own heart—his will to win—was gargantuan.

With Agase the leader of a young line, the Illini pounded South Dakota 46-0 and Butler 67-0 in their first two games. But not even the most optimistic Illini fan expected that streak to go any further. Illinois' third opponent of the year was defending national champion Minnesota, winner of 18 straight games against college competition when the mighty Gophers came to Illinois in early October.

Minnesota was a heavy favorite, but the oddsmakers forgot to tell that to Eliot and his Illini.

Tony "Bronko" Butkovich, the Illini fullback, sat on a

Tony Butkovich predicted the Illinois upset of mighty Minnesota in 1942.

rubdown table in the training room before the start of the game and told a sportswriter, "If the other fellows feel like I do right now, and I'm sure they do, we're going to win. Bet on it. It's a feeling I've never had before with a big game coming up. I wish we were out there right now."

Minnesota, however, had an awesome ground attack led by tackle Dick Wildung and halfback Bill Daley, a pair of All Americans, and Daley exploded early in the game for an 80-yard touchdown run that gave the Gophers a quick 7-0 lead. In the second quarter Agase got his revenge. Daley was hit hard and tried to spin loose, but before he knew what hit him again Agase had the ball and was running 38 yards into the end zone for a touchdown. Jim McCarthy's extra point kick failed, however, and Minnesota still had a 7-6 lead. But it was obvious Bernie Bierman's Gophers had a street fight on their hands.

The Illini emerged from their locker room after the halftime intermission in an emotional frenzy. Soon afterward they grabbed the lead on a razzle-dazzle, double-lateral play that went from blocking back Ray Florek to Butkovich to Don Griffin in Eliot's single-wing formation. Griffin romped in from the three yard line. McCarthy's kick gave the Illini a 13-7 lead.

Minnesota came charging back in the fourth quarter and tied the score on a touchdown pass to Bob Sandberg. The game settled into a trench war that seemed destined to end in a 13-13 tie.

Only four minutes remained in the game, and the Gophers were on their own nine yard line when suddenly the Minnesota center got off a bad snap and the ball was rolling loose in the end zone.

Everyone went for it, but it was a gutty bulldog of a man who got there first. Agase pounced on the loose ball for an Illinois touchdown, his second of the game as a lineman. The fans in Memorial Stadium were still screaming as McCarthy's kick sailed through the uprights for a 20-13 Illini victory. The two-time national champion had fallen. The win streak had ended.

The jubilant Illini players ran into their dressing room, which suddenly became Times Square on New Year's Eve. But nobody could find Eliot. "Somebody go get him," they yelled. Agase and Butkovich tracked him down, still on the field, and rode him back to the locker room on their shoulders. He was

160

bounced around from one set of arms to another. But Eliot was not complaining.

"It's just too good to be true," Agase told reporters, still thunderstruck by the upset. "I still don't believe it. This is the greatest moment of my life.

"That was the longest 38 yards I ever ran," said Agase of the second-quarter steal from Daley. "I saw a good chance to grab the ball when Florek tackled Daley, and I did. The rest was easy. But I didn't wake up until I crossed the goal line."

Griffin, all smiles, chimed in. "He wasn't kidding when he said he didn't know what happened. That's the first thing he said when we caught up with him in the end zone—'What happened?' And you should have seen the look on Daley's face...he had the most amazed look I've ever seen. He didn't know what in the hell happened either."

Butkovich, the brash prophet, was downplaying it all now as he held court in another corner of the locker room. "What a bunch of farmers those Gophers are," he snorted in his Chicago brogue. He peeled off his uniform to show everyone around how he had played the second half without any hip pads. He did not feel like he was getting hit hard enough in the first half to need them and had taken them off at halftime.

A roar broke out again when a smiling Florek displayed the game ball, hand over head.

"I made a dash for it just as the game ended," said Florek. "It was on the ground, and a Minnesota player started for it, too. I said, 'Get the hell out of here, Bud. This is mine.'"

But the game ball on this day belonged to them all—to Agase, Joe Pawlowski, Mac Wenskunas, Mike Kasap, Elmer Engel (all of whom played the full 60 minutes), and even the ones who warmed the bench. Eliot said as much in his post-game comments to the press.

"Do not give me any credit for the victory over Minnesota," he said. "The boys—every one of them on this team—won the game from a championship team which they were given only a slim chance to beat."

Ray returned home after the game expecting a few friends to stop by. Ray's wife, Margaret, had cooked a turkey and made sandwiches. But the Eliots were hardly ready for the hungry throng that would descend on them like locusts after such a victory as this.

In an hour all the turkey was gone, and Eliot went from one house to another in his neighborhood "borrowing everything I could." Before the night was over they would serve over 500 guests—with more than a little help from their friends. The telegrams that flowed in made a small mountain on the living room floor. After all, it was Illinois' first Big Ten win in their last 11 league games.

Fortunately for Maggie, the next Illini game was on the road at Iowa.

Ray stewed all week that his team would be in for a psychological letdown after the win over Minnesota. And he was right about that...for awhile.

Illinois played well...but not as well as Eliot would have liked that day. The Illini went into the fourth quarter with a perilously thin 12-7 lead on touchdowns Butkovich and Griffin had scored in the first and third quarters.

Eliot feared the worst in the final period. He was well aware that Iowa had an excellent passing attack led by Tom Farmer and was capable of a touchdown at the bat of an eyelash. But just as the fourth quarter began, the Illini got an emotional lift from an unexpected source: the Hawkeye public address system announcer made the mistake of announcing that Notre Dame had just beaten the Iowa State Seahawks 28-0. The University of Iowa fans laughed and applauded their approval. But 3,000 Seahawk cadets in the stands for the Illinois-Iowa game in Iowa City sat in stony silence.

"There was no love lost between the Sea Hawks and the Hawkeyes," Eliot laughs, remembering the day. "The Sea Hawks were stationed on the Iowa campus and they were all trying to date the same girls and such.

"The Iowa fans yelling for Notre Dame really made those Sea Hawks at our game mad. They were all sitting together in their uniforms and white hats, and every one of them started cheering for us after what had happened. It was just the emotional charge we needed in the fourth quarter."

Farmer passed three times for 66 yards late in the game, but the Illini turned back the threat without an Iowa score.

Eliot remembers his players coming up to him after the game and saying, "Coach, we couldn't lose that game. We couldn't let those Sea Hawks down."

The first thing Eliot did when he returned to Champaign was sit down at his desk and write a letter to the commanding officer of the Sea Hawks. It said, quite simply, "Thanks."

The Illini had a right to be thankful. It was the first time since 1934 that Illinois had won four straight games.

By now Margaret Eliot was swept up in Illinois' success like everyone else. For the home game to come against Notre Dame she was going to be prepared. She ordered two turkeys, two hams, a barrel of potato salad, and enough shrimp to give a whale indigestion.

Notre Dame, however, had been forewarned about this Illinois team, unlike Minnesota, and the Irish came into Memorial Stadium expecting to have a battle on their hands. They guessed right. Illinois scored first, four minutes after the first quarter began, when Butkovich rambled 24 yards on a reverse. Notre Dame tied it after recovering a fumble on the Illini 20, Corny Clatt carrying it across five plays later. The Illini bounced back in the second quarter on a 24-yard payoff pass from Dick Good to Ray Grierson, but the Irish tied it up again on a one-yard sneak by its great quarterback, Angelo Bertelli. It was 14-14 until Notre Dame's Jerry Cowhig rammed over from the one yard line early in the fourth quarter for what would be the winning touchdown. Any late passing threat the Illini might have mustered was drained by an injury to Good.

Eliot was downcast and disappointed by the loss, but he dutifully returned home soon after the game to help Maggie greet the anticipated multitude.

"It was six o'clock, and there was nobody there, and then it was seven and eight, and the doorbell hadn't rung once," Eliot remembered many years afterward. "I looked at Maggie, and she looked at me. We looked at that turkey, those hams, and all that shrimp. At nine o'clock we said the heck with it and went out to see a movie. Maggie, at least, was very philosophical about it. 'One nice thing,' she said. 'We won't have to go to the grocery store this week.'"

The first-year Illinois coach was starting to learn about the fickleness of the average American football fan; nobody likes to eat with a loser, even if the dinner is free.

Eliot and his 1942 Illini would taste defeat three more

163

times before the season ended: to Michigan the following week 28-14, to powerful Ohio State 44-20, and to Great Lakes 6-0. But they would also add wins over Northwestern 14-7 and Camp Grant 20-0 to finish 6-4 for the year. The 3-2 conference mark was good enough for a tie for third.

The Eliot era was off and rolling. "That Minnesota victory really did it for us," Eliot remembers now. "It attracted the attention not only of our alumni, but the entire nation. I still look back on it as one of the greatest things ever to happen to me at Illinois."

Agase was chosen as a consensus All-American at the season's end, the first sophomore to be so honored in the Big Ten since Bennie Oosterbaan of Michigan in 1925.

Agase would be named to the All-American team two more times during his college career. Unfortunately for the Illini, the second time he was not at Illinois, but at Purdue.

The Vanishing Illini

Only a few weeks after Ray Eliot took over for Bob Zuppke as head football coach at Illinois, the Japanese bombed Pearl Harbor. The war had no effect on Illinois football in 1942, but all that would change before the 1943 season began. Many young men, football players included, were answering the call of their country.

Tony Butkovich and Alex Agase, who starred for the 1942 Illini, had marched off to the Marine Corps. Most Big Ten teams in 1943 were made up of fuzzy-faced 17 and 18-year-olds and 4-F's. Some teams, however, like Purdue and Michigan which had navy-marine training programs, were allowed to use players attached to their schools for that indoctrination.

Michigan, for example, ended up landing the services of Bill Daley of Minnesota and Elroy Hirsch of Wisconsin, two of the league's best ballcarriers. But Purdue gained the most. The Boilermakers gained the talents of half a dozen Illini, including both Agase and Butkovich.

"We got nothing in return," Eliot remembers. "The only military program on our campus was the Navy V-12, a non-collegiate service training, and the boys weren't allowed to go out for football."

The 1943 team became known as "the Vanishing Illini." Eliot lost 25 players to military induction between the start of fall practice and late October.

Eliot was so desperate for players before the season even began that when he saw Eddie Nemeth walking down the street while home on furlough, he grabbed him by the collar, hustled him over to Memorial Stadium, gave him a uniform, and played him in the season opener against Camp Grant. Buck Correll, the Illini punter, had been classified 1-A just a few days before and had gone off to the induction center.

"We never knew who we'd have from one day to the next," Eliot remembers. "That's the main reason why I went to the split-T offense in 1943. In 1942 we'd used Zup's single-wing offense, with some changes, but Don Faurot had introduced the split-T at Missouri, and it seemed like a fairly easy offense to learn. We had so many young and new players that we wanted to have something we could teach in a short period of time and still have reasonably good execution."

The toughest game the Illini played all season, needless to say, was against Purdue. The Boilermakers won the game 40-21, but it was a victory of sorts for the Illini anyway. Fifty of the 61 points racked up by the two teams that day were put on the scoreboard by Illinois or by an Illini playing for Purdue under the lend-lease service rules. Tony Butkovich probably played the greatest game of his college career, running for 207 yards in only 12 carries. Ol' Bronk scored four touchdowns on runs of 80, 27, seven, and two yards. Joe Buscemi, who had spent his freshman year at Illinois, scored on a 16-yard pass. Alex Agase was brilliant on defense. John Genis, Frank Bauman, and Mike Kasap—all members of the team the Champaign-Urbana newspapers referred to as "The Purdue Illini"—also were standouts.

"The thing that I remember most about that game," Eliot says today, "is that Purdue got out to a big early lead, and the Purdue coach, Elmer Burnham, pulled out most of his regulars. Most of the guys who had played for us the previous year at Illinois came over to our side of the field to talk to our players who weren't in the game. Somehow, though, we scored a couple of touchdowns and got back in the game, and I'll never forget Burnham waving frantically for them to come back to their side of the field so he could get them back into the game."

"All right," Eliot yelled to Agase and Butkovich and the others. "Get back over there and...and...and for gosh sakes, don't let down...."

They did not in that game or, apparently, in any other that season. Purdue posted a 9-0 record, shared the Big Ten champi-

ILLINI
FOOTBALL HONOR ROLL

ALEX AGASE	DEE ALBERTS	LEE ALBERTS
DON ANDERSON	FERDY ARAMOVICH	JOE ASTROTH
BOB AULGUR	BOB BABB	ANDY BACEVICH
BOB BAGGOTT	JIM BARTUSEK	BABE BARANOWSKI
MERCER BARNES	RALPH BASSEY	FRANK BAUMAN
BILL BECKER	PAUL BEHAN	CARL BELL
DON BIANCHI	FRANK BUDENBAUM	BOB BURGESS
JOE BUSCEMI	TONY BUTKOVICH	JAMES BUTLER
JACK BUTT	LYLE BUTTON	BILL CHAMBERLAIN
MIKE CHIANAKIS	JACK CHURCHILL	MARVIN CLATT
DON COPELAN	DICK DEPIGIAN	CLARE DE VALK
BILL DICKINSON	JIM DONAHUE	ART DUFELMEIER
LOUIS DUNN	DWIGHT EDDLEMAN	STEVE EDWARDS
WELLS ELLIS	RAY FLOREK	WILLARD FRANKS
LOUIS FRISCH	TOM GALLAGHER	BOB GARDITY
ROY GATEWOOD	DON GAZZANIGA	JOHN GENIS
ART GERONETTA	BOB. GEROMETTA	FRED S. GREEN
J. FRED GREEN	RAY GRIFFSON	DON GRIFFIN
PHIL GUSTAFSON	STEVE HABZANSY	ED HEINE
HEZA HINDMAN	BOB HINKLE	ROY HOPPE
JIM HUDSON	FRANK HURTTE	ELMER HUSS
RAY IRWIN	DON JANSSEN	PHIL JEFFRIES
DON JOHNSON	ED JOHNSTON	JACK KANE
MIKE KASAP	ELIOT KATZ	PETE KEARNEY
LLOYD KELLY	TONY KELLY	CHUCK KOVACH
BILL KRALL	RUDY KRALL	GENE KWASNIEWSKI
JACK LAKE	JACK LARSON	LEE LAUTENSCHLAGER
CHUCK LEISTNER	DON LESHER	LOU LEVANTI
MAX LIPTZMAN	JOHN LUKACHIK	JOHN MAC ARTHUR
RUDY MACCHIONE	DON MAECHTLE	BOB MANNLE
MARIO MAOCHISIO	JOHN MARTIN	DON MATTIAZZA
TOM MAZURA	JOHN McCORMACK	CHUCK MEHMEL
MAC MORRIS	ART MURAKOWSKI	DAVID MURRELL
ED NEMETH	BOB NESWOLD	ERWIN OEHLERKIN
JOHN PAQUEN	ED PALLERIA	RALPH PALMER
AL PARFITT	PAUL PATTERSON	BILL PERRY
GORDON PETERSON	ANDY PHILLIP	AL PIKE,JR
DICK PISKOTY	CHUCK POLLARD	BOB PRYMUSKI
DON RAGGIO	JACK REDMAN	LARRY REED
DAN REED	DICK ROBERTS	BERNIE ROSEN
BOB RUTHER	FRED SCHEID	CHET SAJNAJ
BILL SAMPSEL	DON SHELTON	VINCENT SCHIFFERDECKER
MARVIN SCHULTZ	TOM SMERDEL	CHUCK SHISTROM
MILTON SMAHA	TED SMITHERS	CHUCK SMITH
REX SMITH	BOB STANCIK	JIM SREDNICKI
ED STAAB	STEVE SUCIC	RUSS STEGER
LEONARD STONE	WES TREGONING	BOB THOMPSON
EMIL TOMANEK	HOWARD WEGENER	TONY VAVRUS
BILL VINEVARD	ED WERNER	BERYL WHITE
MAC WENSKUNAS	CHUCK WOOD	BOB WILSON
FRITZ WOETEN		CLAUDE YOUNG

Ray Eliot, right, and Athletic Director Doug Mills look at the list of Illini players serving in the military service during World War II.

onship with Michigan, and in some circles was regarded as the national champion along with Notre Dame. All-American recognition would be accorded to both Agase and Butkovich. Butkovich broke the Big Ten touchdown record with 13 that season in only four conference games. Before the season ended, he was called to active duty and later was killed in action.

With his ragtag band that included quarterback Don Greenwood and two half-pint halfbacks, Eddie Bray and Eddie McGovern, Eliot's Illini were explosive enough on offense to gain a 3-7 record, 2-4 in Big Ten games.

Eliot still believes that team should have been 3-6-1. And it would have been, had it not been for the now-storied "fifth quarter" game with Ohio State.

Illinois went into the Ohio State game with a 2-5 record. The Illini had gotten their first win of the season against Wisconsin 25-7 when Bray teamed up with McGovern, a transfer from Rose Poly, for a five-touchdown outburst. The 17-year-old Bray, just a few months out of LaSalle-Peru High School, scored on runs of 39 and 25, and McGovern escaped on sprints of 65, 13, and 11. But powerful Notre Dame and Michigan teams humbled the Illini before they would win again 19-10 over Iowa.

Ohio State, however, was clearly the favorite as the two teams met in the next-to-last game of the year in Columbus. But the Illini battled the Buckeyes to the wire, and the score was tied 26-26 as the clock ticked away the final seconds. A pass by Dean Sensenbaugher fell incomplete in the Illini end zone on what was believed to be the last play of the game. Both teams ran for their respective dressing rooms, and spectators began filing out of Ohio Stadium. The head lineman, Paul Gobel, however, rushed up to referee Jim Masker to say that he had called Illinois off sides on that final play. Masker ruled that there were two seconds left when the penalty occurred, and he called the players from both teams back on the field. John Stungis kicked a 23-yard field goal when they all returned, to give the Buckeyes a 29-26 victory.

"I still don't believe that one," Eliot says and smiles, now that the pain has subsided. "Players from both teams came back on the field half-dressed. Many of them were in their stocking feet. I'll never forget that Paul Brown, who was coaching Ohio State at the time, was actually in the huddle when they called their last play. Now if that wasn't a penalty, I don't know what was. It was a real disappointment to lose that one like that."

But the war years were not all filled with disappointments for the Illini. If Eliot could not build a football power, he could build character.

"In those days," he once said, "we didn't work just on football; we worked on building the attributes of sportsmanship, self-denial, self-discipline, loyalty, humility, pride, and dedication. We built a big man in every way."

But some of those big men were, again, small of stature.

In 1944 Eliot unveiled one of the smallest but most explosive backs the Big Ten had ever seen. His name was Claude "Buddy" Young.

From Chicago's Phillips High School he came, planning to be only a trackman at Illinois. Eliot convinced him otherwise.

In his first game as a freshman, against Illinois Normal, Young played only nine minutes and carried the ball only four times from scrimmage—but it was for a total of 113 yards. He also ran 22 yards for a touchdown with a fumbled lateral and another 82 yards for a score on a punt return. Alas, he had another 51-yard run into the end zone called back by a clipping penalty. Illinois Normal was thankful for small favors. The final score was *only* 79-0.

Young teamed with another Illini newcomer, Paul Patterson from Aurora, to lead the Illini to a 26-18 victory over Indiana in the second game. Patterson passed to Bray for one score and ran 29 yards for another. The clincher for the Illini came on a 37-yard toss from Greenwood to Young. Young scored on a 93-yard burst the following week against Great Lakes, but the Illini had to settle for a 26-26 tie. Purdue followed, and the Boilermakers were still getting help from outside sources. Bump Elliott (who called Michigan home) was a star on defense for Purdue. Young scored twice and ran for 125 yards, but Purdue prevailed 35-19. Against Iowa, Young electrified the fans with two touchdowns the first two times he carried the ball, rocketing 64 and 30 yards.

Another highlight of the 1944 season was Illinois' first visit to the East in 19 years, the last time being the memorable Red Grange devastation of Penn. The Pitt Panthers were the foe, and the Illini gave eastern football not one running star, but two.

Young rambled for 132 yards, including a 92-yard burst, and Patterson rolled for 102 as the Illini ran up a 39-5 triumph.

But even with Young and Patterson running, Greenwood and Bill Butkovich (the younger brother of Tony) passing, Walt Kersulis and Johnny Orr catching, and Les Bingaman and Ralph Serpico playing brilliantly in the line, the Illini were not able to beat the national powers. Notre Dame, however, barely nosed out the Illini 13-7 as 65,114 jammed Memorial Stadium. The Illini led 7-6 at halftime on Young's 74-yard gallop the first time he touched the football, but he finished the game on the bench with a knee injury. Michigan had its hands full, too, the following week before emerging with a 14-0 victory to dash the Illini Big Ten title hopes. The Les Horvath-led Buckeyes whipped the Illini 26-12 the following week in Cleveland. The Illini ended the season on a winning note by beating Northwestern 25-6, with Young tying Grange's Illinois record of 13 touchdowns and 78 points in a season, a mark that still stands.

The Illini ended the year with a highly respectable 5-4-1 record, and both Young and Serpico were named consensus All-Americans.

The records of the U. of I. athletic association show that before the team left for Pitt, however, Claude A. Young was advanced a token amount of money for use for travel expenses to the naval induction station. It was not likely that someone who could run the 100-yard dash in 9.4 and escape 11 sailors for a 93-yard touchdown against Great Lakes would fail a naval physical.

By the time the 1945 season began, Young had been inducted, along with Patterson and others. Eliot had no Buddy Youngs to unveil in 1945, and the Illini finished 2-6-1 for the year and 1-4-1 in the Big Ten.

But better days were ahead for the Illini and the battle-weary nation.

Time Out: Alex Agase

It is mid-February, and the rolling hills of central Indiana are dotted with clumps of snow which are the melting remains of the most recent howling winter storm.

It is the season for basketball, not football, but Alex Agase, the head coach of the Purdue Boilermakers, is busily making and accepting calls in his Mackey Arena office.

It is a critical time for the college football coach...the countdown to National Letter of Intent Day, when the nation's senior high school football players officially seal their college choices.

Recruiting is the key to success and failure of college coaches today, and they work at it as feverishly as they do the final minutes of a tied-up game.

It was a lot different when Alex Agase enrolled at the University of Illinois in 1941.

"Hardly anybody was recruiting college players in those days," says Agase. "But even if they were, nobody would have recruited me. I wouldn't have recruited me...not in a million years. As a lineman, I was too small to play football in the Big Ten.

"When I came to Illinois, Bob Zuppke was still the head coach, and the first time I ever even talked to him was when I reported for spring football my freshman year. I don't think he even knew I existed until then.

"Recruiting is what it's all about now. Every coach in the country spends hour after hour on it. It's your top priority

171

Alex Agase.

from the time the season ends until you have all your scholarships passed out. I always say that's why Coach Zuppke had
time to do all that painting...he didn't have to worry about
recruiting.

"This year I've already visited with 120 kids either in their
homes or their schools. I know some of them as well as you can
know anybody in four or five meetings."

Agase is a bear of a man, but he has a glowing face that adds
warmth to his personality. And he smiles easily when he recalls
those early days at Illinois.

"I remember the tuition was $35 a semester, and I paid
that myself that first year. I lived in an old warehouse with nine
other guys. It wasn't very comfortable, but we got along all
right. I washed dishes three hours a night for two meals a day."

172

Agase also fondly recalls his association with Ray Eliot, who succeeded Zuppke after Agase's freshman year.

"The thing that Ray taught me that I'll never forget is that the boy is more important than the game," Agase says, speaking with emotion. "I've always appreciated that philosophy, and it's been the singularly most important thing to my own coaching. Every kid is important as a person. I don't think a coach can lose sight of that."

Agase gives Eliot most of the credit for making him the player he was, especially the encouragement he provided in Agase's sophomore year.

"We all loved Ray," said Agase. "I still do. And you can use the word 'love,' because that's the way I felt about the man. That's why I'll never forget the 1942 Minnesota game. It was a great thrill for me as a lineman to score two touchdowns, but it was a bigger thrill to know that we were winning an important game for Ray."

Agase's play at Purdue in 1943 under the wartime V-5 program established friendships that would many years later take him back to the school as its head coach, but once the war ended, Agase returned to Illinois.

"There was never any question about where I'd be playing," said Agase, remembering. "The last thing I told Ray before I left was, 'I'll be back to play for Illinois.' I've always been a man of my word."

There were times during World War II that Agase wondered if he would be able to keep his promise. He was in the thick of combat in the South Pacific as a Marine squad leader. On Okinawa he won a Bronze Star for heroism, along with the Purple Heart.

"The first few days I was in combat, I wondered if I'd ever survive to play football or anything else again," says Agase, "but once I was past that point, I forgot about everything but the fact that I was in a war, and I had a job to do.

"We had a saying in my unit in those days which was, 'If you're on the Lord's roll call in the morning, you'll be there.'"

Amid the whining of bullets and the splitting shrapnel of Okinawa, the Lord did not see fit to call upon Alex Agase. But in 1946, after the winds of war had stilled, Ray Eliot happily did.

Road To The Rose Bowl

They came back in 1946, from places like Bataan and Corregidor, Iwo Jima and Okinawa, to places with names like UCLA and Purdue, Southern Cal and Illinois. The war was over. The nation was ready for a Marshall Plan of the mind, a return from war to fun and games. Football, for fan and player, was both.

Ike Owens had been away from football for five years as an Army Air Corpsman. Art Dufelmeier had spent 11 months in a German prison camp. Alex Agase had lived in the shadow of death during the war in the Pacific. They, and others, returned to the Illinois campus in the summer of 1946, but there was doubt about whether one of their old number would be with them.

Buddy Young had spent most of 1945 playing service football for the naval team at Fleet City in California. His play had been sensational. In one game he scored four times, including twice in two minutes. The little "Mr. Five-by-Five" had become a football hero on the West Coast in the war-torn years. There were rumors that he was being made big offers from pro teams and being lured by the West Coast schools as he prepared for his naval discharge.

The United Press newswire reported: "UCLA has a special welcome mat out with Young's name on it. Uclan officials, of course, deny making any financial offers to Young because such offers are against conference regulations. It is understood, however, that several wealthy and influential Negroes of Los Angeles have sought to persuade Young to come to UCLA."

Such renowned former athletes for the Bruins as Jackie Robinson had taken Young on guided tours of UCLA and attempted to influence him to stay on the West Coast.

It was several weeks before Young made his final decision to return to Illinois. Not long afterward he was quoted: "I went home and talked things over with my mother. We both decided I had a moral obligation to return to Illinois. It's a wonderful school, and I'm out for the best education I can get. Furthermore, I've made some good friends in Champaign, and I couldn't let them down."

Young and the other members of the "Vanishing Illini" joined the young upcoming players, along with a few transfers from other schools, to form the 1946 team.

"We must have had 300 people out for the team at the start of that season," Agase remembers now. "I still don't know how the coaching staff got all those players sorted out. It had to be a tough job. Can you imagine the differences on that team? Some players were 17 years old, and others, like myself, were as old as 24."

One of those transfers was a quarterback by the name of Perry Moss. A year earlier Moss had been a second-string quarterback at Tulsa, but Eliot took a liking to him when he came to the 1945 College All-Star Game in Chicago.

"Henry Frnka of Tulsa was one of my fellow coaches on the All-Star staff in the summer of 1945," Eliot recalls. "One night he was talking about how he had several good quarterbacks at Tulsa. I told him I liked Moss. Henry told me that he doubted that Perry was going to be playing much for him since he had some other good ones, too. I asked, then, if he'd mind if I asked the boy if he would be interested in coming to Illinois. He said no, in fact, he wouldn't, and that's how Moss ended up transferring to Illinois."

It was a good decision for both Moss and Illinois.

Illinois' first game that season was against Pitt, and Young made his postwar debut by circling left end and rolling 46 yards for a touchdown just one minute and 45 seconds into the game, and the Illini throttled Pitt 33-7. But before the Illini could get too heady, Notre Dame, led by Johnny Lujack, delivered a 26-6

1946 Illinois Football Team
Western Conference and Rose Bowl Champions

First row, left to right: Scout Leo Johnson, Head Coach Ray Eliot, Alex Agase, Julie Rykovich, Claude Young, Captain Mac Wenskunas, Lou Agase, Ralph Serpico, Ike Owens, Line Coach Tony Blazino, Trainer Matt Bullock. Second row: Line Coach Burt Ingwersen, Bob Prymuski, Sam Zatkoff, Lou Donoho,

Mike Kasap, Bill Huber, Bill Heiss, Herb Siegert, Al Mastrangeli,
Bill Franks, Backfield Coach Ralph Fletcher, Manager Bill
Buchanan. Third row: Tom Gallagher, Tom Stewart, Gene
Kwasniewski, John Wrenn, Les Bingaman, Ray Florek, Bob
Cunz, Chick Maggioli, Jim Valek, Vern Seliger, Trainer Ike Hill.
Fourth row: End Coach John Tarwain, Paul Patterson, Chuck
Gottfried, Bert Piggott, Art Dufelmeier, Russ Steger, Don
Maechtle, Joe Buscemi, Frank Bauman.

punch. The Illini bounced back to beat Purdue 43-7 the following week. Moss connected with Owens for a touchdown pass on the first play of the game and young Dike Eddleman rambled for 65 yards in four carries, including a 45-yard touchdown run. Eddleman went on to become one of the nation's top punters. But the Illini still wavered between brilliance and mediocrity, and the next weekend Indiana posted a 14-7 upset victory. Ben Riamondi passed for 145 Hoosier yards, and the lone Illini score came on a Moss pass to Paul Patterson.

That loss was a crushing blow to Eliot. It was obvious to him that his team was better than it had been showing. He was downcast and disconsolate.

"I'll never forget what happened after that loss to Indiana. Doug Mills, the athletic director, came to us one night at practice and told us that Ray had submitted his resignation, but that he'd refused to accept it," Agase reveals now. "I think all of us felt that night that we'd let Ray down, and I think we all made up our mind to try to make up for it."

Eliot regained his composure and set out himself to do something about his team's 2-2 record. For one thing it was obvious that opposing defenses had been keying on Young. Eliot sent in motion a new offensive philosophy that would use Young more as a decoy than as a legitimate running threat. He also felt he had to do something to bring the divergent personalities toward a common strength of purpose.

"Frankly," said Eliot, remembering, "some of those players who were older thought they knew more about coaching a football team than I did. I'll admit I was pretty mad after the Indiana game, and I let them know it. I called them all off the practice field one night and put the Indiana film on the projector and showed them that they really hadn't been playing our defense at all in that game. They were all out there playing the kind of defense they wanted to.

"I told them that if they wanted to have a say-so in what defense we were going to use, that was okay. So I told them to get their defense together, and let me know when they were ready. When they were ready, I took them back out on the practice field and called over our freshman team. I told the freshmen exactly what I wanted them to do on offense, and they ran right through that varsity defense like it wasn't even there.

"I didn't say anything. I just walked off the field and went into the locker room. One by one, after the workout was over, they stopped by my office and said that they wanted to go back to playing my defense, and play it the way I wanted it to be played. I knew I had them then. I knew we were on our way."

The next weekend the Illini whipped Wisconsin 27-21 and then turned back three fourth-quarter Michigan drives to stun the Wolverines 13-9. Iowa fell 7-0 on a touchdown by fullback Ruck Steger. That led the Illini to the key conference collision with Ohio State in Champaign.

A festival crowd of 61,519 turned out in Memorial Stadium, and it was the Illini who celebrated a 16-7 victory after it was over.

Jerry Liska of the Associated Press wrote in his deadline-speed dispatch: "Two mud-caked 'forgotten' stars, Julie Rykovich, who streaked 98 yards for one touchdown, and elusive Buddy Young, who set up another on a 34-yard run nearly clinched the title for the Illini." In that fiercely fought contest, Ohio State took a 7-0 lead, but the Illini battled back when Sam Zatoff blocked a kick for a safety, and Moss ran four yards for a touchdown after Young's jaunt.

The Illini claimed the conference championship the following Saturday in Northwestern's Dyche Stadium. Both teams came into the game with 5-1 conference records, but there was no doubt which team was No. 1 after the game ended. The Illini emerged with a 20-0 victory, with Agase, Young, and Dufelmeier leading the way. Young rolled for 83 yards in 12 carries, and Dufelmeier reached the end zone on a 53-yard run, one of 10 he had for a total of 123 yards for the day.

The next week Eliot was on his way to the West Coast to scout UCLA. Rose Bowl teams had traditionally stayed at the Huntington Hotel in Pasadena, so Eliot decided to check in there and drive to Los Angeles to watch UCLA play Colorado. Staying there also seemed sensible since Eliot could also make the necessary housing arrangements for the arrival of his team in December.

Eliot walked up to the manager, introduced himself, told the man that he was the Illinois coach, and said he wanted to make arrangements to house his team there as other Rose Bowl visitors had done.

"Fine," said the manager. "And we'll arrange for housing for your Negro players at another hotel downtown."

Eliot bristled at that suggestion, he recalled once not long ago.

"I don't think you understand," Eliot remembers telling the Huntington manager at the time. "This is a university team."

Eliot strongly emphasized the word "team."

"I told him that on this team everyone stays at the same hotel," Eliot recalled. "If we don't stay together, we don't stay at all."

Eliot remembers the manager saying, "But we've never had colored people stay in our hotel before."

"Well, I tell you this right now," Eliot remembers saying. "We're all 'colored' on this team. Some of us are white, and some of us are black, but we're all colored."

Eliot turned his back to the man, started walking out the door, and barked, "We're finding another place to stay."

According to Eliot's memory, the manager caught Eliot before he had taken more than four or five steps.

"Okay, coach," said the manager. "If you feel that strongly about it, we'll try it."

The Illini broke the racial barrier at the hotel the following December.

"Duck Soup"
And Other Delights

"We were really like neophytes going out there," Ray Eliot remembers, his mind's eye drifting away to 1946 and the rambling train trip to the West Coast that took the team through the dusty flatlands of Texas en route to a January 1 Rose Bowl date with UCLA. "It was the first year of the new bowl pact, and we didn't really know what to expect."

What the Illini found upon arrival in Pasadena was considerable unfavorable publicity from the West Coast's sporting press. The California sportswriters had been busy showing their displeasure with a new Rose Bowl pact with the Big Ten that would bring a team to the foot of Arroyo Seco Canyon which had—heaven forbid—been beaten not only once, but twice. The West Coast press had wanted to see unbeaten Army against the mighty Bruins, and the feeling was hardly hidden.

Eliot remembers that first workout on the West Coast:

"When we ended our practice, and I had talked with the newspapermen, I started back to the clubhouse to change my clothes. One of the newspapermen followed me over and said, 'Coach, I want to help you. I want to tell you what UCLA is doing since I've seen them in practice every day for the last week.'

"I couldn't believe it. We're such big underdogs, I thought to myself, that even the newspapermen are trying to help us out."

Eliot looked at the reporter and said, "Are you sure you're a newspaperman?"

"He opened his wallet and showed me his credentials," Eliot remembers. "I really shouldn't divulge his name. I said, 'Okay, I'm going to give you a scoop. Just write down that all newspapermen from west of the Rocky Mountains will be banned from our practice sessions from now on out!'

"He said, 'Do you really mean that?'

"I said, 'Yes sir, I sure do. If you're willing to tell me what UCLA is doing, I don't think you're going to hesitate a minute to tell UCLA what we're doing. From now on the gates are closed.'

"I couldn't believe it. No newspaperman in my life had ever come up to me and offered to tell me anything about what the opposition was doing, and I'd be the last one in the world to ever ask one of them something like that.".

The closed-practice edict made the California writers even more critical of Illinois.

"The more the West Coast press wrote about how we didn't deserve to be playing in the Rose Bowl and the more they built up this 'great' UCLA team, the madder we got," Eliot recalls. "It became a battle of words. I remember once about a week before the game. Our kids were getting down mentally a little bit so I took out all the clippings I'd been collecting from the West Coast press in a manilla folder. I remember they were saying things like 'Where is Illinois?'

"So I decided that I'd sit all the kids down in the shade near the practice field and just let them start reading them. I remember one clipping in particular that had some quotes from Ray Richards, the UCLA line coach, about how the man playing across from Agase was going to make Alex look sick. I made sure that Alex got that clipping. I remember him starting to read it, and I could see his face getting redder with every word. He started rising to his feet, and he threw the clipping down and yelled, 'All right, it's time we went to work.' That seemed to really get them fired up. They weren't just preparing for a game now, they were preparing for a war. I remember that I had a heckuva time chasing the kids off the practice field every night after that."

Alex Agase (left) signs an autograph for movie star Alan Ladd (right) as Buddy Young looks on during visit by Rose Bowl-bound Illini to a motion picture studio in Hollywood.

Paul Patterson had big day for the Illini in 1947 Rose Bowl game.

Agase remembers that incident and another that helped motivate the Illini.

"I also remember a sports writer by the name of Jack Clowser from the Cleveland Press talking to us one day," says Agase. "He was a great speaker, and his main point was that we weren't just playing for Illinois, but we were carrying the colors of the entire conference. I'd never really thought about it that way before. I think having someone from outside of Illinois tell us that had a lot more effect than, say, if Ray had said it. All I know is that it really sunk in."

It was during that Rose Bowl game preparation that Eliot had to make "one of the toughest coaching decisions I ever made." He sent two players, Ray Florek and Lou Donoho, home for missing curfew. Chuck Flynn, then the Illini sports information director who has since served as the assistant to two university presidents, remembers the incident vividly.

"Ray asked me to call our press together in his room after practice one night," said Flynn. "He said he had something to talk over with them. I remember him saying, 'Men, we've had a couple of boys miss curfew, and I wonder what you think I should do about it?' I remember the writers saying that missing a curfew didn't sound that bad. Ray looked at them and asked, 'For two days?'

"The decision was made."

"I told them that this wasn't the end of the world for them," says Eliot. "I told them I'd bring them back next season. It was a tough decision, but I knew that if I let it go, I would have lost my whole squad. They understood, and I really think that helped to bring us together as a team even more than we already were."

Soon afterward the waiting was over. Game day had arrived.

"I had an awful time sleeping the night before the game," Eliot remembers. "I tossed and turned all night, and finally I went down to the lobby at about 6 o'clock in the morning. I looked around, and half the squad was already there. I could tell then that they were psyched and ready to go."

"Let me tell you, we were ready," remembers Paul Patterson, who joined with Buddy Young to give the Illini a lightning-quick pair of halfbacks. "We had been up-tight in all those pre-game practices, and there was nothing, really, to indicate that we were ready, but we were. Ray had us that way, without us even knowing it.

"Knowing we didn't have Florek probably made us play that much better. He's the guy who had kept us alive in the Iowa and Michigan games in 1946 with his defense at linebacker. He was one of the best."

Ike Owens remembers that it did not take long for him to get ready.

"I had made up my mind to protect my face so that it wouldn't cramp my style in going out on the town after the game," recalls Owens. "So what happened? On the first play— wham!—I got a busted lip. I was hard to handle the rest of the game."

So were the rest of the Illini.

Illinois took the opening kickoff, and on the first play from scrimmage quarterback Perry Moss connected with Julie Rykovich for a 44-yard passing gain. Young ripped through left tackle for six yards and through right tackle on the next play

185

for seven more. Ruck Steger, the sophomore starter at fullback, took it down to the one foot line with a three-yard burst, and Rykovich took it in from there. The extra point kick failed, but Illinois suddenly had a 6-0 lead.

UCLA came back for a touchdown of its own in the first quarter and a slim 7-6 Bruin lead, but that seemed to simply renew Illinois' intensity.

The Illini drove 77 yards in 14 plays for a touchdown soon after the second quarter began. The key play was a third-and-11 situation on the UCLA 38 yard line. Moss took the snap and rifled an overhand lateral back to Young, who waited for the Bruin defense to commit, then zipped 16 yards down the sideline before he was pulled down by Skip Rowland on the UCLA 22.

That play put the Illini drive over the hump, and Rykovich gobbled up seven yards on the next play. Young rambled back around left end for 13 more yards to take it down to the two yard line. You could have driven a tank through the hole Young had over left tackle when he scored on the next play. Don Maechtle's extra point kick made it 13-7.

"I could just see the color go out of those UCLA guys' faces after Buddy made that long run," recalls Patterson, now a member of Illinois' athletic board. "It was a special play, and we called it 'The Young Special.' Ray had put it in especially for UCLA.

"It was all downhill for us after that. And we were already starting to rub it in. Alex Agase and I were the ones who had to block their All-American end, (Burr) Baldwin, and after we did, we'd reach down to help him up and say, 'Hey, has anyone around here seen Baldwin today?'

"I can remember just about everyone now who came off the field was saying, 'Hey, these guys are duck soup.' And they were. I don't think they had really been training for us. They were soft."

It was Patterson who roared four yards over left tackle to rack up Illinois' third touchdown that day, as 93,083 looked on in utter amazement. It was Patterson's brilliant running, too, that set up another Illini touchdown before the second quarter ended. He started the drive rolling with an 18-yard ramble and soon afterward took a handoff from Moss on a fake pass and

Ray Eliot is carried off field on the shoulders of his players after 1947 Rose Bowl victory in Pasadena.

broke around left end for 17 yards to the UCLA one yard line. Moss sneaked for the touchdown on the next play, and Illinois' lead soared to 25-7.

By then, Ike Owens recalls, "We started a chant that lasted through the game, 'You wanted an Army—Well, you got an army today.'"

The margin continued to widen in the second half. Young went over for his second touchdown of the game on the first play of the fourth quarter, on a drive he had keyed along with Rykovich and Steger. It was Steger's pass interception that produced another quick touchdown seconds later. Steger carried it 68 yards for the score. Another pass interception, this one by Stan Green, gave Illinois another TD from 12 yards away, with 5:10 left in the game.

The final score was Illinois 45, UCLA 14. Illinois' 326

yards on the ground erased a 27-year-old Rose Bowl record for rushing yardage.

West Coast sportswriters spent most of the remainder of the New Year's Day on a steady diet of crow.

Sid Ziff in the *Valley Times*: "The Illinois team that wasn't supposed to have an offense, that was supposed to lack a passing attack, that was supposed to have a one-man attack—Buddy Young—turned out to be the best all-around machine we've seen in the Rose Bowl since U.S.C. slugged Pittsburgh 35 to 0 back in 1933."

Dick Hyland in the *Times*: "Four factors entered into the terrific lacing handed the Bruins. Perhaps we may add a fifth—surprise—but the first four are enough. In order they are: (1) the charge of the Illinois line; (2) the Illinois defense as set up by the coaches; (3) the manner in which Quarterback Perry Moss of the Illini called his plays and, lastly but quite important, the manner in which Ernie Case of the Bruins called *his* plays."

George T. Davis in the *Los Angeles Evening Herald-Express*: "Seldom have we witnessed such effective blocking, either at the line of scrimmage or down the turf...As for the two All-Americans, Alex Agase, Illinois guard, and Burr Baldwin, Bruin end, there was no argument—with the visitor having all the better of it despite a knee injury."

Al Santoro in the *Examiner*: "The Illinois sideline running—probably they do it just as a sideline—is fearful to behold. Particularly when Julius Rykovich (Orange Julius, and too bad he couldn't have been in the Orange Bowl) is running with the pill."

It was at least noteworthy at the time that Young, Patterson, and Owens, along with Bob Mike of UCLA, were the first blacks to play in the Rose Bowl since 1923. And when Eliot returned to the hotel after the game, he crossed paths with the manager who had originally wanted to house those three Illini at some other place.

"I just want to tell you, coach, that this is one of the finest groups of young men we've ever had stay at our hotel," said the manager. "And that includes every one of them."

Eliot remembers now, "That made me feel like we'd won the Rose Bowl game all over again."

188

Time Out: Buddy Young

Claude "Buddy" Young was a scared college freshman the first time he went into a Champaign restaurant and ordered a sandwich at the lunch counter in 1944.

"We don't serve Negroes," said the waitress.

Young, as if hit in the heart by the racist's bullet, went back to his dormitory and cried.

He told his coach, Ray Eliot, what had happened the next day at football practice. He could not help but wonder if the scene in the diner might also recur on the football field.

"Get on the scoreboard and see what happens around this town," said Eliot. "And there's something else I want you to remember. We don't have any jobs for whites or Negroes on our football team. We only have jobs for football players. Don't ever forget that."

"Hallelujah!" yelled Young.

Young likes to recall that incident as an example of how sports has set the pace for the rest of society in the battles for individual rights. It also calmed the rising fears of a man who would that same year score 13 touchdowns for Illinois and emblazon his name in the horizon of football as one of the most electrifying little runners the game has ever known.

In 1968 he was inducted into the National Football Hall of Fame. Today he serves as an assistant to National Football League commissioner Pete Rozelle.

Young says that he never once encountered racial prejudice on any team he played, either at Illinois or in the pro ranks.

"We accepted each other as individuals and as football players," he said. "We had a great camaraderie on that 1944 team, in particular. I've always felt a football team is a society within itself—it has to interact. The characteristics of the persons become the characteristics of the team. I have some friends from that 1944 team that I feel so strongly about it's unbelievable."

Young still remembers that freshman year at Illinois as his favorite, more memorable to him at least than the Rose Bowl season of 1946.

"That year was a great one, because I was able to fulfill a desire to prove I could play a big man's game. There had never been a legitimate track sprinter who had been successful in college football at that time.

"I'll always remember our game with Great Lakes that year because Ray (Eliot) was mad about the way we'd been playing, and he started the entire third team. I was on that third unit at the time, and I'll never forget getting away for two long touchdown runs and getting moved up to the first team the next week.

"That had to be one of my proudest times. Don't forget that I had come to Illinois on what amounted to a track scholarship, and I know that Ray probably had some doubts about whether I was college material because of my size."

Two years later, after he starred for Fleet City Naval Base in California during the war years, Young could have had his pick of big-time college football programs, but he decided to return to Champaign-Urbana.

"There was a lot of controversy at the time about whether or not I would come back to the university, but there was nothing in the nature of Buddy Young that would have made him see fit to do anything else. I wasn't that impressed with all the so-called glamour of Los Angeles. If I had been, maybe I would have been more receptive to some of the opportunities that were put before me. But you have got to remember that all my life I'd prepared myself to go to school at Illinois."

Young remembers an amusing story about that fall when he returned to Illinois.

"I kept telling Ray that I wanted to play a little defense,

190

Buddy Young now serves as assistant to NFL Commissioner Pete Rozelle.

Dike Eddleman, now the director of the Illinois grants-in-aid program and one of the school's all-time great athletes, "convinced" Buddy Young he should not try to play defense.

and I became so adamant about it that he decided to give me a chance one day in practice," said Young. "He put me at safety and in single coverage and on the other team he lined up guess who—Dike Eddleman—opposite me."

Eddleman, the school's all-time great all-around athlete, was almost a foot taller than Young and the Big Ten high jump champion as well.

"Ray told Eddleman to run a 15-yard deep route and buttonhook and for Perry Moss to throw the ball to him. Sure enough, Perry threw it about 10 feet in the air, Dike caught it, and that was the end of my defensive days in 1946."

But Young's size never troubled him on offense, and he learned early in his football career not to be troubled by it.

"When I played on the sandlots as a kid, it always seemed like it was the big guys against the little guys," said Young. "And even though I was just five feet, one inch tall when I was 13 years old I still had to compete against boys who were a lot bigger than that at that age on the Chicago Park District teams.

"In the Chicago Park District, we had some great young people who were good teachers. They really taught you fundamentals."

Young remembers being dropped from one high school team in Chicago, though, because of his size.

"I decided to transfer to Wendell Phillips, and I was lucky enough there to have a coach who was a great teacher. It proved to be a tremendous asset to me," said Young.

"I'm reminded of something I saw written once which said if you take a boy as he is, you fail him, but if you take a boy as he ought to be, then you have helped to make him what he can be.

"That's the lesson football has given me."

Sammy Kicked And Hildegarde Sang

The Rose Bowl win at the end of the 1946 season would remain a highlight for four years. In 1947, 1948, and 1949, the Illini posted 5-3-1, 2-6, and 3-4-2 records. The year 1950 brought an upsurge as the team made a run at the title but missed by losing the season finale to Northwestern. Still, the team finished 7-2 (4-2 in the Big Ten), giving Illini fans high hopes for 1951.

And in 1951 a kicker by the name of Sam Rebecca became a never-to-be-forgotten hero with one swing of his leg.

It was Rebecca's 16-yard field goal in the second quarter that stood up for a 3-0 Illinois victory over Northwestern. That win in the final game of the regular season gave the Illini the Big Ten championship, the berth in the Rose Bowl, and Illinois' first undefeated season since 1927. The season still stands as the lone unbeaten Illini campaign of the modern era. The only blemish on Illinois' record that year was a scoreless tie with Ohio State in the next-to-last game of the season.

"I didn't feel any pressure whatsoever because it was early in the game, and at that point it looked like we were going to roll all over them," Rebecca remembers now.

"The field goal really wasn't a big offensive weapon then. It was more of a last-gasp effort. I would love to be a kicker in today's game with the goal posts as wide as they are now. They're six feet wider than they were then. I can tell you those posts lòoked like they were about three feet apart when you were any distance out when I was playing.

"That was the situation in the 1951 game against North-western. One of our drives bogged down to a fourth-and-16, and Ray Eliot told me to try to kick a field goal, so that's what I did. I was happy when I made it because it was a nice thing on a personal basis, but I didn't even have a thought then that it might decide the game. I know I would have been a lot more nervous if I'd had any idea it would have been anything close to as important as it turned out to be."

Illinois dominated the Wildcats that afternoon in Evanston, racking up 310 yards on the ground to just 62 for North-western, but never managed to get the ball in the end zone.

Illinois made it inside the Northwestern 10 yard line three times without scoring and was within the Northwestern 20 twice more without putting a touchdown on the board. The Illini, in fact, had to scramble for their lives defensively in the last quarter to prevent another Northwestern upset for the second straight year. Herb Neathery saved Illinois once when he intercepted a Bill Burson pass on the Illini one yard line after the Wildcats had driven to the 34. Al Brosky came up with another interception in the waning minutes of the game to halt another threat.

Oddly enough, neither Rebecca nor Ohio State's kicker Vic Janowicz had attempted a field goal the week before in the 0-0 deadlock in Columbus.

"That's surprising, isn't it?" said Rebecca when he thought back, "but actually neither team got inside the other team's 30 yard line in that game. It was a defensive battle all the way."

It was also a matter of a rather average Buckeye team rising up to the moment in Woody Hayes' first year as head coach.

Wilfrid Smith expressed that view in the *Chicago Tribune* when he wrote, "The unpredictable Ohio State Buckeyes rose above season-long mediocrity to hold Illinois to a scoreless tie before 81,000 who expected to see the Illini clinch a Rose Bowl bid and at least a tie for the Big Ten title."

Rebecca, now the director of housing for the University of Illinois, with an office just a couple of blocks away from Memorial Stadium, believes he may have been Illinois' first specialist.

"I came to Illinois as a quarterback, but I was awfully small at 5-7 and about 160 pounds, and when Tommy O'Connell transferred to Illinois I could see that I'd better spend more time working on my kicking. The last couple of years on the team that's all I did, although I'd played quarterback some with the jayvees my first two seasons."

O'Connell, strangely enough, became the second transfer quarterback to lead Illinois to a Rose Bowl in his first year at his new school, following in the footsteps of Perry Moss of 1946. O'Connell had originally enrolled at Notre Dame and spent his freshman year there.

"I got a call from Tommy one night, and he expressed the desire to come play for us," Eliot recalled. "I told him that there was nothing that we could do until after he'd talked with his coach, Frank Leahy. He did that, and Frank agreed to allow him to transfer. He sat out one year and was ready to go in 1951.

"Tommy gave our offense the passing dimension that we badly needed. He opened up the game for us. We always like to throw the ball, and I always felt that to make the running game go, you've got to loosen those babies up."

O'Connell blended well into Eliot's offense that boasted Bill Tate, known as the Mattoon Mauler, at fullback and Johnny Karras, who was called the Argo Express, at one halfback. Veteran Don Stevens and newcomer Pete Bachouros alternated at the other halfback behind a smallish but talented line.

That line was led by Chuck Studley, who found being at the bottom of a pileup nothing new after spending two years as a torpedo man in a navy submarine.

The Illini had lost the Big Ten rushing leader, fullback Dick Raklovits, along with stellar linemen like Tony Klimek, Charles Brown, and Leo Cahill, in addition to All-Americans Bill Vohaska and Al Tate, from the 1950 team.

But the Illini still had Karras. As the Illini headed into the 1951 season, Karras was the leading offensive threat on the strength of his strong showings in both 1949 (826 yards) and 1950 (593 yards).

Quarterback Tommy O'Connell led Illini in 1951.

"He was an elusive, will-o-the-wisp who always was a threat anytime he had the ball," is Eliot's memory of the man who scored five touchdowns in the first two games of the 1951 season.

Karras rambled for three touchdowns in the season-opening 27-13 victory over UCLA and then picked up two more when the Illini started league action with a 14-10 victory over Wisconsin the following weekend in Champaign.

The Illini had to rally in the last quarter to nip the Badgers after an early lead of 7-0 on Karras' six-yard touchdown scamper; Wisconsin scraped together a 10-7 halftime lead, and the Illini went into the fourth quarter with their backs to the wall and O'Connell injured and on the bench. Don Engels, who had come in at quarterback, found himself bottled up as he faded to pass in the fourth quarter, but he let the ball fly anyway. It traveled 30 yards in the air, bounced off the hands of end Steve Nosek (the intended receiver), and landed squarely in the outstretched arms of another Illini receiver, Rex Smith, who was tackled on the eight yard line. Pete Bachouros' five-yard run set up Karras' three-yard lunge for the winning touchdown.

That narrow win over Wisconsin, aided by the deflected pass play, proved to be an important one as the season progressed.

O'Connell was still sidelined the next weekend when the Illini took on Eastern power Syracuse, but Engels still had a hot hand, hitting nine of 12 for 180 yards, with Joe Vernasco catching two touchdown passes and Karras tallying two more. Syracuse was bombed 41-20.

The Illini defense began to mature when the Illini reached the fourth game of the year against Indiana, and the Hoosiers were shut out 21-0. Karras continued the pace that would make him an All-American at season's end by scoring all three touchdowns, but the defense drew most of the raves, and Al Brosky bagged two interceptions.

That brought the Illini to a battle for the Big Ten lead against a Michigan team that was unbeaten in four conference

John Karras was three-year, ground-gaining star for Illinois running attack.

1952 Rose Bowl Football Squad—Front row, left to right: Sammy Rebecca, Rex Smith, Charles Ulrich, William Tate, Pete Bachouros, Johnny Karras, Coach Ray Eliot, Charles Studley, Dan Sabino, Robert Weddell, Donald Stevens, Joe Vernasco, Tommy O'Connell, Don Gnidovic. Second row: Assistant Coach Burt Ingwersen, Kenneth Miller, Cliff Waldbeser, Stan Wallace, Robert Lenzini, Elie Popa, Charles Boerio, Rudy Valentino, Al Brosky, Lawrence Stevens, Donald Ernst, Marvin Berschet, Andy Wodziak, Donald Tate. Third row: Assistant

games and loaded with veterans from the 1950 club that had lost to the Illini but won the conference title.

A crowd of 71,119 human icicles braved a driving snowstorm to turn out for the game in Memorial Stadium. A 40-mile gale and two inches of blowing snow neutralized both teams'

Coach Mel Brewer, Herb Neathery, John Ryan, Austin Duke,
Paul Luhrsen, Steve Nosek, Jim Baughman, Claude Taliaferro,
Tom Murphy, Don Henss, Dan Peterson, Richard Jenkins,
George Kasap, Joe Cole, Manager Keith Baumann. Fourth row:
Assistant Coach Bob King, Assistant Coach Ralph Fletcher,
Trainer Ike Hill, John Bauer, Marshall Dusenbury, Herb Bor-
man, Don Engels, Clarence DeMoss, Assistant Coach Lou Agase,
Assistant Coach Chuck Purvis, Scout Elmer Engel.

offenses, and it was a scoreless deadlock as the game entered the
final five minutes.

But suddenly Illinois' offense warmed to the importance
of the game. The Illini took over on their own 16 yard line. At
that point O'Connell had managed just four completions in 12

passing attempts in the miserable conditions, but doggedly he again took to the air. After Karras broke away for 15 yards to get the Illini out of the hole, O'Connell targeted Smith for a 23-yard pickup and then found Smith open again for 14 more. Incredibly O'Connell now could not miss, and the receivers whose hands were cold, numb claws squeezed everything he threw. Vernasco grabbed another for 15, and Tate tore up the middle for 12, to bring the ball to the eight yard line. O'Connell was running the Illini drive now like a man possessed, and he stutter-stepped backward into the pocket and threw again. Smith was almost alone in the end zone, and he cradled the ball like a man handling a newborn. Rebecca's kick split the uprights, and soon it was over. And as the fans filed out of the stadium that day, their bodies were frozen, but their hearts were on fire.

After the 40-13 win over Iowa the following Saturday, it would be up to the defense to carry the Illini to the championship in the last two games. And what a defense it was.

"That three-deep secondary of Al Brosky, Stan Wallace, and Herb Neathery was probably as fine a one as I ever had," Eliot recalled many years later. "Brosky had a great sense of getting to the ball when it went into the air, and so did the others. They really believed in their defense. We never felt at a disadvantage at all when the other team was throwing the football. The more they threw it, the better we liked it. Our defensive game revolved around them and our two linebackers, Chuck Boerio and Elie Popa. Boerio, of course, wasn't the biggest linebacker in the world at 195 pounds, but he was always all over the ball park making tackles. He was one of those people who loved contact."

This was a team that took winning and the game seriously but still had its share of fun.

O'Connell remembered one incident in the Iowa game that almost doubled him up with laughter.

"I walked into the huddle to give the signals, and every player—every doggone one of them—had his eyes crossed. I started laughing so hard I could hardly tell them the next play," he said.

"Then at Indiana late in the game we were ahead 21-0, and Dan Sabino had his hand raised for the huddle and no one

202

would huddle. 'Darn you guys,' he said. 'If you don't huddle, I'm walking off the field.' He was really mad."

But nobody was mad at anybody after the 3-0 win over Northwestern, least of all little Sam Rebecca. Illinois was once again California-bound, this time with an unbeaten team.

In the swank Edgewater Beach Hotel that night Eliot and his friends were still celebrating. The great singer Hildegarde was the entertainer there for the evening.

Eliot, in high spirits, was able to convince her that she needed a new song to dress up her act—something with some class—something like "Illinois Loyalty."

"Ray had the words, and she had the voice," said someone who was there. "They both sang it, and most of the audience joined in. They were a great combination. The whole thing brought down the house. It was a night to end all nights."

"Hey, Are You
Guys As Ready..."

When Illinois arrived in Pasadena in December of 1951, the Pacific Coast had a far different impression of Big Ten football and considerably more respect than it had when the Illini had gone west to open the new Rose Bowl pact five years before.

Big Ten teams had won all five previous games from coast teams, beginning with Illinois' one-sided win over UCLA on New Year's Day, 1947.

"Hey, are you guys as ready as the last Illinois team was?" comedian Bob Hope asked when the Illini went on a tour of the Paramount movie studio shortly after arriving on the West Coast.

Hope admitted that he had made a friendly wager with his buddy Bing Crosby and was picking the Illini to win.

The West Coast sportswriters were not as confident as Hope was that the Big Ten could continue its dominance, however.

"We had another small team and Stanford was big, and I think the West Coast writers decided this was one game the Pac-8 could win after seeing Chuck Studley was playing guard at only 185 pounds and Johnny Karras was just 170," Ray Eliot remembers.

"I guess I made all the West Coast writers mad again because I banned them from our practice sessions, but I'd go downtown for a press conference just about every night. I remember one of the writers asked me if I'd mind if Stanford worked out against one of the pro teams, which apparently was training nearby out there. So I said, 'No, anything Chuck Taylor wants to do to get his team ready is fine with me.' That night I got a call from a writer in San Francisco, and he accused me of encouraging Stanford to practice against that pro team so all their players would be hurt for their game against us. I couldn't win with those West Coast writers no matter what I said out there."

The West Coast questioned Illinois' offensive punch after its late season slide. But the game of football is not won or lost in the newspaper columns. It is what happens on the playing field and in the locker room that counts.

And fullback Bill Tate, who would become the star of Illinois' one-sided 40-7 victory over Stanford, gave his teammates something more important to think about before they took the field that New Year's Day of 1952.

"I was talking with Alex Agase out at practice last week, and he said something I think all of us should hear," Tate told his teammates. "Alex told me that what we'd do today was something we'd remember all our lives. If we go out there and win, it will be something we'll cherish for all time. So let's get out there and do it."

Stanford, however, proved to be a formidable adversary for the first half of the game and led 7-6 at the intermission. The team came into the classic with a 9-1 record, after having its perfect-season hopes wiped out by a 20-7 loss to California in the regular season finale.

Illinois took the opening kickoff and surged 76 yards in six plays for the game's opening touchdown, with halfback Pete Bachouros slashing over left end for the score from seven yards out.

But, for the first time in his college career, Sam Rebecca saw one of his extra-point kicks blocked. The Illini, however, led 6-0 and appeared to be off to the races.

The Indians, surprisingly, came right back with a score of their own, with Harry Hugasian capping an 84-yard Stanford drive and Gary Kerkorian connecting for the extra point and a one-point Stanford edge. Neither team scored in the second quarter, although Rebecca came close but missed on a 37-yard field goal try.

"We decided we had to open our offense up more in the

second half, and that's what we did," Eliot remembers, "but the play that really turned the game around for us was Stan Wallace's pass interception."

Wallace wrestled the Kerkorian pass out of the outstretched hands of Stanford's Bill Storum and ran it back 54 yards to the Indians' 13 yard line in the third quarter. The Illini scored in just three plays. Tate picked up three yards and Johnny Karras picked up five more before Tate took a pitchout and rolled over right end for the score. Rebecca's kick made it 13-7.

Illinois scored almost at will in the fourth quarter against a Stanford team whose spirit had been broken by the sensational defensive play by the Illini sophomore.

The Illini boosted their lead to 20-7 soon after the fourth quarter began, with Karras rolling seven yards over left end for the score.

The next time Stanford had possession, Wallace went to his knees to come up with another interception on the Stanford 44. Illinois needed only four plays to score, with Karras exploding for 15 yards and Tate going the final eight.

Everyone got into the act then, with Eliot substituting freely. The Illini added another score on a seven-yard run by Don Stevens on the heels of a 45-yard escape by freshman halfback Clarence DeMoss.

Don Engels came into the game to replace Tommy O'Connell at quarterback and threw a six-yard scoring pass to sophomore end Rocky Ryan. The ball was thrown in between Ryan and another Illini end, Steve Nosek, but Ryan wrestled him for it and pulled it in.

"No sir," Ryan would say later in the dressing room when asked if he had thought of letting Nosek make the catch. "That play was called for me."

The Illini locker room was filled with chatterboxes and smiling faces after it ended.

"No offense, huh? What jokers," laughed Eliot's backfield coach, Chuck Purvis.

"They just don't hit like they do in the Big Ten," winked linebacker Chuck Boerio.

Al Brosky was telling reporters how he tried to talk Eliot into letting the entire defensive team play on offensive in the

Fullback Bill Tate was an Illini hero in 1952 Rose Bowl game.

last minutes.

"I was ready to go in there and play quarterback," said Brosky. "I would have passed them dizzy. But Ray wasn't having any of that."

Line coach Burt Ingwersen was high in his praise for the men up front.

"You know I became convinced today that I've never seen three better small men on offense in the middle of the line than Don Sabino at center and Chuck Studley and Don Gnidovic at the guards. That Sabino is one of the most underrated players we have. What a job he did today," said Ingwersen.

"Did you see those holes in front of me?" Tate said happily.

The Mattoon Mauler had come out of the game in the fourth quarter with exactly 150 yards gained on the ground, just one shy of the Rose Bowl record set by Bobby Grayson in 1934. Tate could have had the record, too, had he not lost one 11-yard run in the third quarter by a holding penalty.

"We had no way of knowing just how many yards he had, and the only thing we were thinking about then was getting as many kids into the game as we could," Eliot says now. "If we'd known he was that close to the record, we could have broken it by a mile."

Illinois did break the Rose Bowl rushing record the Illini had set in 1947 with 360 yards on the ground. The team which had its problems in its last two games offensively had exploded against Stanford.

"Stanford, according to our scouting reports, liked to use a seven-diamond defense," Eliot remembered, recalling the game not long ago. "They wanted to use seven linemen, one linebacker, and a three-deep secondary against our straight-T and close formations. And they wanted to use a 6-2 when we went into our wide formation. Knowing that, I devised a shift. We'd start in the 'T' to get them in the seven diamond and then shift into a slot formation. Then there were times when we'd slot, they'd go to the 6-2, and we'd shift back to the T. I think those shifts bothered them defensively, especially in the second half."

Bert Bertine, the sports editor of the *Champaign-Urbana Courier* at the time, reflected on the game's one-sided nature in his column the next day and put the differences between the two teams in far more simple terms.

"To our way of thinking," Bertine wrote, "the chief difference between Big Ten and Pacific Coast football remains what might be called 'decadent youth,' as Bob Zuppke would put it.

"The Midwest lads are still the more rugged, the more tough. They'll go out and whale into an opponent with complete abandon, and the West just can't take it. We never saw what you'd call a bone-rattling tackle by Stanford all day. Zuppke, we're sure, would say the California youths are a bit decadent. They are a bit glorified, a bit pampered."

Whatever the reason, thousands of Illinois fans who made the trip to the West Coast had a glorious New Year's Day.

And thousands of others watched the game on television wherever they could find a set as NBC for the first time televised a Rose Bowl game live. It was also the first nationally televised college football game by a major network.

The *Courier*'s Helen Farlow was one of many who made the trip to Chicago to watch the game on television. The next day she wrote:

"If you should chance to see sundry Champaign-Urbana leading citizens (me for instance) wandering the streets Wednesday with shambling gait and bleary eyes, do not scorn them as sodden leftovers from a New Year's Eve revel. Instead, praise them and ask them how was the game. They are high type Illini boosters who traveled to such vantage points as St. Louis or Chicago to see the Rose Bowl on TV."

Illinois was rated No. 2 in the nation behind Kansas in the final Associated Press poll.

But nobody could have convinced Grantland Rice, the legendary sportswriter, that Illinois was not No. 1. In his nationally syndicated column after the Rose Bowl game he wrote:

"I doubt that any other team in the country would have beaten this hard-hitting Illinois squad that Ray Eliot coached and directed so ably. Here was a hard-bitten, fast-moving squad that knew its job. I think it was a much better team than Kentucky and many other bowl winners. The weather was perfect. So was Illinois."

And somewhere that night Hildegarde must have at least hummed one bar of "Illinois Loyalty." Bob Hope certainly did.

Open The Gates,
It's Caroline And Bates

"Where are we on halfbacks?" Ray Eliot wanted to know when he returned from a State Department-sponsored trip to Tokyo in the spring of 1952 after Illinois' victory in the Rose Bowl.

Eliot was asking one of his assistants about recruiting. Eliot found out it was going well, but there was a gnawing need at the halfback position Eliot had been most concerned about.

"What about the guy, Caroline, from South Carolina, they wrote us about?"

"As far as I know he's still available," said one of Eliot's aides.

"All right," said Eliot. "I'm going to write him and offer him a chance with us."

In Columbia, South Carolina, J. C. Caroline happily received the news. He would have his opportunity to play football at Illinois, the chance to follow in the footsteps of his idol, Buddy Young.

Pete Evans, a Columbia grocer and an Illinois fan, along with Bill McCarthy, general manager of the Columbia Reds' minor league baseball team, had written letters to Eliot, as had Caroline's high school coach, John McHugh.

"We had no film on him," Eliot remembers now. "We pretty much had to take their word for it that he was as good as they said he was. We'd never seen him play.

"I remember the first time I saw him when he walked into my office in old Huff Gym that summer. I took one look at those legs, which looked like two pencils, and I wondered what we'd been thinking of."

The bandy-legged Caroline was given a construction job that summer in Champaign to earn his tuition—there still were no NCAA scholarships in those days—and when the fall began, he was given a work-program job helping out in the kitchen of the Inman Hotel under the restaurant's head chef, Herbert Nesbitt. Nesbitt would become a great friend and fan of Caroline's through the years. By washing dishes and doing other assorted odd jobs in the kitchen, Caroline earned enough money for food and for his $10-a-month room with a bed covered by an army blanket.

That fall Caroline was assigned to the freshman team along with more than a hundred others.

The 1952 season turned into a disappointment for the Illini. Despite a good returning nucleus from the 1951 championship squad, the Illini were persistently plagued by injuries and finished 4-5 for the year, 2-5 in the league.

"Things got so bad with injuries by the time we played Michigan in the middle of the year, Ray had to move me from end to the backfield for that game because most all of our backs were hurt," Rocky Ryan remembers.

"That was one of the four games we won that season, though, by a 22-13 score, and Bennie Oosterbaan, the old Michigan coach, told me once that seeing me line up in the backfield messed up their whole defensive game plan."

Tommy O'Connell passed for 1,761 yards in 1952—still a single-season Illini record—and Ryan caught 45 passes for 714 yards and five touchdowns, a school receiving record at the time. Rex Smith also grabbed 45 for 642 yards the same year. But the ground attack sputtered.

Yet, when things were the most discouraging in 1952 and the Illini training room's injury lists were the longest, Eliot and his assistants could find some encouragement from the reports being carried back each night from the freshman practice field.

"I think we may have something after all in this kid Caroline," they would say. "He's been looking good, and there's another good freshman halfback, the kid by the name of Mickey Bates."

"Well, don't let those gol-durned newspapermen know

211

about them so they can blow them up before they've ever gained an inch for Illinois," Ray would say in typical Eliot bluster.

Illinois frosh coaches, true to Eliot's wishes, kept the wraps on Caroline and Bates through the fall and the following spring's workouts.

"We did a pretty good job of keeping them hidden," Eliot says and smiles now. "But I can tell you we had no doubts about what J. C.'s potential was.

"I remember what a scare I got once in spring practice when I looked over and Caroline was down and holding his ankle.

"J. C. had been playing high school and freshman ball at Illinois without a bit of tape on his ankles. The first time I really looked at his ankles closely that spring, I noticed how skinny they were, and so I went to the trainers before practice that day and told them that I wanted a basket-weave on his ankles every day, game or practice. That day they put the basket-weave on, and that was the day he sprained one of his ankles. We never taped his ankles again after that. They were always wrapped but never taped."

By the time the Illini opened the 1953 season, Caroline was in the starting lineup. That year the substitution rules were made more stringent, and the game swung back to one-platoon football.

The Illini opened against Nebraska, and the game ended in a 21-21 tie. Caroline looked good offensively, scoring a touchdown, but had some problems defensively, allowing a Cornhusker touchdown pass to sail over his head into the hands of a wide-open receiver.

"That really wasn't J. C.'s fault," said Eliot, remembering. "We had some other guys back there who just were not accustomed to playing defense and J.C. spent most of the game trying to help them."

The Illini whipped Stanford 33-21 the following weekend, and that set the stage for the first conference game of the year against Ohio State which had unveiled its own sophomore sensation, Howard "Hopalong" Cassady.

"We pointed for the Ohio game from the start of the season," Eliot remembers.

"That was the first game that both Mickey and I started in the backfield," Caroline recalls now. "I remember one thing

Illinois' "big three" offensively in 1953 were quarterback Elry Falkenstein, J.C. Caroline, and Mickey Bates. In those days the two running backs were known as "Mr. Boom" (Bates) and "Mr. Zoom" (Caroline).

that happened the night before the game.

"We were in our room, and we got a telephone call from a young lady who was a student at Ohio State who said she was Dorothy Dandridge's cousin. She invited us to a party they were having.

"We told her we couldn't come, but I used that on Mickey to get him psyched up for the game. I kept telling him that this cousin of the famous movie star was going to be at the game watching him play. I don't know whether it helped or not, but Mickey had a great game."

Eliot particularly remembers an incident that took place just before the game that day with Woody Hayes' Buckeyes.

"Before we'd ever go on another team's field before a game, we'd always try to check with the opposing coach and find how he wanted us to work out on the gridiron. So we started looking for Woody to find out just where he wanted us to go. But I never could find him.

"So we just went out on the field and took the near end zone and started loosening up. We finished that and were passing the ball out on the field, and all of a sudden Ohio State came out and completely encircled us and started doing their exercises when we were passing the ball.

"Ohio State doing something like that really made our kids mad. Burt Ingwersen had our linemen down in the end zone, and some of the Ohio State people came up to him and told him to move to the other end of the field. They said that was their end zone.

"As I recall, Rocky Ryan was the one who was really mad. He had a short temper anyway, and he exploded once we got into the dressing room and had our guys really fired up. Let's just say that we went on the field in the proper state of mind."

The Illini broke loose for three touchdowns in the first 14 minutes of the game, for a 21-0 first-quarter lead, but Ohio State stormed back for 20 points of its own in the second quarter, to make it a tight game again at halftime. But the Illini emerged from their halftime talk in high gear again, rumbling for two more scores in the third quarter and another in the fourth. This time, Ohio State did not bounce back.

Paul Hornung wrote in the *Columbus Dispatch*:

"Illinois employed the old Army game—a relentless infantry attack—Saturday afternoon to send Ohio State's high-riding Buckeyes crashing to the Ohio State turf, 41-20, in football's biggest upset of the 1953 season.

"The season's largest turnout sat unbelieving as the inspired Illini, jet-powered by two driving halfbacks, charged through Buckeye defenses for a fabulous 432 yards in their stunning achievement."

W. W. Hayes stepped before the assembled press corps after it was over and, according to Hornung, said:

"It was pretty obvious. We just weren't able to stop their running attack. They just ran us to death, that's the whole story. They're a great offensive ball club, and the only way you can beat a team like that is keep the ball away from them. We couldn't do that."

Caroline finished the game with a stunning 192 yards and

two touchdowns. Bates racked up 147 yards on the ground and four touchdowns.

"Don't forget that we had one touchdown called back in that game, too," Eliot recalls. "J. C. made another good run in that game for a score that was called back by an offside penalty. Jay had another pass he caught called back that could have given us another one. We missed another touchdown in the game on a fumble on the Ohio one yard line.

"It was just one of those days when just about everything went right for us."

Illinois went on to mow down Minnesota 27-7, Syracuse 20-13, Purdue 21-0, and Michigan 19-3. The Illini headed into the Wisconsin game unbeaten and perhaps a bit overconfident.

The Badgers slugged the Illini with a 34-17 setback.

"We just didn't play a good game, but Wisconsin deserved some of the credit for that," Eliot says now. "The thing that occurred to me most as I looked at the movies afterward was their power. They were just brutal with Alan Ameche coming in there off tackle. We were not a big team. I can still see Don Ernst trying to hold out their left tackle, who looked like a giant. They were a big strong team, and they just beat us."

The loss left Illinois tied for the conference lead with Michigan State, which had seen its 29-game winning streak snapped by Purdue early in the season. MSU, however, bounced back from that setback to win the rest of its games.

Illinois blasted Northwestern 39-14 in the final game of the year, and Caroline, en route to All-American honors, finished the season with 1,256 yards, with 919 in the Big Ten, a conference record that stood for many years.

"We felt confident that we were going to the Rose Bowl again, even though we had tied Michigan State for the conference championship," Eliot remembers now. "It was Michigan State's first year in the conference, and they had been on probation the whole season for something that had happened there before.

"But the faculty representatives took them off probation after the season ended, and the conference voted them as the bowl representative. I've always looked with askance on that decision. It was a great disappointment, both to me and my players, but I called Biggie Munn the night it was decided and congratulated him and wished him and his team well."

Doug Mills, the Illini athletic director at the time, remembers that decision of the other directors that day vividly, too.

215

"They voted by secret ballot, of course," Mills remembers, "but every time they voted it kept ending up in a tie. Neither I nor the Michigan State director voted.

"Fritz Crisler, the Michigan director, wasn't able to make it to the meeting. His plane had been fogged in at Detroit, but he kept calling his vote in on each ballot.

"I have no way of knowing, of course, but I always felt that if Crisler had been at the meeting and had been able to talk to the other directors in person, it would have been different. I don't know how many ballots exactly it took for Michigan State to finally get the bid, but I know it was a lot of them.

"It was as big a disappointment to me as it was to Ray and everyone else connected with Illinois."

It would be the last time the Illini would win the Big Ten title under Eliot. Caroline and Bates would return amid much preseason hoopla in 1954, but that year would prove that even great backs need men up front to block. Most of the experienced linemen of 1953 were missing, and the Illini slid to 1-8.

Time Out: J. C. Caroline

J.C. Caroline today is a living example of how good the game of football can be to a man who played it well.

He was born in a one-room shack in Warrenton, Georgia, into a family of poverty-plagued farm laborers. He spent most of his young life in black Southern ghettos in Georgia; Jacksonville, Florida; and Columbia, South Carolina. He did not know a permanent home until he was in his early teens.

"My grandparents and aunts and uncles took care of me most of the time until I was 13 or 14 years old," said Caroline, in a poignant remembrance. "I went from one place to another until I went to live with my mother and my stepfather in Jacksonville."

But he had found a home in football several years before, playing the game on a windswept dirt field with a bundle of rolled-up rags for a ball.

"We played tackle even though we didn't have any padding to wear," Caroline remembers now. "Most of the guys I played with were older and bigger and I had to learn how to outrun them.

"You had to learn how to dodge when you ran when you played in the places we played. You had to run around clothesline poles, trees, and parked cars, and all kinds of things like that."

It was in Jacksonville, Florida, that Caroline first was introduced to organized football on the junior high school level. He also showed his athletic ability as an unbeaten Golden

Gloves boxer in the 137-pound division.

"Boxing was the only sport my mother didn't want me to be in," Caroline recalls. "She made me give that up, but football replaced it for me."

The family moved to Columbia, South Carolina, and Caroline quickly became an all-around star athlete at Booker T. Washington High School. In four years of running track, Caroline was unbeaten in the 100-, 220- and 440-yard dashes. He also was a four-year starter on the school's basketball team, and in his senior year he was second in the state high school tennis tournament in the singles division. His football career, all the while, was sensational. In his senior season he gained over 2,000 yards and scored 20 touchdowns.

It was when he was in high school that Caroline found out about sports as the great equalizer.

"I'd go to a party and there'd be guys there with nicer clothes and a nice car and such, but it didn't bother me because I knew that I'd done some things in sports they wished they could do," he remembers.

"When I was a kid I had to depend on what other people could do for me. By then, I'd gotten to the point that what happened to me depended on how far my own abilities could carry me, and I liked that.

"Sports were an 'out' for me. There were probably other people in Columbia who were just as good athletes, but they didn't want it as badly as I did. You could look back in my high school yearbook and see that my ambition in life, which I said then, was to be a professional football player."

Caroline, of course, reached that goal. He spent 11 years in the pro ranks, one in the Canadian League and 10 in the NFL as a star defensive back for the Chicago Bears.

But another ambition of Caroline in those high school days was a college education. Football and Illinois helped make that possible.

"My high school coach, John McHugh, made up his mind that he was going to get me to Illinois, and he's the one who wrote Ray Eliot about me. He felt Illinois was a place where a black player could expect to get a fair shake because of the success Buddy Young had. I remember I didn't hear definitely from Illinois that they wanted me until May, and I got on a

218

train and headed for Champaign," he said.

"It must have been a 30-hour trip from Columbia. I remember taking one train from Columbia to Cincinnati and another one to Tolono and then getting on the bus to come to Champaign. I got a job at the Inman Hotel in the kitchen to pay for my room and board."

There were 123 players out for the Illinois freshman team in 1952, Caroline recalls.

"I spent the whole season on anywhere from the sixth to the 10th team," Caroline remembers with a laugh. "But I was still sure I could play on the big-time level, and I felt like it was just a matter of time before I had a chance to prove it.

"I didn't get discouraged because I was happy to be in college, and that was as important to me as anything."

Caroline burst on the college football scene the following year like a meteor, earning All-American honors as a sophomore.

"I've always said that I wished freshmen would have been eligible then the way they are now. I think I could have been a better player as a freshman than I was as a sophomore. I had just come off competing in track in high school and I was really in top shape physically. I was mature enough then to have played," he said.

Caroline played both offense and defense in college but grabbed most of the headlines for his performances as a runner. In pro football he was a defensive specialist.

Looking back, which aspect of the game did he like best?

"That would be hard to say because I enjoyed playing both ways. I think I liked playing defensive back as much as running because it's such a challenge to try to stop a great runner, to try to figure out just what he's going to do. The offensive players, though, got most of the attention when I played in college, so I guess if I had to make a choice then I would have picked offense. I'm glad I had a chance to play both offense and defense in college."

Football has been good to Caroline since his retirement as an active player. He completed work toward his college degree in 1967 and has been an assistant coach at Illinois since that time.

"Yes, I guess I have been lucky, and the game has been

219

good to me," he said. "I've got a super wife (LaVerne) and a great family (Janice, Jayna and JoLynn) and a lot to be thankful for."

A rags-to-riches story?

"I don't know about that," Caroline said and smiled. "I sure was raggy once upon a time, and I'm still not rich from a money standpoint, but we're happy and comfortable, and I guess that's being rich, too."

No Titles–
But A Lot Of Fun

Illinois won no Big Ten football championships in Ray Eliot's last six years as head coach, but that did not mean the Illini did not have some fun.

If the Illini could not win them all, they could win some big ones. Major upsets became Eliot's stock in trade in the late 1950s.

Eliot would also be able to take a bow for producing all kinds of talented individuals–players like Ray Nitschke, the brilliant linebacker for many years with the Green Bay Packers; Bill Brown, who had a long, illustrious career with the Minnesota Vikings; Bobby Mitchell, an All-Pro receiver with the Washington Redskins; Abe Woodson, a star secondary performer for the St. Louis Cardinals and San Francisco 49ers, along with others. One of his quarterbacks in that era, Tom Haller, made his mark in baseball, not football, and had a sparkling career as a catcher with the San Francisco Giants.

But there would also be men of modest athletic ability who would perform to the height of their capabilities–players like John Easterbrook, a quarterback for the Illini in the late 1950s. Eliot remembers the Easterbrooks of those teams just as he does the Nitschkes and the Browns.

"Bill Brown not only was a wonderful athlete, but a remarkable person," Eliot mused on a spring day in 1975. "He wasn't the fastest guy in the world even then, but he was a good, solid, sturdy runner.

"What Bill had that made him great was a great state of

Bill Brown was a bone-jarring ballcarrier for the Illini in 1958, 1959, and 1960.

mind. He worked hard and was dedicated to the game. He got as much out of his body as anyone could. You see so many bodies walking around today that could be super athletes if they had Bill's dedication."

Nitschke came to Eliot as an all-state quarterback.

"He has one of the strongest throwing arms of anyone I've ever seen," Eliot remembers. "He could throw the ball a mile. But we had two seasoned quarterbacks when he came from upstate, and I sat down with him and discussed where we were going to play him in college.

"I told him I felt like he would be a tremendous asset to us as a fullback and as a man to back up our line on defense. I don't think he particularly liked the idea of playing fullback at first, but we gave him a couple of pass plays, and that made him happy.

"I knew from the beginning that this was a guy who came to play. I remember once in a game against Ohio State, one of our players ran off the field and said, 'You'd better get Ray out of there. He's lost some of his teeth, and he's bleeding.'

"Well, we got him out right away and got him over to the doctor, and a little bit later I walked over to check on him. He looked up at me and said, 'Coach, you might as well let me get back in there. They can't hurt me any more. I've already lost my smile.'"

Nitschke has not forgotten the day that he left four front teeth in the turf of Ohio Stadium, either.

"The thing I remember the most was the trip back home," Nitschke said not long ago. "Everyone else was eating steak, and I was sitting there with a straw in my mouth drinking a milk shake. That really made me mad."

But Nitschke has other more fond memories of his playing days at Illinois that he prefers to recall.

"Ray Eliot was one of the most inspirational people I've ever come in contact with," he said.

Nitschke, who played for the late Vince Lombardi for many years at Green Bay during the Packers' pro dynasty, thought for a minute and said, "In some ways, Ray was more inspirational than Lombardi, especially in the locker room right before a big game, because he had that dramatic delivery when he talked to the squad."

Nitschke remembers one time, though, when Eliot's best-laid plans for a big emotional pregame send-off ran into a problem. It was the last game of Nitschke's senior year against Northwestern.

"Ray started his pregame speech by telling all the seniors what a credit we'd been to Illinois and how we'd become a part of a great tradition; and he kept building and building; and just when he'd finished, we could hear the Illini fight song starting on a record player behind us," said Nitschke.

"But not long after it started, we heard this screech com-

Bobby Mitchell was an Illini hero in the 1950s.

ing over the speaker. The needle had slipped, and there was nothing but noise. First, there was a smile. Then somebody laughed, and soon everyone was roaring, Ray included."

The Illini beat Northwestern 27-0 anyway.

"I was satisfied with the way I played defense at Illinois," says Nitschke, "but I always felt I could have done a little bit better on offense than I did. By the time I learned to run out of a three-point stance and block from the fullback spot, my college career was over. But defense was my favorite. I was always naturally aggressive and liked to be close to where the ball was. I had good coaching at Illinois, and we played in a good conference, and all that helped me when I got to the pros."

Mitchell and Woodson, a pair of lightning-quick speed merchants, were both star halfbacks on Eliot's 1956 team that was only 2-5-1 for the season but upset a powerful Michigan State team that came into the game ranked No.1 in the nation.

Woodson scored all three Illini touchdowns that day in a

20-13 triumph. His second, a 70-yard breakaway, tied the score at 13-13, then he took a screen pass and ran 82 yards for the winning tally.

The 1957 team also had a losing record, 4-5, but produced more upset excitement on Homecoming Day by dumping a Minnesota team that was rated No. 3 in the country coming into the game. Illinois posted a one-sided 34-13 triumph.

Wilfrid Smith wrote in the *Chicago Tribune*:

"The Fightin' Illini smashed the myth of Minnesota might this autumn afternoon.

"Before a near-capacity throng of 69,919, Illinois shackled Gopher backs, who had scored 108 points in three previous games, gained 164 yards on three consecutive attacks for three touchdowns and moved easily to the victory.

"Illinois' victory was based on speed and desire. The Illini advantage in mobility was amazing. They set up defenses that invited passes, yet maneuvered to cover passes so well that Bobby Cox, Minnesota quarterback, failed in all attempts in the first half. Minnesota did not complete a pass for three quarters."

Eliot continued to keep the returning alumni happy on Homecoming Day in 1958. He unveiled Bill Brown, who as a sophomore roared for 130 yards in 22 carries in Illinois' 16-0 victory over Michigan State.

Before the 1959 season began, on a day in March, Eliot announced that the coming season would be his last as a coach.

He issued the following statement:

"I suppose every football coach has considered and hoped that his eventual future might be in an administrative role in his university's athletic program. For this reason, I am gratified that Director Douglas R. Mills, Faculty Representative Robert B. Browne, and the Athletic Board have tendered me the position as assistant athletic director.

"My decision to accept was a difficult one—as it is always difficult to decide that one will leave the firing line of the fierce competition which is Big Ten football. But, the choice was made in the off season when unhurried reflection on the future is possible without the heat of battle or influence of a winning or losing season....

"The new position offers a great challenge for achieve-

Bobby Mitchell (22) carries the ball against Michigan State with Bill Burrell (68) providing interference and Ray Nitschke (32)

and Dale Smith (44) throwing blocks.

227

ments by the Fighting Illini, and my hope is that I can fulfill the obligations which I have to the Athletic Association, to the university, and to the traditions of our teams."

That last Eliot team turned out to be one of his best, and it made a run at a Big Ten title despite a rocky start in a season-opening loss to Indiana 20-0.

The second foe of the season was Army, with a nine game unbeaten streak, a national ranking, and a highly publicized "lonesome end" attack featuring Bill Carpenter.

Captain Bill Burrell, whom Eliot would recently call "one of the greatest linebackers I ever saw play the game," turned in a stunning defensive effort that day. Burrell forced two fumbles with bone-rattling tackles and recovered two others.

Sophomore quarterback Mel Myers passed to Johnny Counts, who scored on a 41-yard play, and the brothers Brown—Bill and Jim—each tallied once from the one yard line

Bill Burrell—"one of the greatest linebackers I ever saw play the game," according to Ray Eliot.

as the Illini posted a 20-14 upset win.

The key to the Illini offensive attack was a new formation Eliot put in for the game which had a halfback in motion and two ends on the same side of the formation, one of them split wide.

"I guess," said Eliot, smiling in the locker room afterward, "you could say we had an 'unlonesome' end."

Buoyed by the upset of Army, Illinois would go on to whip Ohio State 9-0 and Minnesota 14-6, but the Illini would be tied by Purdue 7-7 and beaten by Michigan 20-15.

"If one play in the Purdue game had gone differently and one had in the Michigan game, no telling what kind of a year we might have had," Eliot says today.

Kicker Gerald Wood had a chance to win the Purdue game, but his 26-yard boot fell just inches short. Exactly four inches short, some would say in the dressing room later. Illinois had been forced to take a five-yard penalty to get Wood into the game with 18 seconds left, and those five yards might have made a big difference.

"One of those Michigan touchdowns was sort of a fluke," Eliot recalls, remembering the deflected pass that landed in the hands of a prone Michigan receiver, Tony Rio, in the end zone.

The Illini would come back to win a 9-6 defensive duel with Wisconsin and batter Northwestern 28-0, to finish with a 5-3-1 record but 4-2-1 in the conference. Wisconsin won the title and the Rose Bowl bid with a 5-2 record, and Michigan State was second at 4-2. If either the tie with Purdue or the narrow loss to Michigan had gone in Illinois' favor, Illinois could have at least shared the title. Burrell was named the Big Ten's Most Valuable Player at season's end and was accorded All-American honors.

And, despite the might-have-beens, Eliot bowed out of coaching the way he went in—as a winner.

On the occasion of Eliot's retirement, *Chicago Daily News* sports editor John Carmichael remembered something Eliot had said when he had taken over at Illinois in 1942.

"We'll have the will to win," said Eliot, "and if we go down, we'll go down fighting...hard and clean...that's the Illinois way."

Ray Eliot helped to make it "the Illinois way."

229

Time Out: Ray Eliot

Ray Eliot was Illinois' head football coach from 1942 through 1959, second only to Bob Zuppke in terms of longevity.

From the time of his retirement as a coach until 1973 he spread good will as the school's associate athletic director. When he reached the school's mandatory retirement age, Illinois' current athletic director, Cecil Coleman, hired Eliot as an "honorary associate athletic director" at a salary of one dollar per year. In this age of inflation that is like buying Staten Island from the Indians for a bag of beads.

To many thousands of Illinois football fans Ray Eliot is "Mr. Illini."

For many the Illinois athletic program would not be the same, its stature visibly diminished, if Eliot were not somehow associated with it. Eliot still travels widely, spreading the Illini gospel and preaching the values of football. He is an evangelist of sorts, a dynamic spokesman for not only the school but the game.

He is himself dramatic evidence of the virtue of the puritan ethic.

"I worked for my keep the entire time I was in college," said Eliot, remembering his days as a student-athlete at Illinois from 1928 through 1932. "My tuition was only $35, but I worked for every penny of it, taking odd jobs in the summertime. While school was going on, I worked for my room. I lived in the attic of a house on Fourth and Green, and I paid for it by

Illinois' Ray Eliot: they call him "Mr. Illini."

keeping the fires going, the leaves raked, and so on. I don't guess I'll ever forget that old attic room. Was it ever cold. It didn't have any heat. No heat, period. When I wanted to study, I'd go downstairs into one of the other rooms. I remember, too, that my bed was under the eaves of the roof, and every morning I'd bump my head when I got up in the morning. I was convinced that if I didn't die of frostbite, I'd surely have a fatal concussion. Somehow, though, I managed to survive. But it was a struggle at times. I think I set the Big Ten record for most dishes washed during a college career.

231

Cecil Coleman, Illinois' current athletic director, "rehired" Ray Eliot as honorary associate athletic director when he reached retirement.

"Being from the East, as I was, I couldn't afford to go home for the holidays. I remember one Thanksgiving when everyone else went home for the vacation while I stayed alone in that attic room. Most of the restaurants we students could afford closed for the holiday, and I couldn't come close to being able to afford to eat at one of the other restaurants that was open. I remember going to the grocery store and buying a can of sardines and some saltines. That was my Thanksgiving dinner. When my friends came back, I remember them asking if I'd had a nice dinner. 'Oh, wonderful,' I said. 'I had a great meal.' I was too proud to tell them anything else."

A smile lights Eliot's roundish, jack-o-lantern face.

"But you know," he said, "all those hardships you go through in life are 'good-ships,' too. Now if something little goes wrong, I just think back on some of those times."

Eliot, even then, had a burning desire to one day be a football coach.

"I felt I had to do as much as I could to make a name for myself as a player to be able to get a job as a coach later on. It didn't take me long to find out that the way to play football in the Big Ten was to be tough. So much of playing football is mental, and I think I found that out then. I'll never forget the first time they took our freshman team over to scrimmage against the varsity. One of my teammates, (Henry) Steinman, said, 'All right, Ray, let's get in there and tear these guys apart.' Butch Nowack, who was the big star with the varsity at that time, overheard Steinman's remark, took one look at him, and spat tobacco juice right in his face. 'If you come across that line,' Nowack told Steinman, 'I'll tear you apart.' Steinman didn't play very well that night.

"You had to be tough in those days. I was always pleased by the fact that the Ohio State team that won the championship voted me as the toughest lineman they played against that season. I wasn't that big, even in those days, at about 190 pounds playing guard. I guess that's why I've always had a great feeling for the little man in athletics. I still think there's a place for him, and nobody will be able to convince me otherwise."

One of Eliot's most often quoted philosophies is "the boy is more important than the game."

Eliot still believes that whatever success he had as a coach was directly related to his close personal relationship with his players, the knowledge that he was more concerned with their welfare than any other phase of his job.

"Football is, above all else, an educational agency," he said with feeling. "I think a coach has to have a closeness to his players, and I'm afraid a lot of today's coaches have gone down-hill in that regard. They think of themselves, their prestige, their television and radio contracts, where can they go to make more money. But the boy is still the most important part of any coach's job.

"That doesn't mean I'm trying to say that every boy who ever played for me liked me. But I think just about all of them respected me. I don't see how you can possibly have a good team if you don't have the respect of those kids who are playing for you. I always felt I did a better job of coaching off the field than on it.

"I like to meet my players in my office or in their dormi-tory or fraternity and talk to them away from the practice atmosphere. I always tried to relate to them on a personal basis. If they were married, and they had marital problems, I tried to be a little bit of a marital counselor. If they had grade problems, I tried to be a little bit of an academic counselor. I was their father confessor. And if it wasn't me, it was one of my assis-tants.

"I think too many head coaches in the country now are too aloof from their players. Maybe that's where two-platoon football has hurt the game. A lot of coaches have offensive and defensive coordinators, and the head coach hardly ever does any real coaching with an individual boy, much less understand the problems he might have when he's off the football field."

It has never been any secret that the intensified recruiting in college football in the 1950s drove Eliot out of coaching, but he explains that dichotomy explicitly now:

"During the five years I coached under Zup we did very little recruiting; in fact, almost none. It was amazing that we'd go out there on the practice field for the first day of workouts in the fall each year and wonder who we were going to have to play for us that season. I remember very well a player who was brought to me one day...a big red-headed tackle. I took him to meet Zup, and I'll never forget Zup's words to him. 'Young man,' he said, 'we'd like you to come to school here if you can pay your own way.' Zup just shook his hand, and that was it.

"By the time I took over as head coach, more and more schools were working hard to recruit players, and it was pretty obvious to me that you couldn't be any better than the young

Ray Eliot as an Illini player.

men you had playing for you. So we set out to actively interest good players in coming to Illinois, and we spent many hours trying to line up jobs to help them pay their way through school. We tried to get the boy one job during the school year which would pay for his room and board and another one in the summer that would pay for his tuition, books and fees for the coming year.

"The legislative scholarships helped us a lot. At that time each legislator was able to give out four to persons in his district, and I frequently would work closely with them to encourage them to provide one of those to a young man we wanted to play for us. But they still provided only tuition, and we still had to get them jobs to pay for some of their other college expenses.

"The thing that disturbed me most was that, even in those days, there were so many illegal things going on in recruiting, or at least I felt there were. Of course it was very difficult to prove. I suspect that it became gradually worse.

"There is no question that the reason I retired from coaching was the rigors and demands of recruiting. That and the fact that I became increasingly suspicious of the recruiting methods used by some of the other schools. But when I was involved in recruiting, I worked hard at it. Recruiting is the name of the game, but it drove a lot of good men out of college coaching."

The Changing
Of The Guard

Ray Eliot's retirement at the end of the 1959 season left the Illinois football coaching job vacant for only the second time in 47 years. The decision was announced well in advance, giving Illinois ample opportunity to look for a successor.

"We looked over the full coaching field," recalls Doug Mills, who was charged with recommending a successor to Eliot, just as he had done when Bob Zuppke stepped down 18 years before.

As athletic director when Ray Eliot retired, Mills sought out those whose opinion he valued. One of the men he talked with was Oklahoma coach Bud Wilkinson.

"I even asked Bud himself if he would consider moving," Mills recalled not long ago. "When he said he didn't want to leave Oklahoma, I asked him whom he would recommend for the job. He recommended two people, Darrell Royal and Pete Elliott. Royal had just moved to Texas as head coach, and so we started talking to Pete."

Pete Elliott had served as an assistant under Bud Wilkinson for five years at Oklahoma. He spent one year as head coach at Nebraska before moving to California, where he guided the Bears into the Rose Bowl with the help of a quarterback named Joe Kapp in 1958, the second of his three seasons there.

Elliott and Mills came to terms, and on December 22, 1959, the handsome, blond 33-year-old who looked more like a beach boy in a toothpaste commercial than a coach was announced as the successor to Eliot. Yet, everything pointed to

Pete Elliott looked as youthful as his players when he took over as Illinois coach in 1960.

a smooth transition—even the names Eliot to Elliott—and initially it was.

In many ways Pete was a natural for the job.

Elliott was an Illinois native and a Big Ten man, and there is little doubt that he would have been an Illini player had he not been sent to Michigan for military-academic training during World War II. Pete and his brother, Bump, had talked of nothing other than attending Illinois until the war changed their plans. Their father had been a rare breed of man. He was an assistant football coach at Northwestern and coach at Illinois Wesleyan, as well as a prominent ear, nose, and throat specialist in Bloomington. When he retired from coaching, Dr. Elliott finally put his medical training to full use as a practicing physician. At Michigan, Pete had been the only 12-letter man in the school's history. He was the star on the school's unbeaten, conference championship football teams in 1947 and 1948, along with Bump. As quarterback, Pete led Michigan into the Rose Bowl in 1948. His appointment at Illinois followed by only a year Bump's selection as head coach at Michigan. For what may have been the only time it will ever happen in Big Ten annals, two brothers were at the helm of two of the most prestigious football programs in the country. With those kinds of bloodlines, how could either of them fail?

The Big Ten braced for the rush of the golden boys. But it was tough sledding at first for both of them.

Pete inherited a highly capable squad in 1960 at Illinois, even though All-American Bill Burrell and steady guard John Gremer had completed their eligibility, and fleet halfback Johnny Counts had run into scholastic problems. Bill Brown was back for his senior year, along with a stunning tackle Joe Rutgens and a pair of solid ends in Ed O'Bradovich and Ernie McMillan (both of whom would go on to long careers in pro football). But the Illini would be just 5-4 in 1960 and only 2-4 in the Big Ten. Perhaps some found irony in the fact that Michigan, under Bump, also was exactly 5-4 and 2-4 that season.

The next year Michigan continued on its middle-of-the-pack course, but the Illini dipped to the depths of the Big Ten. Illinois was winless in nine games, with only 11 lettermen left from the 1960 team. The Illini would lose five more straight games at the start of the 1962 season, for a string of 15 straight defeats, and the alumni—in Chicago especially—were bitter and inflamed.

At the height of a storm of criticism in early November the Illinois Athletic Board announced that Elliott's contract would definitely be extended after the 1962 season ended. The next day, as if on cue, the long losing streak came to an end with a 14-10 upset of Purdue.

"I can't remember a bigger game in my life," Pete Elliott says now. "We realized, the team and myself, that the end of the drought had come. But I think we all saw it coming the week before when we played Southern Cal a very good football game. We darn near beat them, and they were rated No. 1 or No. 2 in the country at the time. Although we lost that game on the kinds of mistakes that losers make, it sort of set us up a little bit. When we went to Purdue, we were ready to win a game."

Elliott says he never lost faith that the dawn was just beyond the darkness, but he remembers the 1961 season now as "a difficult time."

"Nobody can say losing's fun, and it wasn't. It was hard, and every game was difficult," Elliott recalls. "But I believed in Illinois. But through the coaching transition, a couple of years of recruiting had been lost. We just didn't have much talent. We knew that, and the players knew that down deep. I also knew we could be good, so I wasn't concerned."

Elliott, however, still remembers how many of the Illinois fans did not despair even during that agonizing time.

"I'll never forget the bus ride back from Purdue to Memorial Stadium because there must have been 25,000 fans in the stadium that night just to meet us," said Elliott.

The Illini lost the next weekend to Michigan 14-10 and were dumped by Wisconsin 35-6 a week later, but the 1962 Illini finished the season on a high note with a 7-6 victory over Michigan State.

The win over Michigan State was only the second in a nine-game season, but Elliott believes now it was an important one in providing the right mental attitude for the season to follow.

"I always felt it was an awfully big win for us," Elliott said. "The last game you play is always the one you carry with you all winter. It did one thing that I think was vital and important. It proved to everyone, and to our team, that the Purdue game was no fluke.

"I think that helped us go into the 1963 season with a great deal of confidence that we could play anyone and be successful."

A sophomore on that 1962 team was Dick Butkus, and a 2-7 record did not set well with him in particular. And Butkus did not leave any doubts that he intended to do something about it in 1963.

The next season, help would come from a talented "super-

239

Dick Butkus "set standards that were impossible to follow and not be great," Pete Elliott recalls.

sophomore" class that included players like Jim Grabowski, Sam Price, and Don Hansen.

But it was Butkus who set the course that the others would follow.

"And he set standards for himself," said Elliott, "that were impossible to follow and not be great."

Elliott recalls a spring practice once when the rain came down in torrents and he decided to call off the scheduled workout. Most of the players happily welcomed the one-day respite from the drudgery of the spring, but Elliott looked over and noticed Butkus kicking his locker in contempt.

"I walked over and asked Dick what was wrong," Elliott remembers.

Butkus stood there glaring.

"Coach," he said, "how do you expect us to be ready and play well if we don't practice?"

240

Rags To Roses,
And A Broken Cane

Before the 1963 season began, assistant coach Burt Ingwersen, the grand old man of Illinois football who had remained on Pete Elliott's staff after serving under Ray Eliot, kidded co-captains Mike Taliaferro and Dick Deller.

"If you guys have a good season this year," said Ingwersen, "I'm going to break my cane."

Ingwersen used the cane mainly as a leaning post to rest a hip that had required surgery in his advancing years.

Ingwersen, however, did not spell out at the time just what a good season meant to him, but Elliott did when he met with the touring Big Ten skywriters before the start of the season.

"This team will put Illinois back in the Big Ten," said Elliott.

The Illini not only returned to the respectability that Elliott alluded to in 1963, but vaulted all the way to the conference championship, making a remarkable rise from the rags of eighth place in 1962 to the roses of another trip to Pasadena on January 1, 1964.

The stunning sophomore class—led by a battering ram of a fullback, Jim Grabowski, and a winged-footed halfback, Sam Price—joined with a junior group, led by "Man Mountain" Dick Butkus, and a capable senior class to forge a dramatic run for the title.

Butkus played center on offense, linebacker on defense, under the one-platoon rules of the time and was almost as devastating a blocker as he was a defender. There may have been no

Burt Ingwersen: He broke his cane in delight in 1963.

better college football player in the nation in 1963, as well as in 1964.

"Dick was the greatest asset to a team of anyone I've ever seen," Elliott says now. "He was the best football player I've ever been around and the greatest leader.

"When we recruited him, I felt he was the kind of player who could win the Heisman Trophy, and I was very disappointed when he didn't win it. I don't think anyone deserved it more. I think the Heisman would have been enriched by having a name like Dick Butkus on it."

The Butkus-led Illini defense was spectacular in the opening game of 1963, holding California and superb passer Craig Morton scoreless and logging the first Illinois shutout in 26 games by a 10-0 count. Morton was held to four completions in 15 attempts for 57 yards. Slick work by the three-deep secondary of Mike Dundy, George Donnelly, and Jimmy Warren set the stage for what was to come much of the season.

Ara Parseghian's Northwestern Wildcats, the preseason league favorites, were the opening Big Ten foe the following weekend. Illinois was a decided underdog going in against the bull's-eye passing of Tom "Tommy Gun" Myers, but the Illini defense stopped the explosive Myers with just one scoring toss and put up a touchdown themselves on a 33-yard toss from halfback Ron Fearn to Warren. The decider, though, was a field goal by kicking specialist Jim Plankenhorn. Butkus played his usual game: 17 tackles. There was no question now that Illinois was definitely "back in the Big Ten."

But a strong Ohio State team awaited the next weekend, and the Illini came down from Cloud Nine in a 20-20 tie with the Buckeyes. But it took a Dick Van Raaphorst field goal with 1:53 left to gain a tie for Woody Hayes' warriors after Illini quarterback Mike Taliaferro's passing had set up touchdowns for Price, Warren, and Eddie Russell. And the tie hurt neither team in the eyes of the nation; the following week Ohio State was rated No. 4 in the country and Illinois No. 7.

In fact, when Elliott looks back now, he thinks the tie with Ohio State did as much to build the team's confidence as the win over Northwestern.

"Our players felt they'd outplayed Ohio State even though we were tied, and that game did nothing but give us more confidence," said Elliott. "It helped a lot, too, to beat Northwestern when we knew they were good. I can remember our players drawing Rose Bowl signs on the blackboard after we beat Northwestern. I remember telling them at the time that it was too early to start thinking about anything like that. But from then on, we felt we were good and it was a matter of playing well each week."

As the Illini moved past Minnesota 16-6 and UCLA 18-12, Grabowski began to emerge as a budding superstar, after being slowed early in the season with an injury.

"When he was hurt early in the year, it hurt us," Elliott

reflects now.

Illinois overwhelmed Minnesota (which had a talented defender of its own in Carl Eller) by a 16-6 count the next weekend. Butkus blitzed the Gophers with a 17-tackle outrage. The only time the Gophers were inside the Illini 47 yard line was the lone occasion when they scored. A sophomore quarterback, Fred Custardo, continued to give the Illini a strong one-two punch at the position he shared with Taliaferro. Custardo scored a touchdown in the fourth quarter after the senior signal caller had connected with Gregg Schumacher for a seven-yard payoff early in the game.

After Illinois topped UCLA 18-12, Purdue coach Jack Mollenkopf had more than slight apprehension as he prepared his team for this Illini team at that juncture in the season. A reporter asked him how he planned to steer clear of Butkus.

"How can you do that?" Mollenkopf wondered out loud. "When he's on the field, he's liable to be anywhere." And that Saturday Butkus was everywhere, and the Boilermakers fell 41-21. Grabowski exploded for three touchdowns, bouncing back from the early-season injury.

Ironically, however, in Illinois' best season under Pete Elliott, they did not beat Bump's Michigan Wolverines. Illinois was handed its first league loss by Michigan 14-8, doomed by four lost fumbles. Illinois, ranked second in the nation, suddenly found itself in third place in the Big Ten. Michigan State was 4-0-1, Ohio State 3-0-1, and Illinois 3-1-1.

"The loss to Michigan was a difficult one to face," said Elliott, remembering. "Bump and I never carried the game into the personal atmosphere that many people would like to believe we did. We always kept it as a game between Michigan and Illinois. But we felt like we were kind of charitable in that game. We had it wrapped up and made a fumble on a pitchout. Yet, I don't think that game really destroyed us from a confidence standpoint. In fact, I don't think it changed our course at all."

The Illinois locker room was like a wake after the loss to Michigan, but Elliott went from man to man and kept repeating, "We've still got two more to go. We can still make it."

Jim Grabowski was Illinois' super sophomore in 1963 Rose Bowl year.

But the Illini needed help, and the next weekend they got it. Northwestern knocked off Ohio State 17-8, while the Illini picked off Wisconsin 17-7 with the help of Donnelly's 24-yard interception touchdown that gave the Illini a 14-0 lead after Grabowski's first-quarter score from scrimmage.

The Wisconsin Badgers, however, had done something no other team in the Big Ten managed in 1964. They knocked Butkus off his feet, though Butkus' version makes that a questionable verdict.

"I had jumped off two guys who had tried to block me, and I saw this third one coming. I expected him to go for my knees, but he didn't," said Butkus at the time. "He just sort of bent over, and I flipped right over him. I wish he'd learn how to block."

But the Illini were hardly complaining after the win over Wisconsin. They had the title showdown they had hoped for in the season finale against Michigan State.

But before that game would be played, there would be what Elliott once described as "two of the most confused and hectic days of my coaching career."

The day Illinois flew to East Lansing, Michigan, President John Kennedy was assassinated in Dallas, turning the weekend into a tense, mournful, and uncertain setting. It was not until 10 a.m. on the scheduled day of the game that it was finally postponed until the following Thursday.

"Hearing about President Kennedy was a deep, emotional blow to all our players," Elliott recalls. "I can't think of anything that would even be comparable. I'm glad that the game was postponed, regardless of who won or who didn't, just because it was not the right time to play a football game. Later on, with time to adjust and knowing that things go on, we could face it as a championship game should be faced."

It was not easy for many of the players, but the Illini finally got their minds back on the game. Something assistant coach Gene Stauber said might have shocked their minds back to the battle that lay ahead of them.

Stauber described Michigan State's offense as "80 yards and a cloud of dust"—an obvious reference to the Spartan's home run ground attack triggered by halfback Sherman Lewis, who had scored five times during the season from 80 yards or more. MSU coach Duffy Daugherty called Lewis "the best all-around back I've had in 17 years of coaching."

But on that Thanksgiving Day, Illinois "knocked the treads off the Sherman tank," as guard Ed Washington described it in the dressing room later. Illinois posted an overwhelming 13-0 victory, handing the Spartans their first whitewash in 22 games. The Butkus-led defense jarred the MSU into seven turnovers—four interceptions and three fumbles. A pair of field goals by Plankenhorn and a 14-yard touchdown run by Grabowski provided all the scoring Illinois needed.

"I can still remember that game most vividly, of course," says Elliott.

"They had a special shift to try to goof us up. We had our linebackers go with the strength of the formation, sending Don Hansen to the strong side and Butkus more to the middle so he could go either way. They used the special shift, but we moved our men, too, and they really never got it going.

"Our defense was superb. We never gave them any room to

Happy Illinois players celebrate after victory over Michigan State that sent the Illini to the 1964 Rose Bowl game.

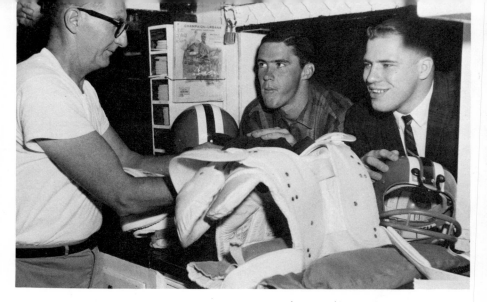

Co-captains in 1963, Mike Taliaferro (center) and Dick Deller (right) draw their gear from long-time Illini equipment manager Paul Schaede.

run, and when they tried to throw the ball, we were all over them.

"As we went into the game, we felt like we had to have some variety in our offense, but the thing we felt we really had do was run Grabowski up the middle or off-tackle. We established that Jim could make yardage this way. The offensive line really gave him daylight, and Jim really took advantage of it. Our squad never let up. It was one of the most satisfying games ever played by a team I coached."

And Illinois was on the way to its third appearance in the Rose Bowl, with a mark of 5-1-1, edging Ohio State and the Spartans who had identical 4-1-1 records.

But even before the win over Michigan State, Ingwersen had let this team know, in his way, that he was proud of its comeback.

After the win over Wisconsin, Ingwersen had offered the cane to Taliaferro and Deller and said, "You guys are going to have to break it for me."

They did, and each took a piece.

"Some day our grandchildren will ask Mike and I about these pieces of wood," said Deller that day, "and we can tell them the whole story about this team.

"I'll bet nobody else ever had a trophy like this."

One More Time, With Feeling

An icy wind blasted across the barren prairie of east-central Illinois in December of 1963, bringing with it a mountain of snowfall.

"It was the coldest, snowiest December I can ever remember," said Pete Elliott.

It was not the ideal atmosphere to prepare a football team for playing against Washington a few weeks later in the Rose Bowl game.

"There was snow all over our field just about every day during the time we were allowed to practice at home before going to the West Coast," Elliott recalls. "So we'd all go over to the stock pavilion of the agriculture school and work out there.

"But we really couldn't do much inside. It was dusty, and there was a lot of sawdust all over the floor, and we certainly couldn't scrimmage. So what we did most of the time was run. We ran around that cow barn every day, and I think it got our players into great shape.

"I think it turned out to be a blessing because when we got to Pasadena, we had to work very quickly to learn new things we wanted to put in for the game. I'm kind of a believer, though, that you learn quicker if you have a limited amount of time to do so. I think hurrying to get ready made us that much sharper when the game came around."

The team Illinois would meet in the Rose Bowl was a spirited Washington squad that prided itself on conditioning.

"They called us 'The Big, Fat Big Ten,'" Elliott says now with a smile.

One of the things that Elliott and his assistants had noticed as they studied Coach Jim Owens' team on film was the way its offensive line had continually outcharged opposing defenses.

"Washington used a multiple-type offense, and they'd come out with a great variety of formations and then go very quick at the line of scrimmage," Elliott recalls.

"We decided that on the first play when they were on offense that as soon as their quarterback put his hands under the center, we were going to go and come just as hard as we could, right or wrong, even if we were offside.

"As it turned out, they did go on a quick count, and we were right there as the ball was snapped. I think that helped set the momentum of the game. Our squad felt that it could beat them to the charge. And Washington wasn't sure just when we were going to come. They went on later counts after that, and they were not quite as aggressive. I felt that was a factor in the game, although not the most important, which was the way the whole team played."

Still, Washington came at Illinois with both barrels in the first quarter. A pair of sparkling defensive plays by guard Wylie Fox seemed to save the day for the Illini. He recovered one fumble after Washington had driven to the Illinois nine yard line and stole the ball from Husky quarterback Bill Siler late in the period with Washington on the Illini 27.

Then, an Illini fumble set up a Washington score in the second quarter. The Huskies took over on the Illini 27 and scored in four plays, halfback Dave Kopay going in on a pitchout.

The Illini battled back late in the second quarter and had to settle for a 22-yard field goal by Jim Plankenhorn that left them on the short end of a 7-3 halftime score—but only for the moment.

"Plankenhorn's field goal put us in the locker room feeling that things were starting to go our way," Elliott remembers, "and we really dominated the second half."

An interception by safety George Donnelly, a future All-American, turned the momentum of the game in Illinois' favor in the third quarter. He winged 19 yards after the steal to the Washington 33; the Illini scored five plays later with Mike Taliaferro's 11-yard run setting up his pitchout play to Jimmy Warren for the final two yards.

But Donnelly was not through yet. He saved a potential Washington score later in the quarter by intercepting a Siler pass after Washington had driven to the Illini 14.

The Illini took over and marched 85 yards in 18 plays for an insurance touchdown. Jim Grabowski exploded early for two 11-yard pickups, and Taliaferro passes to Ron Fearn kept the Huskies off balance. The Illini went the final 19 yards on Grabowski's brute strength, with the soph fullback finally bulling across from the one foot line for the score. Plankenhorn's kick made it 17-7 with 8:01 gone in the period.

Illinois' first touchdown in the 1964 Rose Bowl game came on this play as quarterback Mike Taliaferro (19) pitched out to halfback Jimmy Warren (not shown), who roared into the corner of the end zone. The Illini beat Washington, 17-7.

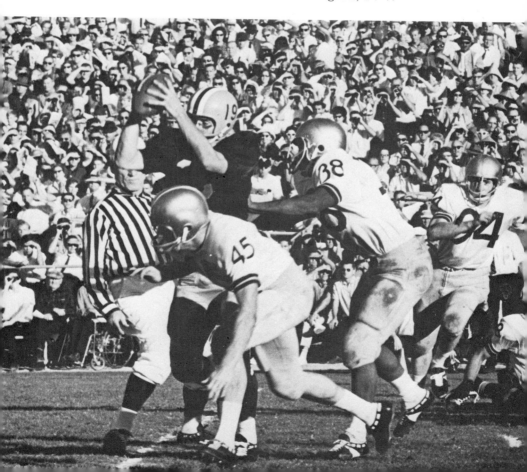

An interception by Dick Butkus, five Washington plays later, iced it for Illinois.

Grabowski finished with 125 yards in 23 carries, was named the game's top player, and Illinois remained unbeaten in Rose Bowl play.

From there Grabowski became the all-time leading ground gainer in Illini history with 2,878 yards in his three-year career. He was consensus All-American in both his junior and senior years.

Butkus was an All-American selection in 1963 and 1964, before moving to an illustrious career in the National Football League with the Chicago Bears.

Donnelly also gained All-American status the season after his Rose Bowl heroics in 1964.

It is nice to be a Rose Bowl hero as George Donnelly (left) and Dick Butkus found out. Here they pose with Judy Percival, Miss Illinois County Fair of 1964.

With three All-Americans in the lineup in 1964, the Illini again had a good year with a 6-3 record, but losses to Ohio State, Purdue, and Michigan cost the Illini a shot at the title.

"It was the time of the no-repeat rule in the Big Ten," Elliott remembers, "and there was a letdown. It had happened to others to some degree. Although we realized the big thing was to win the championship, the goal of most young men was to go to a Rose Bowl game. While 6-3 was a good season, it wasn't a great one because I don't think we had the goals ahead of us that are the intangible ones but important for a team to look forward to."

In many ways the high point had been reached on New Year's Day in bright, sunny California. The team had proven that the so-called "Big, Fat Big Ten" was big but certainly not fat.

Elliott says that he will never forget something that happened when the gun sounded the end to that Rose Bowl game in 1964.

"I don't know whose idea it was," said Elliott. "I like to think it was Butkus'. Regardless, our entire squad ran a lap around the field at the Rose Bowl just after the game ended.

"It was their symbol of what they'd accomplished."

Time Out: Jim Grabowski

Jim Grabowski looks like he could still run the football a mile, and he probably could unless someone cracked him across the knees.

When his legs went out on him a few years ago, Jim gave up the game and entered private business after some glory days in the National Football League during the reign of Vince Lombardi's Green Bay Packers.

He still wears the NFL's World Championship ring with considerable pride, as he does the Rose Bowl watch he latched onto after Illinois' 1964 victory over Washington in Pasadena.

As Illinois' all-time leading ground gainer, "Grabo's" mark of 2,878 yards, along with Red Grange's 31 touchdowns, ranks as the most prestigious in the Illini record books.

But Grabowski was not exactly treated like a future all-time great when he arrived on the Illinois campus in 1962.

"I had been the *Chicago Sun-Times'* prep Player of the Year in 1961, and I was starting to believe I was pretty good," Grabowski smiles now. "I reported for freshman ball, and they put me on the fourth team. I kept telling myself that they were just doing that to show me that I wasn't as good as I probably thought I was, but I now think they put me there because that's probably where they thought I belonged."

Grabowski proved as a freshman, however, that he was the best fullback among the recruits, and when the squad reported in the fall of 1962 Grabowski found himself listed No. 1 at the spot on the varsity.

Jim Grabowski, now a business executive, still holds record as Illinois' all-time top career ground gainer.

"It was picture day, and afterward Buck McPhail, our backfield coach, had all the backs line up and run a sprint for time. As I recall, I finished next-to-last, and they dropped me down to the third team. I guess I'm the only guy who ever went from the first to the third team without an official day of practice. I never was a great practice player anyway. I always said when the band played, I played."

After overcoming early-season ankle and hip injuries, Grabowski moved into the starting lineup but almost became a goat in his first game, the match against preseason conference favorite Northwestern.

"We were driving for a touchdown, and I took the ball from about the 20 to the 17, but I fumbled. Being a rookie, I was absolutely petrified by that. I remember how I kept hoping they wouldn't score after that fumble. Fortunately for me, our defense stopped them," said Grabowski.

"The next game was with Ohio State, the 20-20 tie, and I remember after that game we voted on who were the Most Valuable Players on Ohio State's team. As it turned out, Freddie Custardo, our sophomore quarterback, was named the No. 1 Most Valuable Player for Ohio State that day, and I was voted second Most Valuable. As I recall, Dick Fitzgerald finished third in the voting. Freddie had gone into the game with the ball on our own 20 and immediately threw a strike to their halfback, Matt Snell, and he ran it from there for a touchdown. On the next kickoff, the ball came to me. I ran a few yards and fumbled. And the reason I fumbled was that Fitzgerald, my own teammate, had run into me and knocked the ball out of my hands."

Grabowski says he was always nervous and tightly wound before any game he played.

"I spent most of the time in the bathroom of the locker room," he laughs now. "I never could eat the pregame meal because I was so nervous. I'd try to throw up, but nothing would come out. I was always casual about it in practice, but just before a game I was always nervous. That was just my nature. After the first series of downs, I was all right."

Grabowski says he was never more tense than before the 1963 championship game with Michigan State.

"The thing that I remember most about that game, along

with the touchdown I scored, was the way Dick Butkus played that day, the way he was all over the field," said Grabowski.

"Butkus was the greatest player I've ever seen. It's hard to judge positions, of course, but if I were going to pick a team I'd take him No. 1. Forget the quarterback. I'll take him.

"I think I even had more respect for him after playing against him when we were in the pros. I know how we had to prepare for a team like the Bears when Butkus was playing. We prepared ourselves for Butkus. He was probably the best tackler I've ever seen, especially when his legs were good, and they were always good when he was in college. I remember my junior year when Dick was a senior, and we got beat by Ohio State. Out of respect for Dick, they had a lot of counter plays to get Dick moving. They ran away from us most of the day and we got beat 26-0. But I remember there were a couple of pro scouts watching the game, and they were quoted in the paper that we'd have gotten beat 56-0 if it hadn't been for Butkus, which may have been the truth."

When the Illini headed into the Rose Bowl game on January 1, 1964, Grabowski had no doubt about who would be selected as the game's Most Valuable Player.

"I knew that they had the award, and I felt certain that Butkus would win it going away," Grabowski remembers. "I knew he was the best player on the field. I guess I was lucky in that we did play a ball-control kind of game, and that always worked to my personal advantage."

It was Grabowski, of course, who won the award.

Grabowski remembers the 1964 season as something of a disappointment, although the Illini were 6-3. However, he turned in one of the most phenomenal performances of his career that season against Wisconsin when he ran for 239 yards in 33 carries.

"I remember once in that game when I'd carried three straight times, and we'd gotten the ball down to the six yard line, and Custardo said he was going to give me a rest and call a play for somebody else," said Grabowski.

"But when Fred got up to the line, Wisconsin had shifted defenses, and so he had to call an audible and checked off with another play to me.

"I still remember the thought that went through my head

257

at the time: Grabowski, you've got to make it this time or you won't have the strength to run again. All I could think about was how embarrassing it would be to be carried off the field without scoring.

"But I did score on the play, and I just laid there in the end zone after it was over. I remember the picture the photographer took of me just lying there. Bob Trumpy, one of our receivers, was beating me on the helmet with his hand and saying, 'Way to go Jim.'

"I remember looking up at him and saying, 'The hell with that, Bob, just help me stand up.'"

The next year, after picking up 1,004 yards as a junior, Grabowski gained 1,258 as a senior and moved past Grange first and then Johnny Karras to become the career rushing leader. Grabowski acknowledges now that he felt a sense of football history when he passed Grange.

"It was because of who Grange was," said Grabowski. "It may have been that same year, but it was along about that time, that they had a poll, and people were asked to name the most famous college football player of all time, and the person the most people named was Red Grange."

Grabowski remembers once in that senior year when he and Custardo, who passed for 1,124 yards as a senior, tried to insure some touchdown glory for their buddy, Ron Acks.

"Ronnie came to Illinois as an outstanding high school quarterback, but he suffered a broken finger his freshman year and was switched to defensive back," said Grabowski. "Ronnie played a little bit of offensive back his senior year, too, and most of the time he was a blocker, not a runner.

"Anyway, the season was almost over, and Freddie and I decided we were going to make sure Ronnie scored a touchdown. We had taken the ball down to about the two yard line, and we decided this was the time. But when Fred called the play he didn't realize that Ronnie had been knocked ding-dong on the play before and was on the sidelines. Tony Parola had come in for him and Parola scored the touchdown. I'm not sure Ronnie ever did get one. I don't feel too sorry for him now, though. He's still playing in the NFL as a linebacker and has had a great career."

While Grabowski was the running star, he did his share of

Long-time Illinois ticket manager George Legg made money on Jim Grabowski's big family.

blocking, too, especially in practice.

"Buck McPhail was on me all the time about my blocking," Grabo remembers. "He used to have blocking drills just for me. They'd alternate three or four people for me to block, and I'd still be blocking in practice. I was always thankful that Buck made me work on it because the last three years in pro football just about all I did was block."

Football was always a family affair for the Grabowski clan. "I don't think there were ever any less than 10 people from family at a game that I played at home," Grabowski recalls with a smile, "and when I closed out my career at Northwestern, there were 47 of my relatives at the game.

"I still remember the look George Legg, the ticket manager, gave me when I told him I wanted 47 tickets for the Northwestern game. The color came back to his face after I told him I was planning to pay for them.

"Both my father and mother and two of my brothers made the trip to California to see the Rose Bowl game, and they did it at some personal sacrifice. But they enjoyed the trip. There was a party after the game, and I remember how I played 'The Great McGaffer' and poured champagne for them all.

"My father was a butcher in Chicago, and he never made a lot of money. He was a guy who said he never went around bragging about what I'd done in football, but he always seemed to get around to it. People tell me they'd be introduced to him, and there'd be a minute or two of small talk, and then he'd say, 'By the way, do you follow football?' He'd be so corny about it you could really appreciate it. He was a good person."

The Rose Bowl MVP award was Grabowski's biggest thrill at Illinois because of what it meant to his father, who died in 1975.

"They gave me the award in the locker room right after the game, and my dad was there. I'll never forget the picture they took. People sent me copies of it out of newspapers from all over. I had a towel wrapped around my neck and my father was giving me a big hug. I had a great feeling for him, a guy who worked hard for everything he had, and you could just see the pride that was in his face," said Grabowski. "That minute was worth everything I ever put into playing football."

The Troubled Times

The resignation of Pete Elliott as Illinois' football coach was part of one of the most agonizing, tumultuous times any major university ever experienced in its athletic program.

Elliott was set to ascend to the athletic directorship upon the retirement of Doug Mills in December 1966. But the very day the announcement of Elliott's appointment was being prepared, it was brought to the attention of Illinois president David Dodds Henry that a special fund existed with the knowledge of some in the athletic department which provided monies for athletes in particular need above that allowed under Big Ten rules. Elliott's alleged knowledge of the so-called Illinois "slush fund" made him vulnerable, as it did others.

The announcement of Elliott's appointment was withdrawn, and Dr. Henry went before the Big Ten with the information he had received. Little did anyone anticipate the kind of actions from the Big Ten fathers that would follow.

On February 11, 1967, Big Ten athletic directors, acting under the recommendation of Commissioner Bill Reed, voted 8-1 to demand that Illinois fire Elliott, along with basketball coach Harry Combes and basketball assistant Howie Braun. Illinois appealed that decision at a meeting of the conference faculty representatives, but again the decision was affirmed. In each case Michigan cast the opposing vote to the most stringent penalty.

On March 18, Dr. Henry appeared again before the faculty representatives, pleading that the penalty was "too severe." The decision, however, remained unchanged, and Illinois was given three days either to dismiss the coaches or be "indefinitely suspended from the conference."

The next day Elliott, Combes, and Braun resigned rather than, in the words of their prepared statement, place Illinois "in an impossible position."

Eight athletes who allegedly benefited financially from the existence of the fund lost all or part of their remaining eligibility, three of whom were football players.

The NCAA placed Illinois on two years of probation with sanctions which prohibited participation in postseason games and from appearances in NCAA-sanctioned television coverage.

Elliott went on to work for several years in private business before returning to athletics as head football coach at the University of Miami in Coral Gables, Florida. He is now athletic director there and has retired from coaching.

Not long ago when he looked back on those dark days amid the upheaval at Illinois, he said, "Never were there any extra inducements offered to any young man to get him to come to Illinois. This, to me, is cheating. This is something we did not do. Any violation that did occur happened only after a young man was coming or was already there in a case of special need."

Did the punishment fit the violation? The Illinois fans never believed so. The state's sports press generally agreed with the fans, and *Chicago Tribune* columnist David Condon wrote that Illinois "went before two separate kangaroo courts and drew penalties that would have to enrage any citizen with a sense of fair play."

In a front-page editorial, the *Chicago Tribune* said in part: "The self-righteous rules of Big Ten sports could have decided, in good conscience, that the Illinois coaches were not guilty of breaking any law, but had only violated a house rule, and the university could have been placed on probation. But to put the university in the position of having to fire three of its faculty members, on penalty of being suspended indefinitely from the conference, was high-handed bulldozing."

The slush fund episode and the raging controversy that followed left deep scars on the Illinois football program. The entire 1967 recruiting season had been lost in the tidal wave of

There were happy days, like this one after an Illini victory, for Jim Valek as head coach, but there were troubled times, too.

uncertainties connected with the battle with the Big Ten.

Illinois did not name a new football coach until late March, 1967. Gene Vance, the man who eventually succeeded Mills as athletic director, recommended former Illinois star Jim Valek for the job, and he was hired. Valek had played for Ray Eliot in the mid-1940s and had coached briefly under him at Illinois. He had also served under Paul Dietzel at Army and South Carolina.

In less troubled times, Valek might have been a highly successful head coach. His first team was 4-6, upsetting Ohio State in Columbus 17-13, as fleet split end John Wright wound up a three-year career in which he finished as the school's all-time leading receiver with 159 catches for 2,284 yards. Quarterback Dean Volman passed for 1,004 yards for the season.

But Illinois' talent level suffered a marked drop after the 1967 season, and two consecutive sub-par recruiting years eventually sealed Valek's doom as head coach. The specter of the NCAA and Big Ten penalties hung heavily over the Illinois program.

The Illini won only once in 1968, beating Northwestern 14-0 in the next-to-last game of the season. The 1969 season was winless.

Illinois won two of its first three games in 1970, but a 48-0 setback in the fourth game of the year against Northwestern was a crushing blow. A 30-25 loss to Indiana the next weekend amid rumors of mounting player discontent brought the school's Athletic Board to an unprecedented mid-season firing of Valek.

But in retrospect it soon was obvious that the Athletic Board had acted hastily. The Illini players learned of Valek's firing just before they went on the field to play Ohio State, and they rallied behind their coach for an emotional performance that had Woody Hayes furiously pacing the sidelines much of the day before the nationally top-ranked Buckeyes finally emerged with a 48-29 victory.

In a seething Illini locker room afterward, the players threatened a walkout en masse unless Valek was allowed to finish the season. The Athletic Board, realizing that the feelings of the majority of the players had been misjudged, agreed to reinstate Valek for the rest of the season. But the die has been cast. Valek's firing was reaffirmed at the end of the schedule.

Hindsight always has 20-20 vision, but it seems unlikely that anyone who could not walk on water could have pulled Illinois up by its bootstraps at the time Valek came on the scene. He was a good, capable football man and has proved it since in pro football in a front-office capacity with the Dallas Cowboys and most recently as a top assistant under Chuck Fairbanks for the New England Patriots. But Valek was no miracle worker, as few coaches are.

Illinois football badly needed someone with a miracle-worker reputation to heal the old wounds and bring the fans back into historic Memorial Stadium. The school reached out for a man who had performed Lazarus-like feats elsewhere and landed Bob Blackman.

Bob Blackman's
Brave New World

"The joy is not in sustaining, but in creating."

That was Vince Lombardi's simple explanation in 1969 for his decision to leave behind the dynasty he had built with the Green Bay Packers and seek a new challenge as coach of the Washington Redskins. Cancer struck down Lombardi only a year after he took over at Washington, ending a noble attempt to prove beyond question that he was the master architect in the history of professional football.

Men change jobs every day, you say. They leave behind the patterns of the past and scan the horizon with new hopes and new goals, shedding a tired and tattered world that, at times—at least to them—seems to be only a treadmill into oblivion. But mostly they are men young in years, men with still more to gain than to lose.

But there are other men like Lombardi. Bob Blackman, when he became head coach at Illinois in 1971, began his own Lombardi-like adventure. He left behind the comfortable, pillowy life of a coach who had established himself as one of the most successful in college football to accept a demanding new challenge at the age of 53.

Blackman's record for 16 years as head coach at Dartmouth was unparalleled in the Ivy League: 104 victories, 37 defeats, three ties; three undefeated conference champions, seven titles in all; and two teams which claimed the Lambert Trophy, symbol of football supremacy in the East. In his first 22 years of college coaching, Blackman's teams won 150 games, lost only 49, and tied eight.

But statistics do not always reveal what motivates a man. On a chill December night in a house on a hill in Hanover, New Hampshire, Blackman was weighing a decision. The wind whipped across the slopes where Dartmouth students ski during the bright, sunny New England days. But inside the Blackman home that night, the fire was burning brightly. It was one of those nights when you are happy you are inside, and you can care less if the snow piles high against the door and the roads that wind among the pines are clogged with the misery that can be winter. It is not an atmosphere in which new challenges are easily accepted. But it was on such a night that Blackman decided to leave behind the warm fire—to leave behind gracious little Hanover—to leave behind the dynasty he had built at Dartmouth. It was obvious that night that there was a flame burning in a man as well as between the stucco and brick below the mantle.

The day before, Blackman had visited the University of Illinois, where its football program was once again in a state of disarray. When the Illinois Athletic Board invited Blackman to come to Champaign-Urbana for an interview they had serious doubts that he would be willing to leave Dartmouth. Most of the speculation in the press had centered on Lou McCullough, who was the chief recruiter and defensive coordinator for Woody Hayes at the time. Just a few days earlier McCullough turned down the coaching job at Texas Christian because he had felt confident that the Illini job was his. When McCullough walked out of his interview, he was so convinced that he was the leading candidate for the job that he began making telephone calls to put together his own coaching staff. It was Blackman, however, who was eventually offered the job and accepted it, and McCullough moved on to become athletic director at Iowa State.

It was a telephone call from his old friend Ray Eliot, then the associate athletic director at Illinois, that first interested Blackman in the Illinois job.

Blackman recounted the timing of those events not long after he took over as the new coach. "Ray called me and told me of the position and wanted to know if I'd come out for an interview. I told him that I had speaking commitments for

266

Illini coach Bob Blackman.

several weeks and just didn't see any way I'd be able to do so. I thought that would be the end of it. But Ray told me they would wait until my schedule would allow me to come. And the more I thought about it, the more I became interested.

"I knew all about the great legends of Illinois, Bob Zuppke and Red Grange, and all, and I'd watched Buddy Young play on the West Coast when I was in the Navy. When I was in the service, my wife Kay and I really skimped in the days of gas rationing to go to see him play.

"Since I'd spent most of the first six years of my life in Illinois and Chicago before my family moved to the Los Angeles area, I felt like coaching at Illinois would sort of be like going back home. Even the name 'Fighting Illini' is something that always intrigued me."

Blackman admitted at the time that the key factor in his decision was the fact that there was "little else I could do at Dartmouth." It was a matter of "if we lost one game next season, it would be a bad year," according to Blackman.

"When I went to Dartmouth, I never thought for a minute I'd stay there as long as I did," Blackman remembered. "But I had 16 very happy years there, and we made many friends. You'd have a tough time finding a better place to raise a family than in a small college town where everything is centered around the school. But with both my son and daughter gone from home, I was no longer concerned about this aspect, and my wife, the wonderful person she is, was willing to go anywhere I felt I would be happy."

The possibility of being able to take a team to a bowl game—particularly to the Rose Bowl, where he had played in high school while in Long Beach, California, and had coached in while at Pasadena City College—loomed important in his decision to make the move he did. Ivy League teams, of course, are not allowed postseason competition by conference rules.

"In the first week of December there's almost always snow on the ground at Dartmouth, and it would be awfully hard for Dartmouth or any other New England team to prepare for a bowl game at home. But there's no question that for a coach and his players, a bowl game is a special honor and challenge."

Ivy League rules also prohibited Blackman from coaching in any of the postseason college all-star games.

"On several occasions I was offered the opportunity to coach one of the all-star teams, but under Ivy League rules I had to decline those invitations."

Blackman also saw greater potential in Illinois once again

becoming a national power in football.

"I've never had any doubt that the schools which are going to be on top are the state universities, where the entire state takes pride in their team. I can see that kind of situation at Illinois," said Blackman.

But it would not happen overnight, even under a coach who had built a reputation as a miracle worker at Monrovia, California, High School; at Pasadena City College; at Denver; and at Dartmouth.

Blackman's first team in 1971 got off to a rocky start, losing its first six games and suffering shutouts in its first three at the hands of Michigan State, North Carolina, and nationally prominent Southern Cal (the new Illini coach's alma mater).

Center Larry McCarren was twice elected Illinois' offensive captain in the early 1970s.

Quarterback Mike Wells became Illinois' all-time leading passer in 1972 season.

"An Ivy League Lombardi Gets A Big Ten Jolt," said the headline on a story in *Sports Illustrated*.

But once past the expected losses to Big Ten superpowers Ohio State and Michigan, and with the players now adjusting to a different system, the 1971 team caught fire and won its last five games over Purdue 21-7, Northwestern 24-7, Indiana 22-21, Wisconsin 35-27, and Iowa 31-0. The 5-3 conference record boosted Illinois into a tie for third place. The five league victories were the most for an Illinois team since the Rose Bowl year of 1963 and the first time in 25 years Illinois had won five straight Big Ten games.

Junior quarterback Mike Wells bounced back from only 20 completions in 48 passes and 199 yards in his first four games to pass for 1,007 yards for the season, and sophomore Garvin Roberson had come on strong as a receiver after an early-season hand injury. Junior co-captain and center Larry McCarren led a "Kiddie Korps" offensive line to rapid maturity.

"It looked like we had the momentum built up to really move after that," Blackman reflected once not long ago. But Blackman could hardly have anticipated the ill fortune that would befall the Illini before the start of the 1972 season. Roughly a dozen key players would become academically ineligible between the end of the 1971 campaign and the start of the one in 1972. The Illini never recovered from the blow, and the once-bright hopes faded into a 3-8 season against a man-eater of a schedule. There was another late-season resurgence to finish 3-5 in the league, but it was hardly the kind of year for which Blackman had hoped.

Wells salvaged some personal glory out of the ill-fated year. His 837 yards passing boosted him to a career total of 2,750 yards through the air and 3,204 yards in career total offense, both all-time school records. Larry Allen and Tab Bennett turned in yeoman efforts defensively, but the defensive unit in particular paid the price much of the year for the academic shortcomings of the missing.

Blackman had some major patchwork to do before the

Tab Bennett (75), one of Illinois' premier defensive linemen, celebrates downing a ball carrier in the end zone for a safety.

1973 season began after losing Wells and others. But the Illini bounced back to 5-6, thanks in no small measure to a late-summer decision to award a scholarship to a kicking specialist, Dan Beaver, who had learned to boot soccer-style when his father was a church missionary in Africa.

Illinois whipped Indiana 28-14 in the opener in a good show of strength and blasted California 27-7 in the second game behind the running of halfback George Uremovich; but West Virginia whipped the Illini 10-7 on a 55-yard scoring pass to Danny "Lightning" Buggs with 3½ minutes to play, and Stanford posted a 24-0 blitz a week later.

Then, along came Beaver at a time when the offensive punch was sagging from early-season backfield injuries. The freshman's Big Ten record-tying five field goals, including a 52-yarder, provided all the points in a 15-13 win over Purdue. Two more field goals by Beaver produced a 6-3 win over the Spartans. The Illini, amazingly, were 3-0 in the Big Ten without scoring a touchdown in two of the three games. The Illini took out their vengeance on Iowa in a 50-0 romp the next weekend, to build a 4-0 conference mark. However, Ohio State and Michigan brought Illinois down to earth in back-to-back games, and the Illini did not recover. Minnesota nipped Illinois 19-16, and Northwestern pulled off a 9-6 ambush in the season finale.

The Illini had let their first winning season since 1965 slip through their fingers in each of the last two games, and Illinois fans were beginning to wonder if the ice would ever be broken again.

But it was. A gutty team, with a quarterback who was short on speed but big in inspiration, would provide that long-awaited winner and etch its place among the most memorable in Illini history in 1974.

Dan Beaver carried Illinois offensively with his field goal kicking in 1973 season.

"The Building Blocks"

On November 23, 1974, in the Illinois locker room at Memorial Stadium, there was a mini-celebration going on.

For the first time since 1965, Illinois was celebrating an honest-to-goodness winning football season. The Illini had just hammered Northwestern 28-14 to finish 6-4-1 for the year.

Quick-minded safety Bill Kleckner said it best for the rest of his senior teammates when he thought for a few seconds and remarked, "We didn't accomplish what we set out to do when we came here four years ago...to win the conference championship and go to the Rose Bowl...but we were the building blocks."

There was no doubt that this group of seniors—Kleckner, Mike Gow, Ty McMillin, Tom Hicks, Bill Uecker, Revie Sorey, Joe Hatfield, Roy Robinson, and others—had played key roles in the return of Illini football to its tradition as a winner after the dark days of the late 1960s.

But none played a more important role in the Illini success of 1974 than a slow-footed senior quarterback who made up for whatever talent he lacked as a runner with pinpoint passing, a ton of inspiration, and icy nerves in the clutch.

His name? Jeff Hollenbach, but call him "Beat the Clock" Hollenbach because that was what he did more than once in the 1974 season.

Hollenbach was Illinois' third-string quarterback at the start of the 1974 season, after starting most of the year in 1973. Sophomore Mike McCray started the opening game against

Illini quarterback Jeff Hollenbach was the key man in the late-game heroics of the 1974 season.

Indiana at quarterback, but an injury took him out of the game early, leaving coach Bob Blackman with junior Jim Kopatz and Hollenbach at the position. The Illini rolled past an outclassed Indiana team 16-0 without much problem.

But with Lonnie Perrin, the team's top-rated runner, sidelined for the season with torn knee ligaments before the year ever began, the picture did not look particularly bright for the Illini. They were heading into the second game of the year against a Stanford team that was 19th-ranked in the nation at the time.

Hollenbach, however, took over at quarterback and directed the Illini to a surprising 41-7 romp over the favored Cardinals. Gow set a school record by intercepting four Stanford passes before leaving the game.

On the plane flight back to Champaign that night, Hollenbach explained how his strong religious beliefs helped him through his personal disappointment at the beginning of the year.

"If you don't have faith, it's easy to get down on yourself and down on others," he said. "I'm actively involved in the Fellowship of Christian Athletes, and my faith in my religion has sustained me. I've felt peaceful about the whole situation."

Coach Blackman added: "Our players who are members of the Fellowship of Christian Athletes meet with Rev. (Jerry) Gibson each Friday night before the game, and each of them says a prayer. The night before our opening game with Indiana, Jeff's prayer was that both Jim Kopatz and Mike McCray would play great games the next day. That really told me a lot about him.

"You might expect some sour grapes from most players in his situation at that time because you expect a quarterback to have a great deal of pride. But Jeff never said a word; he just hustled and worked that much harder to improve."

Hollenbach's "you gotta believe" attitude became contagious.

And in the third game of the season, the Illini trailed Washington State 19-14 with three minutes left. Kopatz had been directing the Illini offense in the second half, but with an all-out passing attack the only hope for an Illini victory, Blackman looked down the sidelines for Hollenbach.

"Jeff," yelled Blackman, "get in there, and move that football."

Hollenbach snapped on his helmet and did just as ordered, driving the Illini to the shadow of the visitors' end zone. It was third-and-one on the five yard line, and Hollenbach connected with an open Joe Smalzer in the end zone for what appeared to be the winning touchdown. However, the officials called the Illini for holding, wiping out the score and pushing the ball back to the Washington State 22 with time rapidly fading.

Orange-clad Illini players kicked at the turf in disappointment, but Hollenbach calmed them as they returned to the huddle.

"All right," he said, calling a signal. "We can still do it."

Hollenbach took the snap, churned backward, and let another pass fly—this one to Jeff Chrystal in the other corner of the end zone. There were 34 seconds left on the clock when Chrystal caught the game-winner. This time there was no flag.

Illinois could have folded up a half-dozen times in that

game. The offense fumbled twice in its first three plays. There was a psychological setback for everyone when star fullback Steve Greene was carried from the field with torn knee ligaments during the game and was lost for the rest of the year. But Hollenbach and the others who remained would not let it happen, not even after a crucial scoring pass was nullified.

"When I saw that flag fall, I knew it was holding," said Hollenbach after that game. "I had some doubts then, I'll tell you that, but I guess the Good Lord was with us today. I thought we had a better football team than they did, and I'm just glad we were able to win it."

California stopped the three-game winning streak 31-14 the following weekend behind the passing of Steve Bartkowski, but the Illini bounced back to win a hard-fought 27-23 game with Purdue the following Saturday.

With Perrin and Greene sidelined, the Illini had found a new running star. Sophomore Jim "Chubby" Phillips had averaged 100 yards per game through the first five outings.

Although the Illini had to settle for a 21-21 tie the next weekend against Michigan State, the comeback kids had Illinois fans on their feet again late in the fourth quarter. Hollenbach moved the Illini 45 yards with three passes in just 18 seconds after the Illini took over on their own 31 yard line with just 21 seconds left. With three seconds left, Illinois was safely within Dan Beaver's field goal range, but a wobbly snap and a troubled hold aborted his 41-yard kick, denying the redheaded sophomore a chance to beat the Spartans for the second year in a row. (Beaver had kicked two field goals in a 6-3 triumph over MSU in 1973.)

The next week the Illini were upset by Iowa 14-12, and after a 49-7 loss to Ohio State in Columbus, it began to look like the Illini's "you gotta believe" magic had run its course.

Just before the Illini took the field for the homecoming game against Michigan a week later, the players learned that a popular teammate, Greg Williams, had been fatally shot in an incident at his fraternity house early that same morning. Williams had been injured on the gridiron and had not made the trip with the team that night before to its traditional pregame quarters at secluded Allerton House.

Despite their shock and sorrow, the Illini turned in a stun-

Joe Smalzer caught 10 passes for 162 yards in crucial Illini win over Minnesota in 1974.

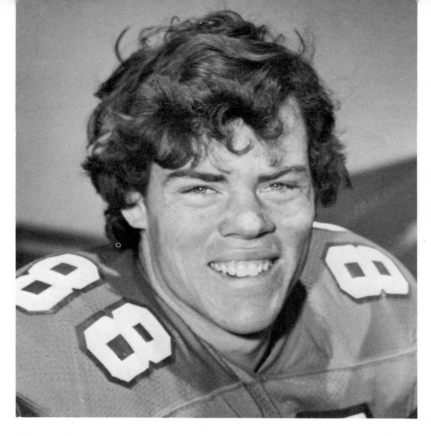

Marty Friel caught the game-winning pass against Minnesota in 1974.

ning performance against eventual Big Ten co-champion Michigan before losing 14-6. Michigan scored twice against the emotion-drained Illini in the first half, but in the second half Illinois battled back. Gow returned a punt 45 yards for a touchdown with 2:10 left. But the two-point running try failed. The Illini, however, miraculously regained possession on an onside kick, and Hollenbach set out to try to rally the team. Three straight completions and a pass interference penalty put the Illini on the Michigan nine yard line. Hollenbach's first pass from there was pulled down by a leaping Smalzer at the corner of the end zone, but officials ruled that he was out of bounds on the catch.

But the Illini would play "beat the clock" one more time in 1974 and win. It would top anything that had come before in the season. With Minnesota leading 14-10 and just two minutes left, Hollenbach drove the Illini 87 yards for the game-winning touchdown. He completed five passes in as many tries in the surge, Smalzer catching three of them for a game total of 10 completions for 162 yards.

The winning score in the 17-14 game would come with 45 seconds left—on a 25-yard Hollenbach pass to reserve tight end Marty Friel, in for one play to replace the winded Smalzer.

"I really don't know what to say," Friel said in the happy locker room afterward. "I haven't caught many passes."

But Hollenbach did.

"We've been there before," he smiled. "Haven't we?"

For the sake of the long-awaited winning season, it was the game Illinois had to win. The icing would be added to the cake the following Saturday, at home in Memorial Stadium against Northwestern.

And when the season was finally over—they had dressed and the fans had left—Kleckner, Hollenbach, and the others walked away with the flash of a smile.

"The Building Blocks" had done their job.

The following season, 1975, the Illini finished with a 5-6 over-all record and wound up in a tie for third place in the Big Ten with a 4-4 record, their fourth first-division finish in five years under Blackman. Halfback Lonnie Perrin bounced back from missing the 1974 campaign with a big year, gaining 907 yards for the year even though he was again sidelined part of the early season with a leg ailment. One of the highlights of 1975 was the emergence of a flashy, whip-armed quarterback, sophomore Kurt Steger, who showed indications of being a key man in Illini fortunes in the years ahead. Steger threw for 1,136 yards and eight touchdowns, third best single-season yardage total in Illinois history and best ever by a sophomore.

But the best indication that the Illini football program had again been rebuilt probably came in that 1974 season when Illini fans once again celebrated a winning year.

And there, on that day, in the gathering twilight, a historic old stadium, which has been a showcase for some of the greatest players and some of the most renowned coaches the game has ever known, was again filled with pride.

And pride, in victory and defeat, is really what it is all about.

ACKNOWLEDGMENTS

A story about a football tradition is not written by just one person; it is written by a lot of people as it happens day-by-day. The reportage of many outstanding newspapermen contributed to the production of this book, either directly or indirectly. Articles written by the late Bert Bertine provided a wealth of information.

Two earlier books, *Zuppke of Illinois* by Red Grange and *The Big Ten* by Tug Wilson and Jerry Brondfield, were especially helpful in providing background and insights. The *Big Ten Record Book* provided an additional ready reference source.

But a book of this type would not have been possible except for the meticulous record-keeping, the collections and writings of the school's sports information directors through the years: L. M. Tobin, Chuck Flynn, Charles Bellatti, Norm Sheya and Tab Bennett along with their staff. Flynn, in particular, contributed greatly. He read the manuscript for accuracy and offered numerous excellent editing suggestions. I also am grateful to Athletic Director Cecil Coleman for his support; to Ray Eliot, in particular, for his inspiration; and to the Illinois players and coaches, past and present, who gave of their time generously.

Several of my colleagues at the *Courier* also were of special assistance. Photographers Phil Greer and Curt Beamer supplied pictures as did the Illinois Sports Information Office. Staff writers Dave French and Reed Schreck also assisted. Don Lindsay, D. G. Schumacher and Jerry Dunning also were supportive.

And for the patience and understanding of my wife, Kathleen; my son, Shawn; and my daughter, Heather, I am especially thankful.

Lon Eubanks

Appendix

(ILLINOIS ATHLETIC DEPARTMENT DATA)

ALL-TIME ILLINOIS MARKS

CONSECUTIVE GAME STREAKS

Games Unbeaten	15	(13-0-2, 1914-16)
	14	(13-0-1, 1923-24)
	13	(13-0-0, 1909-11)
Home Games Unbeaten	17	(16-0-1, 1927-30)
	16	(16-0-0, 1902-03)
	12	(11-0-1, 1899-1901)
Conference Games Unbeaten	11	(9-0-2, 1914-15)
	8	(8-0-0, 1919-20)
	8	(7-0-1, 1923-24)
Home Conference Games Unbeaten	10	(10-0-0, 1907-11)
	7	(7-0-0. 1927-29)
	7	(6-0-1, 1923-24)
Games Won	13	(1923-24)
	13	(1909-11)
	9	(1927-28)
	9	(1914-15)
Home Games Won	16	(1902-03)
	14	(1927-30)
	11	(1923-24)
	11	(1900-01)
Conference Games Won	9	(1909-10)
	8	(1919-20)
Home Conference Games Won	10	(1907-11)
	7	(1927-29)
	6	(1950-52)

Highest Scoring Illinois Victories

87-3	over Illinois Wesleyan	1912
80-0	over Iowa	1902
79-0	over Illinois College	1895
79-0	over Illinois Normal	1944

Largest Illinois Defeats

63-0	to Chicago	1906
62-0	to Purdue	1890
58-0	to Iowa	1899
57-0	to Michigan	1969

Illinois All-American Football Players

Ralph Chapman, guard 1914
Perry Graves, end 1914
Bart Macomber, halfback 1915
John Depler, center 1918
Charles Carney, end 1920
Jim McMillen, guard 1923
Harold E. "Red"Grange, halfback 1923-24-25
Bernie Shively, guard 1926
Russ Crane, guard 1927
Robert Reitsch, center 1927
A.J. "Butch" Nowack, tackle 1928
Leroy Wietz, guard 1928
Lou Gordon, tackle 1929
Jim Reeder, tackle 1939
Alex Agase, guard 1942-43-46
Claude "Buddy" Young, halfback 1944
Ralph Serpico, guard 1944
William Vohaska, center 1950
Albert Tate, tackle 1950
Al Brosky, safety 1951
Johnny Karras, halfback 1951
Charles Ulrich, tackle 1951
Charles Boerio, linebacker 1951
J.C. Caroline, halfback 1953
Bill Burrell, guard 1959
Dick Butkus, center 1963-64
Jim Grabowski, fullback 1964-65
George Donnelly, safety 1964

Other Players Who Ranked High Nationally

F.C. Van Hook, guard 1906-07-08
J.F. Twist, center 1910
G.D. Butzer, guard 1910
Otto Seiler, quarterback 1910
Harold Pogue, halfback 1914
J.W. Watson, center 1915
C.K. Squier, end 1915
C.O. Applegran, guard 1919
Burt Ingwersen, tackle 1919
Jack Crangle, fullback 1920
C.E. Kassel, end 1925
J.A. Timm, halfback 1928
Gilbert Berry, halfback 1932
Charles Galbreath, tackle 1934
Lester Lindberg, halfback 1935
James McDonald, center 1938

Ike Owens, end. 1947
Richard Raklovits, fullback. 1950
Tommy O'Connell, quarterback. 1952
Rich Kreitling, end 1958
Joe Rutgens, tackle 1960
Archie Sutton, tackle. 1964
Tab Bennett, tackle 1972
Lonnie Perrin, halfback 1975
Dan Beaver, kicker 1975

FIGHTING ILLINI INDIVIDUAL RECORDS

SCORING

Total Points:

Career — Harold 'Red' Grange (1923-'24-'25) 186
Season — Harold 'Red' Grange (1924) 78
　　　　　Claude 'Buddy' Young (1944) 78
　　　　　*John Karras (1951) 78
Game — Harold 'Red' Grange
　　　　　(vs. Michigan, Oct. 18, 1924) 30

Touchdowns:

Career — Harold 'Red' Grange (1923-'24-'25) 31
Season — Harold 'Red' Grange (1924) 13
　　　　　Claude 'Buddy' Young (1944) 13
　　　　　*John Karras (1951) 13
Game — Harold 'Red' Grange
　　　　　(vs. Michigan, Oct. 18, 1924). 5

*Karras' season records for 1951 include 1952 Rose Bowl game.

TOTAL OFFENSE

Plays
Career — Mike Wells (1970-'71-'72) 758
Season — Bob Naponic (1968) 360
Game — Mike Taliaferro
           (vs. Minnesota, Oct. 20, 1962) 49
           (seven runs, 42 passes)

Yards Gained
Career — Mike Wells (1970-'71-'72) 3204
Season — Tommy O'Connell (1952) 1724
Game — Harold 'Red' Grange
           (vs. Pennsylvania, Oct. 31, 1925) 413

RUSHING

Attempts
Career — *Jim Grabowski (1963-'64-'65) 579
Season — Jim Grabowski (1964) 252
Game — Darrell Robinson
           (vs. Ohio State, Oct. 1970) 43

Yards Gained
Career — *Jim Grabowski (1963-'64-'65) 2878
Season — Jim Grabowski (1965) 1258
Game — Harold 'Red' Grange
           (vs. Pennsylvania, Oct. 31, 1925) 363
           (36 attempts)

*Grabowski's career records include 1964 Rose Bowl game.

PASSING

Attempts:
Career — Mike Wells (1970-'71-'72) 507
Season — Tommy O'Connell (1952) 224
Game — Mike Taliaferro
           (vs. Minnesota, Oct. 20, 1962) 42

Completions:
Career — Mike Wells (1970-'71-'72) 231
Season — Tommy O'Connell (1952) 133
Game — Tommy O'Connell
           (vs. Iowa, Nov. 8, 1952) 22

Interceptions:
Career — Mike Wells (1970-'71-'72) 32
Season — Tommy O'Connell (1952) 17
         Mike Taliaferro (1962) 17
Game — Tommy O'Connell
           (vs. Iowa, Nov. 8, 1952) 6

Yards Gained
Career — Mike Wells (1970-'71-'72) 2750

```
Season — Tommy O'Connell (1952) . . . . . . . . . . . . 1761
Game  — Tommy O'Connell
         (vs. Iowa, Nov. 8, 1952) . . . . . . . . . . . . 306
         (34 attempts, 22 completions)
Play   — Mike Taliaferro
         (to Mike Yavorski, vs Ohio State)
         (Oct. 13, 1962) . . . . . . . . . . . . . . . . . 90
```

Touchdowns

```
Career  — Mike Wells (1970-'71-'72) . . . . . . . . . . . . 21
Season  — Tommy O'Connell (1952) . . . . . . . . . . . . . 12
          Fred Custardo (1965) . . . . . . . . . . . . . . 12
Game    — Tommy O'Connell
          (vs. Washington, Oct. 11, 1952) . . . . . . . . . 5
```

RECEIVING
Receptions:

```
Career  — John Wright (1965-'66-'67) . . . . . . . . . . . 159
Season  — John Wright (1966) . . . . . . . . . . . . . . . 60
Game    — Rex Smith
          (vs. Iowa, Nov. 8, 1952) . . . . . . . . . . . . 11
          John Wright
          (vs. Stanford, Oct. 22, 1966) . . . . . . . . . . 11
```

Yards Gained

```
Career  — John Wright (1965-'66-'67) . . . . . . . . . . 2284
Season  — John Wright (1966) . . . . . . . . . . . . . . . 831
Game    — Rex Smith
          (vs. Iowa, Nov. 8, 1952) . . . . . . . . . . . . 190
          (11 receptions)
Play    — Mike Yavorski
          (from Mike Taliaferro, vs. Ohio State)
          (Oct. 13, 1962) . . . . . . . . . . . . . . . . . 90
```

PASS INTERCEPTIONS
Interceptions:

```
Career  — *Al Brosky (1950-'51-'52) . . . . . . . . . . . . 28
Season  — Al Brosky (1950 and 1951) . . . . . . . . . . . . 10
          Mike Gow (1973) . . . . . . . . . . . . . . . . . 10
Game    — Mike Gow
          (vs. Stanford, Sept. 21, 1974) . . . . . . . . . . 4
```

Yards Returned

```
Career  — *Al Brosky (1950-'51-'52) . . . . . . . . . . . 313
Season  — Ron Bess (1967) . . . . . . . . . . . . . . . . 198
Game    — Ron Bess
          (vs. Notre Dame, Oct. 21, 1967)
          (2 interceptions) . . . . . . . . . . . . . . . . 152
Play    — Julius Rykovich
          (vs. Ohio State, Nov. 16, 1946) . . . . . . . . . 98
          Bruce Sullivan
          (vs. Michigan, Nov. 5, 1966) . . . . . . . . . . . 98
```

Willie Osley
(vs. Washington, Oct. 2, 1971) 98

Most Consecutive Games with at Least One Pass Interception.
Al Brosky (during 1950 and 1951 seasons). . . 15

*Brosky records include 1952 Rose Bowl game.

PUNTING

Punts:
Career — Terry Masar (1969-'70-'71) 198
Season — Terry Masar (1971) 85
Game — Charlie Bareither
(vs. Missouri, Sept. 28, 1968). 13

Yards
Career — *Dwight 'Dike' Eddleman (1946-'47-'48) . 6128.5
Season — Charlie Bareither (1968) 2639
Game — Charlie Bareigher
(vs. Missouri, Sept. 28, 1968). 494
(13 punts)
Play   — Dwight 'Dike' Eddleman
(vs. Iowa, Nov. 6, 1948) 88
*Eddleman record includes 1947 Rose Bowl Game.

Average
Career — Bill Brown (1958-'59-'60) 40.2
(40 punts, 1610 yards)
Season — Dwight 'Dike' Eddleman (1948). 42.9
(59 punts, 2535 yards)
Game — Bill Brown
(vs. Michigan, Nov. 8, 1958) 54.3
(3 punts, 163 yards)

SCORING PLAYS

Longest Kickoff Return
Lonnie Perrin (11 yards), lateral to George Uremovich
(87 yards) (vs. Indiana, Nov. 11, 1972) 98

Longest Touchdown Punt Return
Dwight 'Dike' Eddleman
(vs. Western Michigan, Nov. 8, 1947) 92

Longest Touchdown Run with Recovered Fumble
Cliff Waldbeser
(vs. Iowa State, Sept. 27, 1952) 72

Longest Touchdown Run with Pass Interception
Julius Rykovich
(vs. Ohio State, Nov. 16, 1946) 98
Bruce Sullivan
(vs. Michigan, Nov. 5, 1966) 98
Willie Osley
(vs. Washington, Oct. 2, 1971) 98

Longest Touchdown Run from Scrimmage
Claude 'Buddy' Young
(vs. Great Lakes, Sept. 30, 1944) 93

Longest Touchdown Pass
Mike Taliaferro to Mike Yavorski
(vs. Ohio State, Oct. 13, 1962 90

Longest Field Goal
Dan Beaver
(vs. Purdue, Oct. 18, 1975) 57

SINGLE PLAYS
Longest Kickoff Return
Lonnie Perrin (11 yards), lateral to George Uremovich
(87 yards) (vs. Indiana, Nov. 11, 1972) 98

Longest Punt Return
Dwight 'Dike' Eddleman
(vs. Western Michigan, Nov. 8, 1947) 92

Longest Run with Recovered Fumble
Cliff Waldbeser
(vs. Iowa State, Sept. 27, 1952) 72

Longest Run from Scrimmage
Claude 'Buddy' Young
(vs. Great Lakes, Sept. 30, 1944) 93

Longest Pass
Mike Taliaferro to Mike Yavorski
(vs. Ohio State, Oct. 13, 1962). 90
Dan Beaver
(vs. Purdue, Oct. 18, 1975) 57

Illinois Football Captains

1890—Scott Williams—QB
1891—R.W. Hart—FB
1892—R.W. Hart—FB
1893—George H. Atherton
    —E
1894—J.E. Pfeffer—T
1895—Robert J. Hotchkiss
    —FB
1896—Charles E. Beebe—G
1897—Don Sweney—T
1898—Arthur R. Johnson
    —FB
1899—E.C. McLane—C
1900—Arthur R. Hall
    —E-HB
1901—Justa M. Lindgren
    —T
1902—Garland (Jake) Stahl
    —T
1903—Claude J. Rothbeg
    —G-E
1904—C.A. Fairweather—G
1905—C.J. Moynihan—T-HB
1906—Ira T. Carrithers—HB
1907—Lion Gardiner—HB
1908—F.C. VanHook—G
1909—Benjamin F. Baum
    —E
1910—G.D. Butzer—G
1911—Chester C. Roberts
    —HB
1912—William H. Woolston
    —FB-HB
1913—Enos M. Rowe—FB
1914—Ralph D. Chapman
    —G
1915—John W. Watson—C
1916—Frank B. Macomber
    —QB
1917—Reynold R. Kraft—E
1918—B.A. Ingwersen—T
    (Acting)
1919—William K. Kopp—FB
1920—John C. Depler—C
1921—Lawrence W. Walquist
    —HB
1922—David D. Wilson—E
1923—James W. McMillen
 —   —G

1924—Frank E. Rokusek
    —E-T
1925—Harold E. (Red) Grange
    —HB
1926—Charles E. Kassel
    —E
1927—Robert Reitsch—C
1928—Albert J. Nowack —T
1929—Russell J. Crane —G
1930—Olaf E. Robinson
    —FB
1931—Gilbert Berry
    —HB (Honorary)
1932—Gilbert Berry—QB
1933—Herman Walser—FB
1934—Charles Bennis—G
    —Jack Beynon—QB
1935—Charles S. Galbreath
    —T
1936—Elvin C. Sayre—C
1937—Lowell Spurgeon
    —HB
1938—James W. McDonald
    —C
1939—Melvin Brewer—G
1940—Thomas J. Riggs
    —T
1941—captain-elect ineligible
1942—James Smith—FB
1943—John Genis—
    in service
1944—appointed for each
    game
1945—Ralph Serpico—T
1946—Mac Wenskunas
    —C
1947—Art Dufelmeier
    —HB
1948—Herb Siegert—G
1949—Lyle Button—T
1950—Bill Vohaska—C
1951—Charles Studley—G
1952—Alfred Brosky—HB
1953—Robert Lenzini—T
1954—Jan Smid—G
1955—captain-elect
    ineligible
1956—James Minor—C
1957—Dale Smith—HB

1958– Jack Delveaux
  –FB
1959–Bill Burrell–G
1960–Bill Brown–FB
1961–Gary Brown–T
1962–Bob Scharbert–T
  –Ken Zimmerman–HB
1963–Mike Taliaferro–QB
  –Dick Deller–G
1964–Dick Butkus–C
  –George Donnelly–HB
1965–Jim Grabowski–FB
  –Don Hansen–LB
1966–Bo Batchelder–E
  –Kai Anderson–C
1967–Ron Bess–HB
  –Ken Kmiec–E

1968–Carson Brooks–E
  –Tony Pleviak–T
1969–Doug Redmann–G
  –Bruce Erb–LB
1970–Kirk McMillin–G
  –Doug Dieken–E
1971–Glenn Collier–E
  –Larry McCarren–C
1972–Larry McCarren–C
  –John Wiza–LB
1973–John Gann–G
  –Ken Braid–rover
1974–Ty McMillin–LB
  –Revie Sorey–G
1975–Dean March–DE
  –Stu Levenick–OT
1976–Dean March–DE
  –Scott Studwell–LB
  –Marty Friel–E

Illinois Most Valuable Players

1930–Stan Bodman–G
1931–Fred Frink–E
1932–Gil Berry–HB
1933–Dave Cook–FB
1934–Les Lindberg–HB
1935–Ed Gryboski–G
1936–Cliff Kuhn–G
1937–Jack Berner–QB
1938–James Hodges–G
1939–Bill Lenich–C
1940–George Bernhardt–FB
1941–Nate Johnson–T
1942–Elmer Engel–E
1943–Eddie Bray–HB
1944–Buddy Young–HB
1945–Mac Wenskunas–C
1946–Alex Agase–G
1947–Ike Owens–E
1948–James Valek–E
1949–John Karras–HB
1950–Tony Klimek–E
1951–Charles Boerio–LB
1952–Al Brosky–HB
1953–Don Ernst–T
1954–Jack Chamblin–C

1955–Em Lindbeck –QB
1956–Dave Walker–G
1957–Rod Hanson–E
1958–Gene Cherney–C
1959–Bill Burrell–G
1960–Joe Rutgens–T
1961–Tony Parrilli–G
1962–Ken Zimmerman–HB
1963–Dick Butkus–C
1964–Dick Butkus–C
1965–Jim Grabowski–FB
1966–Ron Guenther–G
1967–John Wright–E
1968–Rich Johnson–FB
1969–Doug Dieken–E
1970–Doug Dieken–E
1971–Terry Masar–P-HB
1972–Larry McCarren–C
  –Larry Allen–DE
1973–Eddie Jenkins–HB
  –Octavus Morgan–DE
1974–Tom Hicks –LB
  –Jeff Hollenbach–QB
1975–Stu Levenick–OT
  –Bruce Beaman–DB

FIGHTING ILLINI CAREER LEADERS

SCORING

	Player	Years	TD's	X-1	X-2	FG	Total
1.	Harold 'Red' Grange	1923-25	31	0	0	0	186
2.	Dan Beaver	1973-75	0	60	0	29	147
3.	Jim Grabowski	1963-65	24	0	0	0	144
	Johnny Karras	1949-51	24	0	0	0	144
5.	Mike Wells	1970-72	10	45	0	11	139

TOTAL OFFENSE

	Player	Years	Rush	Pass	Plays	Total
1.	Mike Wells	1970-72	454	2750	748	3204
2.	Fred Custardo	1963-65	516	2415	481	2931
3.	Jim Grabowski	1963-65	2878	0	594	2878
4.	Harold 'Red' Grange	1923-25	1071	643	430	2714
5.	Tom O'Connell	1951-52	-29	2453	254	2424

PASSING

	Player	Years	Att.	Comp.	Int.	Yds.	TD's	Ave.
1.	Mike Wells	1970-72	505	231	32	2750	21	.457
2.	Tom O'Connell	1951-52	344	195	29	2453	18	.566
3.	Fred Custardo	1963-65	389	204	23	2416	5	.524
4.	Jeff Hollenbach	1972-74	304	142	15	1953	9	.467
5.	Bob Naponic	1966-68	404	166	19	1937	7	.411

RUSHING

	Player	Years	Att.	Net	TD's	Ave.
1.	Jim Grabowski	1963-65	579	2878	24	4.9
2.	Johnny Karras	1949-51	403	2077	22	5.1
3.	Harold 'Red' Grange	1923-25	388	2071	26	5.1
4.	Rich Johnson	1966-68	521	2058	13	3.9
5.	Lonnie Perrin	1971-75	367	1771	10	4.8

RECEIVING

	Player	Years	No.	Yds.	TD's	Ave.
1.	John Wright	1965-67	159	2284	12	14.4
2.	Doug Dieken	1968-70	89	1246	7	14.0
3.	Garvin Roberson	1971-73	84	1357	10	16.1
4.	Rex Smith	1951-52	69	1011	5	14.6
5.	John 'Rocky' Ryan	1952-53	61	1022	9	16.7

PUNTING

	Player	Years	No.	Yds.	Ave.
1.	Terry Masar	1969-71	198	7586	38.3
2.	Phil Vierneisel	1973-75	173	6882	39.8
3.	Dwight 'Dike' Eddleman	1946-48	161	6310	39.2
4.	Charlie Bareither	1967-68	115	4062	35.3
5.	Ken Miller	1951-53	102	3975	38.1

FIGHTING ILLINI SEASON LEADERS

SCORING

	Player	Year	TD's	X-1	X-2	FG	Total
1.	Harold 'Red' Grange	1924	13	0	0	0	78
	Claude 'Buddy' Young	1944	13	0	0	0	78
	John Karras	1951	13	0	0	0	78
4.	Harold 'Red' Grange	1923	12	0	0	0	72
5.	Mickey Bates	1953	11	0	0	0	66

OFFENSE

	Player	Year	Rush	Pass	Plays	Total
1.	Tom O'Connell	1952	-37	1761	260	1724
2.	Harold 'Red' Grange	1924	1164	524	*27	1688
3.	Harold 'Red' Grange	1925	1213	119	*15	1332
4.	Kurt Steger	1975	163	1136	232	1299
5.	Mike Taliaferro	1962	126	1139	283	1265

*Grange plays are based on passing only, rushing attempts were not recorded in early '20's.

PASSING

	Player	Year	Att.	Comp.	Int.	Yds.	TD's	Ave.
1.	Tom O'Connell	1952	224	133	17	1761	12	.599
2.	Mike Taliaferro	1962	212	80	17	1139	5	.377
3.	Kurt Steger	1975	166	80	14	1136	8	.482
4.	Fred Custardo	1965	170	90	10	1124	2	.529
5.	Fred Custardo	1964	159	86	11	1012	3	.547

RUSHING

	Player	Year	Att.	Net.	TD's	Ave.
1.	Jim Grabowski	1965	252	1258	7	5.0
2.	J. C. Caroline	1953	194	1256	5	6.5
3.	Jim Grabowski	1964	186	1004	10	5.4
4.	Rich Johnson	1968	243	973	5	6.5
5.	Lonnie Perrin	1975	171	907	6	5.3

RECEIVING

	Player	Year	No.	Yds.	TD's	Ave.
1.	John Wright	1966	60	831	4	13.8
2.	John Wright	1967	52	698	4	13.4
3.	John Wright	1965	47	755	4	16.1
4.	John 'Rocky' Ryan	1952	45	714	5	15.8

ILLINI TEAM RECORDS

Most Points, One Game
Non-Conference 87, Illinois vs. Illinois Wesleyan (3), 1912
Conference 80, Illinois vs. Iowa (0), 1902
Most Points, One Season (Average Per Game)
Full season, 380, 1902, (28.8), 13 games
Full season, 229, 1975, (20.8), 11 games
Full season, 273, 1944, (27.3), 10 games
Full season, 228, 1953, (25.3), 9 games
Conference, 149, 1971, (18.6), 8 games
Conference, 155, 1965, (22.1), 7 games
Conference, 154, 1953, (25.7), 6 games
Most Touchdowns, One Game
*Non-conference, 12, Illinois vs. Illinois Normal, 1944
Conference, 7, Illinois vs. Iowa, 1973
Conference, 7, Illinois vs. Wisconsin, 1966

Most First Downs, One Game (Since 1924)
25 vs. Ohio State, 1929
25 vs. California, 1955
25 vs. Colgate, 1957
25 vs. Minnesota, 1957
Most Consecutive Wins Without Ties
13, 1909-1911, 1923-1924
Most Consecutive Conference Wins
8, 1919-1920
Most Consecutive Losses
15, 1960-61-62
Most Total Net Offensive Yards
3669 (2330 rushing, 1339 passing) 1975, 11 games
3555 (2927 rushing, 628 passing) 1944, 10 games
Most Yards Rushing, One Game
Non-Conference, 562, Illinois vs. Illinois Normal, 1944
Conference, 467, Illinois vs. Iowa 1973
Most Net Yards Rushing, One Season
11 games, 2340, 1971
10 games, 2927, 1944
Most Rushing Plays, One Season
593, 1973 (11 games)
504, 1968 (10 games)
Most First Downs Rushing
125, 1972 (11 games)
117, 1968 (10 games)
Most Touchdowns Rushing, One Season
19, 1975 (11 games)
13, 1968 (10 games)
Most Passes Attempted, One Game
42, Illinois vs. Minnesota, 1962
Most Passes Attempted, One Season
245 (141 completed), 1952
Most Passes Completed, One Game
22, Illinois vs. Iowa, 1952
Most Passes Completed, One Year
141 (245 attempted), 1952
Most Yards Passing, One Game
306 , Illinois vs. Iowa, 1952
Most Yards Passing, One Year
1929 (141 of 245) 1952
Most First Downs Passing, One Game
13, Illinois vs. Minnesota, 1974
Most First Downs Passing, One Season
65, 1974
Most Passes Had Intercepted, One Season
20, 1952
Best Passing Completion Percentage, One. Game
.750, 18 of 24 for 212 yards, Illinois vs. Purdue, 1952
Best Passing Completion Percentage, One Season
.575, 141 of 245, 1952

*Most Punts, One Game
  14, Illinois vs. Missouri, 1968
*Most Punts, One Season
  86, 1971
*Most Yardage Punting, One Game
  521, Illinois vs. Missouri, 1968
*Most Average Yardage Punting, One Season
  40.7, 1975 (54 punts)

(*since 1949)

YEARLY STATISTICAL LEADERS
(SINCE 1946)

SCORING
	Points
1946 Perry Moss	36
1947 Dike Eddleman	42
1948 Paul Patterson, Bernie Krueger	24
1949 John Karras	42
1950 Dick Raklovits	48
1951 John Karras	78
1952 Rocky Ryan	36
1953 Mickey Bates	66
1954 Abe Woodson	42
1955 Bob Mitchell	30
1956 Abe Woodson	36
1957 Ray Nitschke	30
1958 Rich Kreitling	30
1959 Bill Brown	36
1960 Marchall Starks	42
1961 Jim Plankenhorn	11
1962 Dave Pike	12
1963 Jim Grabowski	42
1964 Jim Grabowski	60
1965 Fred Custardo	43
1966 Bob Naponic	36
1967 Rich Johnson	36
1968 Rich Johnson	34
1969 Dave Jackson, Steve Livas, Doug Dieken, Bob Bess	18
1970 Mike Wells	57
1971 John Wilson	42
1972 Mike Wells	51
1973 Dan Beaver	50
1974 Chubby Phillips	56
1975 Dan Beaver	45

RUSHING
	Yards
1946 Buddy Young	456
1947 Ruck Steger	447
1948 Ruck Steger	265
1949 John Karras	826
1950 Dick Raklovits	709

TOTAL OFFENSE
	Yards
1946 Buddy Young	456
1947 Perry Moss	726
1948 Bernie Krueger	709
1949 John Karras	832
1950 Dick Raklovits	709
1951 Tom O'Connell	700
1952 Tom O'Connell	1724
1953 J.C. Caroline	1256
1954 Em Lindbeck	476
1955 Em Lindbeck	664
1956 Abe Woodson	599
1957 Tom Haller	724
1958 John Easterbrook	762
1959 Mel Meyres	565
1960 John Easterbrook	890
1961 Ron Fearn	292
1962 Mike Taliaferro	1265
1963 Mike Taliaferro	619
1964 Fred Custardo	1163
1965 Jim Grabowski	1290
1966 Bob Naponic	1223
1967 Dean Volkman	995
1968 Bob Naponic	984
1969 Steve Livas	679
1970 Mike Wells	859
1971 Mike Wells	1221
1972 Mike Wells	1124
1973 Jeff Hollenbach	857
1974 Jeff Hollenbach	973
1975 Kurt Steger	1299

PASSING
	Yards
1946 Perry Moss - 23	298
1947 Perry Moss - 71	719
1948 Bernie Krueger - 52	703

1951 Bill Tate 684
1952 Pete Bachouros . . 484
1953 J.C. Caroline . . .1256
1954 J.C. Caroline . . . 440
1955 Harry Jefferson . . 514
1956 Abe Woodson . . . 599
1957 Ray Nitschke . . . 514
1958 Marshall Starks . . 303
1959 Bill Brown. 504
1960 Bill Brown. 531
1961 Al Wheatland . . . 230
1962 Ken Zimmerman . 225
1963 Jim Grabowski . . 616
1964 Jim Grabowski . .1004
1965 Jim Grabowski . .1258
1966 Bill Huston 420
1967 Rich Johnson . . . 768
1968 Rich Johnson . . . 973
1969 Dave Jackson . . . 465
1970 Darrell Robinson . 749
1971 John Wilson 611
1972 George Uremovich .611
1973 George Uremovich .519
1974 Chubby Phillips . .772
1975 Lonnie Perrin . . . 907

1949 Bernie Krueger - 42 . . 477
1950 Fred Major - 32. 464
1951 Tom O'Connell - 62 . . 692
1952 Tom O'Connell - 133 .1761
1953 Elry Falkenstein - 36. . 577
1954 Em Lindbeck - 38 . . . 476
1955 Em Lindbeck - 39 . . . 588
1956 Hiles Stout - 20. 278
1957 Tom Haller - 51. 675
1958 John Easterbrook - 34 . 656
1959 Mel Meyers - 32. 495
1960 John Easterbrook - 40 . 538
1961 Dave McGann - 27 . . . 269
1962 Mike Taliaferro - 80 . .1139
1963 Mike Taliaferro - 35 . . 450
1964 Fred Custardo - 86 . . .1012
1965 Fred Custardo - 90 . . .1124
1966 Bob Naponic - 70. . . . 998
1967 Dean Volkman - 77 . .1005
1968 Bob Naponic - 83. . . . 813
1969 Steve Livas - 42. 705
1970 Mike Wells - 71 906
1971 Mike Wells - 84 . .   1007
1972 Mike Wells - 76 837
1973 Jeff Hollenbach - 78 . . 916
1974 Jeff Hollenbach - 64 . .1037
1975 Kurt Steger - 80 1136

PASS RECEIVING

	Catches	Yards
1946 Bill Heiss - 5		132
Sam Zatkoff - 5		60
1947 Sam Zatkoff - 13		147
1948 Walt Kersulis - 22		329
1949 Ronnie Clark - 11		105
1950 Tony Klimek - 13		200
1951 Rex Smith - 22		243
1952 Rocky Ryan - 45		714
Rex Smith - 45		642
1953 Rocky Ryan - 16		308
1954 Dean Renn - 17		246
1955 Bob DesEnfants - 12		206
1956 Abe Woodson - 12		257
1957 Rich Kretling - 12		203
1958 Rich Kreitling - 23		688
1959 John Counts - 19		314
1960 Ed O'Bradovich - 21		233
1961 Dick Newell - 16		184
Gary Hembrough - 16		170
1962 Jim Warren - 18		230
1963 Jim Warren - 10		121
Sam Price - 10		98
1964 Bob Trumpy - 28		428
1965 John Wright - 47		755
1966 John Wright - 60		831
1967 John Wright - 52		698
1968 Doug Dieken - 21		223
1969 Doug Dieken - 29		486
1970 Doug Dieken - 39		537
1971 Garvin Roberson - 28		372
1972 Garvin Roberson - 31		569
1973 Garvin Roberson - 25		416
1974 Joe Smalzer - 29		525
1975 Jeff Chrystal - 22		261

PUNTING
(Minimum of 10 punts)

	Ave.
1946 Dike Eddleman . . 37.7
1947 Dike Eddleman . . 36.3
1948 Dike Eddleman . . 42.9
1949 John Vukelich . . 34.6
1950 Don Laz 37.0
1951 Ken Miller. 36.8
1952 Ken Miller. 39.9
1953 Ken Miller. 37.6
1954 J.C. Caroline . . 40.4
1955 Abe Woodson . . 39.6
1956 Abe Woodson . . . 37.7
1957 Jack Delveaux . . 33.9
1958 Bill Brown. 40.2
1959 Bill Brown. 39.3
1960 Ed O'Bradovich. . 31.1
1961 Doug Mills   37.1
1962 Mike Taliaferro . . 33.2
1963 Mike Taliaferro . . 36.3
1964 George Donnelly . 38.2
1965 Terry Miller 35.0
1966 Terry Miller 35.5
1967 Terry Miller 36.6
1968 Charlie Bareither . 36.2
1969 Terry Masar 38.2
1970 Terry Masar 38.8
1971 Terry Masar 38.3
1972 Jim Rucks. 36.3
1973 Phil Vierneisel . . 37.3
1974 Phil Vierneisel . . 39.0
1975 Phil Vierneisel . . 40.7

ALL-TIME RECORD

FIRST GAME - LAST GAME	OPPONENT	GAMES
1898-1899	Alumni	3
1929-1959	Army	7
1892	Baker U.	1
1892	Beloit	1
1891	Bloomington	1
1891	Bloomington Swifts	1
1927-1940	Bradley	8
1922-1942	Butler	9
1955-1974	California	6
1917	Camp Funston Kansas	1
1942-1943	Camp Grant	2
1897-1898	Carlisle Indians	2
1918	Chanute Field	1
1892-1939	Chicago	44
1893-1895	Chicago Athletic Association	3
1903	Chicago Dentistry	1
1914	Christian Brothers	1
1926-1932	Coe	3
1916-1957	Colgate	2
1936-1938	DePaul	3
1892-1924	DePauw	6
1892	Doane College	1
1910-1941	Drake	4
1958-1965	Duke	2
1892-1903	Englewood High School	4
1891-1897	Eureka College	3
1967	Florida	1
1918-1945	Great Lakes	4
1902-1915	Haskell	2
1895	Illinois College	1
1944	Illinois Normal	1
1890-1912	Illinois Wesleyan	7
1899-1974	Indiana	37
1894	Indianapolis Artillery	1
1899-1975	*IOWA	42
1943	Iowa Seahawks	1
1927-1969	Iowa State	6
1892-1968	Kansas	5
1892	Kansas City Athletic Club	1
1948	Kansas State	1
1909-1913	Kentucky	2
1891-1905	Knox	8
1891-1897	Lake Forest	5
1900-1903	Lombard College	2
1901	Marion Sims	1
1908	Marquette	1
1932-1941	Miami of Ohio	2
1898-1975	*MICHIGAN	60
1955-1975	*MICHIGAN STATE	15
1909-1911	Millikin	3

AGAINST OPPONENTS   (* 1976 Opponents)

WON	LOST	T	PTS F.	PTS A.	ILL. WIN %
1	1	1	27	29	.500
3	3	1	65	66	.500
1	0	0	26	10	1.000
1	0	0	(won by forfeit)		1.000
1	0	0	20	12	1.000
1	0	0	26	0	1.000
7	0	1	208	13	.938
8	1	0	307	53	.889
5	1	0	113	85	.833
1	0	0	28	0	1.000
1	1	0	20	23	.500
0	2	0	6	34	.000
1	0	0	3	0	1.000
23	17	4	550	417	.570
0	3	0	4	32	.000
1	0	0	54	0	1.000
1	0	0	37	0	1.000
3	0	0	71	0	1.000
1	1	0	46	7	.500
2	0	1	53	13	.833
6	0	0	193	4	1.000
1	0	0	20	0	1.000
4	0	0	123	6	1.000
1	1	0	41	29	.500
4	0	0	131	5	1.000
3	0	0	72	0	1.000
0	1	0	0	14	.000
0	3	1	32	51	.125
2	0	0	60	10	1.000
1	0	0	79	0	1.000
1	0	0	79	0	1.000
6	1	0	188	29	.857
24	11	2	584	350	.676
0	1	0	14	18	.000
26	14	2	806	464	.643
0	1	0	18	32	.000
3	1	2	132	86	.667
3	2	0	93	73	.600
1	0	0	42	0	1.000
1	0	0	40	0	1.000
1	1	0	23	6	.500
8	0	0	223	9	1.000
4	0	1	138	24	.900
2	0	0	78	0	1.000
1	0	0	52	0	1.000
0	0	1	6	6	.500
2	0	0	65	7	1.000
18	43	0	503	1137	.295
7	7	1	154	218	.500
3	0	0	69	0	1.000

FIRST GAME - LAST GAME	OPPONENT	TOT. GAMES
1898-1975	*MINNESOTA	37
1923	Mississippi A & M	1
1896-1975	*MISSOURI	7
1902-1908	Monmouth	2
1918	Municipal Pier	1
1892-1953	Nebraska	8
1971	North Carolina	1
1902	North Division	1
1892-1975	*NORTHWESTERN	69
1904-1905	Northwestern College	2
1898-1968	Notre Dame	12
1893-1896	Oberlin College	2
1902-1975	*OHIO STATE	64
1935-1950	Ohio University	4
1917	Oklahoma	1
1970	Oregon	1
1965	Oregon State	1
1902-1903	Osteopaths	2
1893-1894	Pastime Athletic Club	2
1925-1926	Pennsylvania	2
1954-1972	Penn State	4
1897-1905	Physicians & Surgeons	7
1943-1967	Pittsburgh	6
1890-1975	*PURDUE	57
1915	Rolla Mines	1
1900	Rose Poly	1
1895-1903	Rush Lake Forest	2
1921-1942	South Dakota	2
1935-1972	Southern California	8
1965-1966	Southern Methodist	2
1951-1974	Stanford	6
1899-1931	St. Louis U.	4
1909-1970	Syracuse	6
1975-1975	*TEXAS A & M	1
1970	Tulane	1
1946-1964	UCLA	7
1893-1926	Wabash College	8
1950-1972	Washington	9
1969-1975	Washington State	3
1892-1936	Washington (St. Louis)	9
1947	Western Michigan	1
1960-1973	West Virginia	2
1895-1975	*WISCONSIN	48

WON	LOST	T	PTS F.	PTS A.	ILL. WIN %
16	20	1	445	543	.446
1	0	0	27	0	1.000
2	5	0	104	166	.286
2	0	0	50	6	1.000
0	1	0	0	7	.000
2	5	1	62	110	.313
0	1	0	0	27	.000
1	0	0	34	6	1.000
34	31	4	1051	846	.522
2	0	0	34	0	1.000
0	11	1	68	312	.968
1	1	0	46	40	.500
19	41	4	671	1145	.328
2	2	0	48	20	.500
1	0	0	44	0	1.000
1	0	0	20	16	1.000
0	1	0	10	12	.000
2	0	0	58	0	1.000
2	0	0	28	16	1.000
2	0	0	27	2	1.000
1	3	0	48	77	.250
6	1	0	137	11	.858
6	0	0	176	49	1.000
27	24	6	848	868	.526
1	0	0	75	7	1.000
1	0	0	26	0	1.000
2	0	0	102	0	1.000
2	0	0	98	0	1.000
1	7	0	78	188	.125
1	1	0	48	26	.500
3	3	0	119	77	.500
4	0	0	70	12	1.000
6	0	0	142	47	1.000
0	1	1	13	43	.000
0	1	0	9	23	.000
5	2	0	150	86	.714
7	0	1	221	27	.937
4	5	0	164	213	.444
2	1	0	66	59	.667
9	0	0	205	26	1.000
1	0	0	60	14	1.000
1	1	0	43	17	.500
21	22	5	683	702	.490

ANNUAL ILLINI TEAM RECORD

OVERALL BIG TEN

Year	W	L	T	W	L	T	Finish	Coach
1890	1	2	0					Scott Williams
1891	6	0	0					Robert Lackey
1892	9	3	2					E.K.Hall
1893	3	2	3					E.K.Hall
1894	5	3	0					Louis D. Vail
1895	4	2	1					George Huff
1896	4	2	1	0	2	1	Sixth-T	George Huff
1897	6	2	0	1	1	0	Fourth	Fred L. Smith
1898	4	5	0	1	1	0	Fourth	Fred L. Smith
1899	3	5	1	0	3	0	Sixth-T	Neilson Poe
1900	7	3	2	1	3	2	Eighth	Fred L. Smith
1901	8	2	0	4	2	0	Fourth	Edgar G. Holt
1902	10	2	1	4	2	0	Fourth	Edgar G. Holt
1903	8	6	0	1	5	0	Seventh	George Woodruff
1904	9	2	1	3	1	1	Fourth	Alumni
1905	5	4	0	0	3	0	Sixth-T	Fred Lowenthal
1906	1	3	1	1	3	0	Fifth	Justa Lindgren
1907	3	2	0	3	2	0	Third	Arthur R. Hall
1908	5	1	1	4	1	0	Second	Arthur R. Hall
1909	5	2	0	3	1	0	Third	Arthur R. Hall
1910	7	0	0	4	0	0	FIRST-T	Arthur R. Hall
1911	4	2	1	2	2	1	Fourth-T	Arthur R. Hall
1912	3	3	1	1	3	1	Sixth-T	Arthur R. Hall
1913	4	2	1	2	2	1	Fifth	Robert C. Zuppke
1914	7	0	0	6	0	0	FIRST	Robert C. Zuppke
1915	5	0	2	3	0	2	FIRST-T	Robert C. Zuppke
1916	3	3	1	2	2	1	Fourth-T	Robert C. Zuppke
1917	5	2	1	2	2	1	Fifth-T	Robert C. Zuppke
1918	5	2	0	4	0	0	FIRST	Robert C. Zuppke
1919	6	1	0	6	1	0	FIRST	Robert C. Zuppke
1920	5	2	0	4	2	0	Fourth	Robert C. Zuppke
1921	3	4	0	1	4	0	Eighth-T	Robert C. Zuppke
1922	2	5	0	2	4	0	Sixth	Robert C. Zuppke
1923	8	0	0	5	0	0	FIRST	Robert C. Zuppke
1924	6	1	1	3	1	1	Second-T	Robert C. Zuppke
1925	5	3	0	2	2	0	Fourth-T	Robert C. Zuppke
1926	6	2	0	2	2	0	Sixth-T	Robert C. Zuppke
1927	7	0	1	5	0	0	FIRST-T	Robert C. Zuppke
1928	7	1	0	4	1	0	FIRST	Robert C. Zuppke
1929	6	1	1	3	1	1	Second	Robert C. Zuppke
1930	3	5	0	1	4	0	Eighth	Robert C. Zuppke
1931	2	6	0	0	6	0	Ninth-T	Robert C. Zuppke
1932	5	4	0	2	4	0	Seventh	Robert C. Zuppke
1933	5	3	0	3	2	0	Fifth	Robert C. Zuppke

Year	W	L	T	W	L	T	Finish	Coach
1934	7	1	0	4	1	0	Third	Robert C. Zuppke
1935	3	5	0	1	4	0	Ninth-T	Robert C. Zuppke
1936	4	3	1	2	2	1	Sixth	Robert C. Zuppke
1937	3	3	2	2	3	0	Eighth	Robert C. Zuppke
1938	3	5	0	2	3	0	Seventh	Robert C. Zuppke
1939	3	4	1	3	3	0	Sixth	Robert C. Zuppke
1940	1	7	0	0	5	0	Ninth	Robert C. Zuppke
1941	2	6	0	0	5	0	Ninth	Robert C. Zuppke
1942	6	4	0	3	2	0	Third-T	Ray Eliot
1943	3	7	0	2	4	0	Sixth	Ray Eliot
1944	5	4	1	3	3	0	Sixth	Ray Eliot
1945	2	6	1	1	4	1	Seventh	Ray Eliot
1946	8	2	0	6	1	0	FIRST	Ray Eliot
1947	5	3	1	3	3	0	Third-T	Ray Eliot
1948	3	6	0	2	5	0	Eithth	Ray Eliot
1949	3	4	2	3	3	1	Fifth-T	Ray Eliot
1950	7	2	0	4	2	0	Fourth	Ray Eliot
1951	9	0	1	5	0	1	FIRST	Ray Eliot
1952	4	5	0	2	5	0	Sixth-T	Ray Eliot
1953	7	1	1	5	1	0	FIRST-T	Ray Eliot
1954	1	8	0	0	6	0	Tenth	Ray Eliot
1955	5	3	1	3	3	1	Fifth	Ray Eliot
1956	2	5	2	1	4	2	Seventh-T	Ray Eliot
1957	4	5	0	3	4	0	Seventh	Ray Eliot
1958	4	5	0	4	3	0	Sixth	Ray Eliot
1959	5	3	1	4	2	1	Third-T	Ray Eliot
1960	5	4	0	2	4	0	Fifth-T	Pete Elliott
1961	0	9	0	0	7	0	Ninth-T	Pete Elliott
1962	2	7	0	2	5	0	Eighth	Pete Elliott
1963	8	1	1	5	1	1	FIRST	Pete Elliott
1964	6	3	0	4	3	0	Fourth-T	Pete Elliott
1965	6	4	0	4	3	0	Fifth	Pete Elliott
1966	4	6	0	4	3	0	Third-T	Pete Elliott
1967	4	6	0	3	4	0	Fifth-T	Jim Valek
1968	1	9	0	1	6	0	Eighth-T	Jim Valek
1969	0	10	0	0	7	0	Tenth	Jim Valek
1970	3	7	0	1	6	0	Ninth-T	Jim Valek
1971	5	6	0	5	3	0	Third-T	Bob Blackman
1972	3	8	0	3	5	0	Sixth-T	Bob Blackman
1973	5	6	0	4	4	0	Fourth-T	Bob Blackman
1974	6	4	1	4	3	1	Fifth	Bob Blackman
1975	5	6	0	4	4	0	Third-T	Bob Blackman

TOTALS

Overall	W - 397	L - 308	T - 41
Big Ten	W - 209	L - 224	T - 23

ILLINI SCORES THROUGH THE YEARS

National Championships: 1914 (tied with Army): 1919 (tied with Harvard and Notre Dame): 1923; 1927. Authority, Parke H. Davis in Spalding's Guides. Rose Bowl Appearances: 1947, 1952, 1964.

*Home Games
Illini Scores are First

1890
Coach: Scott Williams
Captain: Scott Williams

O 2- 0	Ill. Wesleyan	16
N 22- 0	Purdue	62
*N 27-12	Ill. Wesleyan	6
12	(1-2-0)	84

1891
Coach: R. A. Lackey
Captain: Robert W. Hart

+O 1- 0	Lake Forest	8
*O 12-26	Bloomington Swifts	0
*N 7-40	Eureka Coll.	0
*N 13-44	Ill. Wesleyan	4
*N 21-12	Knox Coll.	0
N 26-20	Bloomington	12

+Lake Forest later forfeited game for using ineligible players
Illinois was champion of Illinois Intercollegiate Football League

142	(6-0-0)	24

1892
Coach: E. K. Hall
Captain: Robert W. Hart

*O 8- 6	Purdue	12
*O 12-16	Northwestern	16
O 21-22	Washington (St. Louis)	0
O 22-20	Doane Coll. (Omaha)	0
O 24- 0	Nebraska	6
O 26-26	Baker U (Baldwin.Kan.)	10
O 27-4	Kansas	26
O 29-42	Kansas City A. C.	0
*N 1-	Wisconsin (Forfeited)	
*N 5-38	Englewood H.S. (Chicago	0
N 16- 4	Chicago	4
N 17-	Beloit (Forfeited)	
*N 18-34	DePauw	0
*N 24-28	Chicago	12
240	(9-3-2)	96

1893
Captain: George H. Atherton

*S 30-60	Wabash	6
O 7-14	DePauw	4
O 21- 0	Northwestern	0
O 28- 4	Chi.Ath.Assn.	10
*N 6-24	Oberlin	34
+N 11-18	Pastime Ath. Club	16
N 25-26	Purdue	26

*N 30-10	Lake Forest	10
+ at St. Louis,Mo.		
156	(3-2-3)	106

1894
Coach: Louis D. Vail
Captain: J.E. Pfeffer

O 6-36	Wabash	6
O 13- 0	Chicago A.C.	14
*O 20-54	Lake Forest	6
*N 3-66	Northwestern	0
*N 17- 2	Purdue	22
N 21	Chicago (Forfeit)	
*N 24-14	Indianapolis Artillery	18
+N 29-10	Pastime Ath. Club	0
+ at St. Louis, Mo.		
282	(5-3-0)	66

1895
Coach: George A. Huff
Captain: R. J. Hotchkiss

*O 5-48	Wabash	0
O 12- 0	Chicago A.C.	8
*O 19-79	Illinois Coll.	0
O 26-10	Wisconsin	10
*N 2-38	Rush - Lake Forest	0
*N 23-38	Northwestern	4
N 28- 2	Purdue	6
215	(4-2-1)	28

1896
Captain: C. D. Beebe

*O 3-38	Lake Forest	0
*O 10-70	Knox	4
+O 17-10	Missouri	0
*O 21-22	Oberlin	6
O 31- 0	Chicago	12
*N 7- 4	Northwestern	10
N 26- 4	Purdue	4
+ at St. Louis, Mo.		
148	(4-2-1)	36

1897
Captain: Don Sweney

*O 2-26	Eureka	0
*O 9- 6	Physicians- Surgeons	0
*O 16-36	Lake Forest	0
*O 23-34	Purdue	4
*O 30-12	Chicago	18
*N 12-74	Knox	0
+N 20- 6	Carlisle Indians	23
++N 25-6	Eureka	0

+at Chicago Coliseum in first night and indoor game
++at Peoria

194	(6-2-0)	45

1898

Captain: A. R. Johnston

*S 28-18	III. Wesleyan	0
*O 1- 6	Physicians-Surgeons	11
*O 8- 0	Notre Dame	5
*O 15-16	DePauw	0
*O 22-10	Alumni	6
*N 4-17	Alumni	23
+N 12- 5	Michigan	12
++N 19- 0	Carlisle Indians	11
N 24-11	Minnesota	10

+ at Detroit
++ at Chicago

72	(4-5-0)	78

1899

Captain: E. C. McLane

*S 30- 6	III. Wesleyan	0
O 7- 5	Knox	0
*O 14- 0	Indiana	5
*O 28- 0	Michigan	5
*N 6- 0	Alumni	0
+N 11- 0	Wisconsin	23
N 22- 0	Purdue	5
N 25-29	St. Louis U	0
++N 30- 0	Iowa	58

+ at Milwaukee
++ at Rock Island

40	(3-5-1)	96

1900

Coach: F. L. Smith
Captain: A. R. Hall

*S 29-26	Rose Poly	0
*O 3-63	DePauw	0
*O 6-21	III. Wesleyan	0
*O 10- 6	Physicians-Surgeons	0
*O 13-16	Knox	0
*O 16-35	Lombard	0
O 20- 0	Northwestern	0
+O 27- 0	Michigan	12
*N 3-17	Purdue	5
N 10- 0	Minnesota	23
++N 17- 0	Indiana	0
N 24- 0	Wisconsin	27

+ at Chicago
++ at Indianapolis

184	(7-3-2)	67

1901

Coach: E. G. Holt
Captain: J. M. Lindgren

*S 28- 3	Englewood H.S.	0
*O 5-52	Marion Sims	0
*O 11-23	Physicians Surgeons	0
*O 12-21	Washington (St. Louis)	0
O 19-24	Chicago	0
*O 26-11	Northwestern	17
+N 2-18	Indiana	0
N 9-27	Iowa	0
N 16-28	Purdue	6
*N 28- 0	Minnesota	16

+ at Indianapolis

207	(8-2-0)	39

1902

Captain: Garland Stahl

*S 20-34	North Div.	6
*S 27-45	Englewood H.S.	0
*O 1-22	Osteopaths	0
*O 4-33	Monmouth	0
*O 8-24	Haskell	10
*O 11-44	Washington (St. Louis)	0
*O 18-29	Purdue	5
O 25- 0	Chicago	6
*N 1-47	Indiana	0
N 8- 5	Minnesota	17
N 15- 0	Ohio State	0
N 22-17	Northwestern	0
*N 27-80	Iowa	0

380	(10-2-1)	44

1903

Coach: George Woodruff
Captain: C. J. Rothgeb

*S 19-45	Englewood H.S.	5
*S 26-43	Lombard	0
*S 30-36	Osteopaths	0
*S 3-29	Knox	5
*O 7-40	Physicians-Surgeons	0
*O 10-64	Rush	0
*O 14-54	Chicago Dentistry	0
O 17-24	Purdue	0
O 24- 6	Chicago	18
*O 31-11	Northwestern	12
N 6- 0	Indiana	17
*N 14- 0	Minnesota	32
N 21- 0	Iowa	12
N 26- 0	Nebraska	16

352	(8-6-0)	1 17

1904

Coach: Graduate coaching system used until 1912
Captain: C. A. Fairweather

*S 24-10	Northwestern Coll.	0
*S 28-23	Wabash	2
*O 1-11	Knox	0
*O 5-26	Physicians-Surgeons	0
O 8-31	Washington (St. Louis)	0
*O 15-10	Indiana	0
O 22-24	Purdue	6

O 29- 6 Chicago   6
N 5-46 Ohio State   0
N 12-   Northwestern   12
*N 19-19 Iowa   0
N 24-10 Nebraska   16

| 232 | (9-2-1) | 42 |

1905

Captain: C. J. Moynihan

*S 30- 6	Knox	0
*O 4- 6	Wabash	0
*O 7-24	Northwestern Coll.	0
*O 14-12	St. Louis	6
*O 21- 0	Purdue	29
*O 28-30	Physicians Surgeons	0
*N 4- 0	Michigan	33
N 18- 0	Chicago	44
N 30- 0	Nebraska	24

| 78 | (5-4-0) | 136 |

1906

Captain: L. T. Carrithers

*O 13- 0	Wabash	0
O 27- 9	Michigan	28
*N 10- 6	Wisconsin	16
N 17- 0	Chicago	63
N 24- 5	Purdue	0

| 20 | (1-3-1) | 136 |

1907

Captain: Lion Gardiner

*O 19- 6	Chicago	42
O 26-15	Wisconsin	4
*N 2-21	Purdue	4
N 9-12	Iowa	25
N 22-10	Indiana	6

| 64 | (3-2-0) | 81 |

1908

Captain: F. C. Van Hook

*O 3-17	Monmouth	6
*O 10- 6	Marquette	6
O 17- 6	Chicago	11
*O 31-10	Indiana	0
*N 7-22	Iowa	0
N 14-15	Purdue	6
*N 21-64	Northwestern	8

| 140 | (5-1-1) | 37 |

1909

Captain: B. F. Baum

*O 2-23	Millikin	0
*O 9- 2	Kentucky	6
O 16- 8	Chicago	14
*O 30-24	Purdue	6
*N 6- 6	Indiana	5
N 13-35	Northwestern	0

N 20-17 Syracuse   8

| 140 | (5-2-0) | 39 |

1910

Captain: G. D. Butzer

*O 1-13	Millikin	0
*O 8-29	Drake	0
+*O 15- 3	Chicago	0
O 29-11	Purdue	0
N 5- 3	Indiana	0
N 12-27	Northwestern	0
*N 19- 3	Syracuse	0

+*First College Homecoming
First Western Conference title, undefeated, untied and unscored upon

| 224 | (7-0-0) | 22 |

1911

Captain: C. C. Roberts

*O 7-33	Millikin	0
*O 14- 9	St. Louis	0
O 21- 0	Chicago	24
*N 4-12	Purdue	3
N 11- 0	Indiana	0
*N 18-27	Northwestern	13
*N 25- 0	Minnesota	11

| 81 | (4-2-1) | 51 |

1912

Captain: W. H. Woolston

*O 5-87	Ill. Wesleyan	3
*O 12-13	Washington St. Louis	0
*O 19-13	Indiana	7
N 2- 0	Minnesota	13
N 9- 9	Purdue	9
*N 16- 0	Chicago	10
N 23- 0	Northwestern	6

| 122 | (3-3-1) | 48 |

1913

Coach: Robert Zuppke
Captain: E. M. Rowe

*O 4-21	Kentucky	0
*O 11-24	Missouri	7
*O 18-37	Northwestern	0
O 25-10	Indiana	0
N 1- 7	Chicago	28
*N 15- 0	Purdue	0
*N 22- 9	Minnesota	19

Zuppke's first team

| 108 | (4-2-1) | 54 |

1914

Captain: R. D. Chapman

| *O 3-37 | Christian Bros. | 0 |
| *O 10-51 | Indiana | 0 |

*O 17-37 Ohio State 0
O 24-33 Northwestern 0
O 31-21 Minnesota 6
*N 14-21 Chicago 7
N 21-24 Wisconsin 9

224 (7-0-0) 22

1915

Captain: J.W.Watson
*O 2-36 Haskell Indians 0
*O 9-75 Rolla Mines 7
O 16- 3 Ohio State 3
*O 23-36 Northwestern 6
*O 30- 6 Minnesota 6
*N 13-17 Wisconsin 3
N 20-10 Chicago 0

183 (5-0-2) 29

1916

Captain: F. B. Macomber
*O 7-30 Kansas 0
*O 14- 3 Colgate 15
*O 21- 6 Ohio State 7
O 28-14 Purdue 7
N 4-14 Minnesota 9
*N 18- 7 Chicago 20
N 25- 0 Wisconsin 0

74 (3-3-1) 56

1917

Captain: R. R. Kraft
*O 6-22 Kansas 0
*O 13-44 Oklahoma 0
*O 20- 7 Wisconsin 0
*O 27-27 Purdue 0
N 3- 0 Chicago 0
N 17- 0 Ohio State 13
*N 24- 6 Minnesota 27
N 29-28 Camp Funston, Kansas 0

134 (5-2-1) 40

1918

Captains: E. C. Sternaman
B. A. Ingwersen
O 4- 3 Chanute Field 0
*O 12- 0 Great Lakes 7
*O 26- 0 Municipal Pier 7
N 2-19 Iowa 0
N 9-22 Wisconsin 0
*N 16-13 Ohio State 0
N 23-29 Chicago 0

86 (5-2-0) 14

1919

Captain: W. K. Kopp
O 11-14 Purdue 7
*O 18- 9 Iowa 7
*O 25-10 Wisconsin 14
*N 1-10 Chicago 0
N 8-10 Minnesota 6
*N 15-29 Michigan 7

N 22- 9 Ohio State 7

91 (6-1-0) 48

1920

Captain: J. C. Depler
*O 9-41 Drake 0
*O 16-20 Iowa 3
O 23- 7 Michigan 6
*O 30-17 Minnesota 7
N 6- 3 Chicago 0
N 13- 9 Wisconsin 14
+*N 20- 0 Ohio State 7
*+First College Dad's Day

97 (5-2-0) 37

1921

Captain: L. W. Walquist
*O 8-52 South Dakota 0
O 15- 2 Iowa 14
*O 22- 0 Wisconsin 20
*O 29- 0 Michigan 3
*N 5-21 DePauw 0
*N 12- 6 Chicago 14
N 19- 7 Ohio State 0

88 (3-4-0) 51

1922

Captain: D. D. Wilson
*O 14- 7 Butler 10
*O 21- 7 Iowa 8
O 28- 0 Michigan 24
*N 4- 6 Northwestern 3
N 11- 3 Wisconsin 0
N 18- 0 Chicago 9
*N 25- 3 Ohio State 6

26 (2-5-0) 60

1923

Captain: J. W. McMillen
*O 6-24 Nebraska 7
*O 13-21 Butler 7
O 20- 9 Iowa 6
+O 27-29 Northwestern 0
++*N 3- 7 Chicago 0
*N 10-10 Wisconsin 0
*N 17-27 Miss. A & M 0
N 24- 9 Ohio State 0

+ at Chicago
++*First game played in Memorial Stadium

136 (8-0-0) 20

1924

Captain: F. E. Rokusek
O 4- 7 Nebraska 6
*O 11-40 Butler 10
+*O 18-39 Michigan 14
*O 25-45 DePauw 0
*N 1-36 Iowa 0

N 8-21 Chicago 21
N 15-7 Minnesota 20
*N 22- 7 Ohio State 0
+* Memorial Stadium dedicated

202 (6-1-1) 71

1925
Captain: H. E. Grange
*O 3- 0 Nebraska 14
*O 10-16 Butler 13
O 17-10 Iowa 12
*O 24- 0 Michigan 3
O 31-24 Pennsylvania 2
*N 7-13 Chicago 6
*N 14-21 Wabash 0
N 21-14 Ohio State 9

98 (5-3-0) 59

1926
Captain: C. E. Kassel
*O 2-27 Coe 0
*O 9-38 Butler 7
*O 16-13 Iowa 6
O 23- 0 Michigan 13
*O 30- 3 Pennsylvania 0
N 6- 7 Chicago 0
*N 13-27 Wabash 13
*N 20- 6 Ohio State 7

121 (6-2-0) 46

1927
Captain: Robert Reitsch
*O 1-19 Bradley 0
*O 8-58 Butler 0
*O 15-12 Iowa State 12
O 22- 7 Northwestern 6
*O 29-14 Michigan 0
N 5-14 Iowa 0
*N 12-15 Chicago 6
N 19-13 Ohio State 0

152 (7-0-1) 24

1928
Captain: A. J. Nowack
*O 6-33 Bradley 6
*O 13-31 Coe 0
*O 20-13 Indiana 7
*O 27- 6 Northwestern 0
N 3- 0 Michigan 3
N 10-14 Butler 0
N 17-40 Chicago 0
*N 24- 8 Ohio State 0

145 (7-1-0) 16

1929
Captain: R. J. Crane
*O 5-25 Kansas 0
*O 12-45 Bradley 0
O 19- 7 Iowa 7
*O 26-14 Michigan 0
N 2- 0 Northwestern 7
*N 9-17 Army 7
*N 16-20 Chicago 6
N 23-27 Ohio State 0

155 (6-1-1) 27

1930
Captain: O. E. Robinson
*O 4- 7 Iowa State 0
*O 11-27 Butler 0
*O 18- 0 Northwestern 32
O 25- 7 Michigan 15
*N 1- 0 Purdue 25
+N 8- 0 Army 13
N 15-28 Chicago 0
*N 22- 9 Ohio State 12
+ at New York

78 (3-5-0) 97

1931
Captain: Gil Berry
*O 3-20 St. Louis 6
O 10- 0 Purdue 7
*O 17-20 Bradley 0
*O 24- 0 Michigan 35
O 31- 6 Northwestern 32
*N 7- 6 Wisconsin 7
*N 14- 6 Chicago 13
N 21- 0 Ohio State 40

58 (2-6-0) 140

1932
Captain: Gil Berry
*O 1-20 Miami of Ohio 7
*O 1-13 Coe 0
*O 8-20 Bradley 0
*O 15- 0 Northwestern 26
O 22- 0 Michigan 32
O 29-13 Chicago 7
O 5-12 Wisconsin 20
*N 12-18 Indiana 6
*N 19- 0 Ohio State 3

96 (5-4-0) 101

1933
Captain: H. Walser
*S 30-13 Drake 6
O 7-21 Washington
(St. Louis) 6
*O 14-21 Wisconsin 0
+O 21- 0 Army 6
*N 4- 6 Michigan 7
N 11- 3 Northwestern 0
*N 18- 7 Chicago 0
N 25-6 Ohio State 7
+ at Cleveland

77 (5-3-0) 32

1934
Captains: C. Bennis
J. Beynon
*S 29-40 Bradley 7
O 6-12 Washington
(St. Louis) 7
O 13-14 Ohio State 13
O 27- 7 Michigan 6
*N 3- 7 Army 0
N 10-14 Northwestern 3
N 17- 3 Wisconsin 7
N 24- 6 Chicago 0

103 (7-1-0) 43

1935

Captain: Charles S. Galbreath Jr.

*S	28- 0	Ohio Univ.	6
*O	5-28	Washington (St. Louis)	6
O	12-19	Southern Cal.	0
*O	26- 0	Iowa	19
N	2- 3	Northwestern	10
*N	9- 3	Michigan	0
N	16- 0	Ohio State	6
*N	23- 6	Chicago	7

59	(3-5-0)	54

1936

Captain: Elvin C. Sayre

*S	26- 9	DePaul	6
*O	3-13	Washington (St. Louis)	7
*O	10- 6	Southern Cal.	24
O	17- 0	Iowa	0
*O	24- 2	Northwestern	13
O	31- 9	Michigan	6
*N	14- 0	Ohio State	13
N	21-18	Chicago	7

57	(4-3-1)	76

1937

Captain: Lowell Spurgeon

*S	25-20	Ohio Univ.	6
*O	2- 0	DePaul	0
*O	9- 6	Notre Dame	6
O	16- 6	Indiana	13
*O	30- 6	Michigan	7
N	6- 6	Northwestern	0
N	13- 0	Ohio State	19
N	20-21	Chicago	0

65	(3-3-2)	51

1938

Captain: James W. McDonald

*S	24- 0	Ohio Univ.	6
*O	1-44	DePaul	7
*O	8-12	Indiana	2
O	15- 6	Notre Dame	14
*O	22- 0	Northwestern	13
O	29-0	Michigan	14
*N	12-14	Ohio State	32
N	19-34	Chicago	0

110	(3-5-0)	88

1939

Captain: Melvin C. Brener

*S	30- 0	Bradley	0
O	14- 0	Southern Cal.	26
*O	21- 6	Indiana	7
O	28- 0	Northwestern	13
*N	4-16	Michigan	7
*N	11- 7	Wisconsin	0
N	18- 0	Ohio State	21
N	25-46	Chicago	0

75	(3-4-1)	74

1940

Captain: Thomas J. Riggs

*O	5-31	Bradley	0
*O	12- 7	Southern Cal	13
O	19- 0	Michigan	28
*O	26- 0	Notre Dame	26
N	2- 6	Wosconsin	13
N	9-14	Northwestern	32
*N	16- 6	Ohio State	14
N	25- 7	Iowa	18

71	(1-7-0)	144

1941

Captain: Selected Each Game

*O	4-45	Miami of Ohio	0
O	11- 6	Minnesota	34
*O	18-40	Drake	0
O	25-14	Notre Dame	49
*N	1- 0	Michigan	20
*N	8- 0	Iowa	21
N	15- 7	Ohio State	12
N	22- 0	Northwestern	27

112	(2-6-0)	163

1942

Coach: Ray Eliot
Captain: James Smith

*S	26-46	South Dakota	0
*O	3-67	Butler	0
*O	10-20	Minnesota	13
O	17-12	Iowa	7
*O	24-14	Notre Dame	21
O	31-14	Michigan	28
N	7-14	Northwestern	7
+N	14-20	Ohio State	44
*N	21- 0	Great Lakes	6
++N	28-20	Camp Grant	0

+ at Cleveland
++ at Rockford

Ray Eliot's first team

227	(6-4-0)	126

1943

Captain: Selected Each Game

*S	11- 0	Camp Grant	23
*S	18-18	Iowa Seahawks	32
O	2-21	Purdue	40
O	9-25	Wisconsin	7
*O	16-33	Pittsburgh	25
O	23- 0	Notre Dame	47
*O	30- 6	Michigan	42
N	6-19	Iowa	10
N	13-26	Ohio State	29
N	20- 6	Northwestern	53

154	(3-7-0)	308

1944

Captain: Selected Each Game

*S	16-79	Ill. Normal	0
*S	23-26	Indiana	18
S	30-26	Great Lakes	26

```
*O  7-19 Purdue              35
*O 14-40 Iowa                 6
 O 21-39 Pittsburgh           5
*O 28- 7 Notre Dame          13
 N 11- 0 Michigan            14
+N 18-12 Ohio State          26
 N 25-25 Northwestern         6
+ at Cleveland

   273      (5-4-1)         149
```

1945

Captain: Ralph Serpico
```
*S 22-23 Pittsburgh           6
 S 29- 0 Notre Dame           7
*O  6- 0 Indiana              6
 O 20- 7 Wisconsin            7
*O 27- 0 Michigan            19
*N  3- 6 Great Lakes         12
*N 10-48 Iowa                 7
 N 17- 2 Ohio State          27
 N 24- 7 Northwestern        13

    93      (2-6-1)         104
```

1946

Captain: Mac Wenskunas
```
 S 21-33 Pittsburgh           7
*S 28- 6 Notre Dame          26
*O  5-43 Purdue               7
 O 12- 7 Indiana             14
*O 19-27 Wisconsin           21
 O 26-13 Michigan            21
 N  2- 7 Iowa                 0
*N 16-16 Ohio State           7
 N 23-20 Northwestern         0
+J  1-45 UCLA                14
+ 1947 Rose Bowl

   217      (8-2-0)         105
```

1947

Captain: Art Dufelmeier
```
*S 27-14 Pittsburgh           0
 O  4-35 Iowa                12
+O 11- 0 Army                 0
*O 18-40 Minnesota           13
 O 25- 7 Purdue              14
*N  1- 7 Michigan            14
*N  8-60 W. Michigan         14
 N 15-28 Ohio State           7
*N 22-13 Northwestern        28
+ at New York City's
  Yankee Stadium

   204      (5-3-1)         102
```

1948

Captain: Herbert Siegert
```
*S 25-40 Kansas State         0
 O  2-16 Wisconsin           20
*O  9-21 Army                26
 O 16- 0 Minnesota            6
*O 23-10 Purdue               6
 O 30-20 Michigan            28
*N  6-14 Iowa                 0
```

```
*N 13- 7 Ohio State          34
 N 20- 7 Northwestern        20

   135      (3-6-0)         140
```

1949

Captain: Lyle Button
```
*S 24-20 Iowa State          20
*O  1-13 Wisconsin           13
 O  8-20 Iowa                14
*O 15-20 Missouri            27
 O 22-19 Purdue               0
*O 29- 0 Michigan            13
*N  5-33 Indiana             14
 N 12-17 Ohio State          30
*N 19- 7 Northwestern         9

   149      (3-4-2)         140
```

1950

Captain William Vohaska
```
*S 30-28 Ohio Univ            2
*O  7- 6 Wisconsin            7
 O 13-14 UCLA                 6
*O 21-20 Washington          13
*O 28-20 Indiana              0
 N  4- 7 Michigan             0
 N 11-21 Iowa                 7
*N 18-14 Ohio State           7
 N 25- 7 Northwestern        14

   137      (7-2-0)          56
```

1951

Captain: Charles Studley
```
*S 29-27 UCLA                13
*O  6-14 Wisconsin           10
 O 13-41 Syracuse            20
 O 20-27 Washington          20
 O 27-21 Indiana              0
*N  3- 7 Michigan             0
*N 10-40 Iowa                13
 N 17- 0 Ohio State           0
 N 24- 3 Northwestern         0
+J  1-40 Stanford             7
+ at 1952 Rose Bowl

   220      (9-0-1)          83
```

1952

Captain: Alfred Brosky
```
*S 27-33 Iowa State           7
 O  4- 6 Wisconsin           20
*O 11-48 Washington          14
 O 18- 7 Minnesota           13
*O 25-12 Purdue              40
 N  1-22 Michigan            13
 N  8-33 Iowa                13
*N 15- 7 Ohio State          27
*N 22-26 Northwestern        28

   194      (4-5-0)         175
```

1953

Captain: Robert Lenzini
```
*S 26-21 Nebraska            21
*O  3-33 Stanford            21
 O 10-41 Ohio State          20
*O 17-27 Minnesota            7
*O 24-20 Syracuse            13
```

*O 31-21 Purdue 0
*N 7-19 Michigan 3
N 14- 7 Wisconsin 34
N 21-39 Northwestern 14

228 (7-1-1) 133

1954
Captain: Jan Smid
*S 25-12 Penn State 14
O 2- 2 Stanford 12
*O 9- 7 Ohio State 40
O 16-6 Minnesota 19
*O 23-34 Syracuse 6
O 30-14 Purdue 28
N 6- 7 Michigan 14
*N 13-14 Wisconsin 27
*N 20- 7 Northwestern 20

103 (1-8-0) 180

1955
Captain: Robert Rousch
S 24-20 California 13
*O 1-40 Iowa State 0
O 8-12 Ohio State 27
*O 15-21 Minnesota 13
O 22- 7 Michigan State 21
*O 29- 0 Purdue 13
*N 5-25 Michigan 6
N 12-17 Wisconsin 14
N 19- 7 Northwestern 7

149 (5-3-1) 114

1956
Captain: James Minor
*S 29-32 California 20
O 6-13 Washington 28
*O 13- 6 Ohio State 26
O 20-13 Minnesota 16
*O 27-20 Michigan State 13
N 3- 7 Purdue 7
N 10-7 Michigan 17
*N 17-13 Wisconsin 13
N 24-13 Northwestern 14

124 (2-5-2) 154

1957
Captain: Dale Smith
S 27- 6 UCLA 16
*O 5-40 Colgate 0
O 12- 7 Ohio State 21
*O 19-34 Minnesota 13
O 26-14 Michigan State 19
*N 2- 6 Purdue 21
*N 9-20 Michigan 19
N 16-13 Wisconsin 24
*N 23-27 Northwestern 0

167 (4-5-0) 133

1958
Captain: Jack Delveaux
*S 27-14 UCLA 18
O 4-13 Duke 15
*O 11-13 Ohio State 19
O 18-20 Minnesota 8
*O 25-16 Michigan State 0
N 1- 8 Purdue 31
N 8-21 Michigan 8

*N 15-12 Wisconsin 31
*N 22-27 Northwestern 20

144 (4-5-0) 150

1959
Captain: William Burrell
S 26- 0 Indiana 20
*O 3-20 Army 14
O 10- 9 Ohio State 0
*O 17-14 Minnesota 6
+O 24- 9 Penn State 20
*O 31- 7 Purdue 7
*N 7-15 Michigan 20
N 14- 9 Wisconsin 6
*N 21-28 Northwestern 0
+ at Cleveland

111 (5-3-1) 93

1960
Coach: Pete Elliott
Captain: William Brown
*S 24-17 Indiana 6
*O 1-33 West Virginia 0
*O 8- 7 Ohio State 34
O 15-10 Minnesota 21
*O 22-10 Penn State 8
O 29-14 Purdue 12
N 5- 7 Michigan 8
*N 12-35 Wisconsin 14
N 19- 7 Northwestern 14
Pete Elliott's first team

140 (5-4-0) 117

1961
Captain: Gary Brown
*S 30- 7 Washington 20
*O 7- 7 Northwestern 28
O 14- 0 Ohio State 44
*O 21- 0 Minnesota 33
O 28-10 Southern Cal. 14
*N 4- 9 Purdue 23
*N 11- 6 Michigan 38
N 18- 7 Wisconsin 55
N 25- 7 Michigan State 34

53 (0-9-0) 289

1962
Captains: Bob Scharbert
Ken Zimmerman
S 29- 7 Washington 28
O 6- 0 Northwestern 45
*O 13-15 Ohio State 51
O 20- 0 Minnesota 17
*O 27-16 Southern Cal. 28
N 2-14 Purdue 10
N 10- 0 Michigan 14
*N 17 6 Wisconsin 35
*N 24- 7 Michigan State 6

75 (2-7-0) 234

1963

Captains: Mike Taliaferro
Dick Deller

*S 28-10	California	0
*O 5-10	Northwestern	9
O 12-20	Ohio State	20
*O 19-16	Minnesota	6
O 25-18	UCLA	12
*N 2-41	Purdue	21
*N 9- 8	Michigan	14
N 16-17	Wisconsin	7
N 28-13	Michigan State	0
+J 1-17	Washington	7
+ at 1964 Rose Bowl		

170   (8-1-1)   82

1964

Captains: Dick Butkus
George Donnelly

S 26-20	California	14
O 3-17	Northwestern	6
+O 10- 0	Ohio State	26
O 17-14	Minnesota	0
*O 24-26	UCLA	7
O 31-14	Purdue	26
N 7- 6	Michigan	21
*N 14-29	Wisconsin	0
*N 21-16	Michigan State	0

142   (6-3-0)   100

1965

Captains: Jim Grabowski
Don Hansen

*S 18-10	Oregon State	12
*S 25-41	Southern Methodist	0
O 2-12	Michigan State	22
O 9-14	Ohio State	28
*O 16-34	Indiana	13
*O 23-28	Duke	14
*O 30-21	Purdue	0
*N 6- 3	Michigan	23
N 13-51	Wisconsin	0
N 20-20	Northwestern	6

234   (6-4-0)   118

1966

Captains: Kai Anderson
Bo Batchelder

S 17- 7	Southern Methodist	26
*S 24-14	Missouri	21
*O 1-10	Michigan State	26
*O 8-10	Ohio State	9
O 15-24	Indiana	10
*O 22- 3	Stanford	6
O 29-21	Purdue	25
N 5-28	Michigan	21
*N 12-49	Wisconsin	14
N 19- 7	Northwestern	35

173   (4-6-0)   193

1967

Coach: Jim Valek
Captains: Ken Kimec
Ron Bess

S 23- 0	Florida	14
*S 30-34	Pittsburgh	6
*O 7- 7	Indiana	20
*O 14- 7	Minnesota	10
*O 21- 7	Notre Dame	47
O 28-17	Ohio State	13
*N 4- 9	Purdue	42
*N 11-14	Michigan	21
N 18-27	Northwestern	21
N 25-21	Iowa	19
Jim Valek's first Team		

143   (4-6-0)   213

1968

Captains: Carson Brooks
Tony Pleviak

*S 21- 7	Kansas	47
*S 28-10	Missouri	44
O 5-14	Indiana	28
O 12-10	Minnesota	17
O 19- 8	Notre Dame	51
*O 26-24	Ohio State	31
N 2-17	Purdue	35
N 9- 0	Michigan	36
*N 16-14	Northwestern	0
*N 23-13	Iowa	37

117   (1-9-0)   326

1969

Captains: Bruce Erb
Doug Redmann

*S 20-18	Washington State	19
S 27- 6	Missouri	37
*O 4-20	Iowa State	47
*O 11- 6	Northwestern	10
O 18-20	Indiana	41
O 25- 0	Ohio State	41
*N 1-22	Purdue	49
*N 8- 0	Michigan	57
N 15-14	Wisconsin	55
*N 22- 0	Iowa	40

106   (0-10-0)   396

1970

Captains: Doug Dieken
Kirk McMillin

*S 19-20	Oregon	16
*S 26- 9	Tulane	23
*O 3-27	Syracuse	0
O 10- 0	Northwestern	48
*O 17-24	Indiana	30
*O 24-29	Ohio State	48
O 31-23	Purdue	21
N 7- 0	Michigan	42
*N 14-17	Wisconsin	29
N 21-16	Iowa	22

165   (3-7-0)   279

1971

Coach: Bob Blackman
Captains: Glenn Collier
Larry McCarren

S 11- 0	Michigan State	10
*S 18- 0	North Carolina	27
S 25- 0	Southern Cal.	28
*O 2-14	Washington	52
*O 9-10	Ohio State	24
O 16- 6	Michigan	35
*O 23-21	Purdue	7
*O 30-24	Northwestern	7
N 6-22	Indiana	21
N 13-35	Wisconsin	27
*N 20-31	Iowa	0

Bob Blackman's first team

163	(5-6-0)	228

1972

Captains: Larry McCarren
John Wiza

*S 16- 0	Michigan State	24
*S 24-20	Southern Cal.	55
S 30-11	Washington	52
*O 7-17	Penn State	35
O 14- 7	Ohio State	26
*O 21- 7	Michigan	31
O 28-14	Purdue	20
N 4-43	Northwestern	13
*N 11-37	Indiana	20
*N 18-27	Wisconsin	7
N 25-14	Iowa	15

197	(3-8-0)	272

1973

Captains: Ken Braid
John Gann

S 15-28	Indiana	14
S 22-27	California	7
*S 29-10	W. Virginia	17
*O 6- 0	Stanford	24
*O 13-15	Purdue	13
O 20- 6	Michigan State	3
*O 27-50	Iowa	0
*N 3- 0	Ohio State	30
N 10- 6	Michigan	21
*N 17-16	Minnesota	19
N 24- 6	Northwestern	9

164	(5-6-0)	157

1974

Captains: Ty McMillin
Revie Sorey

*S 14-16	Indiana	0
S 21-41	Stanford	7
*S 28-21	Washington State	19
*O 5-14	California	31
O 12-27	Purdue	23
+*O 19-21	Michigan State	21
O 26-12	Iowa	14
N 2- 7	Ohio State	49
*N 9- 6	Michigan	14
N 16-17	Minnesota	14
N 23-28	Northwestern	14

+* Memorial Stadium's
Golden Anniversary Game

210	(6-4-1)	206

1975

Captains: Dean March
Stu Levenick

S 13-27	Iowa	12
*S 20-20	Missouri	30
S 27-13	Texas A & M	43
*O 4-27	Washington State	21
*O 11-42	Minnesota	23
*O 18-24	Purdue	26
O 25-21	Michigan State	19
N 1-9	Wisconsin	18
*N 8-3	Ohio State	40
*N 15-15	Michigan	21
N 22-28	Northwestern	7

229	(5-6-0)	260

313

ALL-TIME ILLINOIS MARKS
CONSECUTIVE GAME STREAKS

Games Unbeaten . . . . 15 . . . . . (13-0-2, 1914-16)
. . . . 14 . . . . . (13-0-1, 1923-24)
. . . . 13 . . . . . (13-0-0, 1909-11)
Home Games Unbeaten . . . . 17 . . . . . (16-0-1, 1927-30)
. . . . 16 . . . . . (16-0-0, 1902-03)
. . . . 12 . . . . (11-0-1, 1899-1901)
Conference Games Unbeaten . 11 . . . . . . (9-0-2, 1914-15)
. . . . .9 . . . . . . (9-0-0, 1909-10)
. . . . .8 . . . . . . (8-0-0, 1919-20)
. . . . .8 . . . . . . (7-0-1, 1923-24)
Home Conference Games
Unbeaten . . . . 10 . . . . . (10-0-0, 1907-11)
. . . . .7 . . . . . . (7-0-0. 1927-29)
. . . . .7 . . . . . . (6-0-1, 1923-24)
Games Won . . . . 13 . . . . (1923-24)
. . . . 13 . . . . (1909-11)
. . . . .9 . . . . (1927-28)
. . . . .9 . . . . (1914-15)
Home Games Won . . . . 16 . . . . (1902-03)
. . . . 14 . . . . (1927-30)
. . . . 11 . . . . (1923-24)
. . . . 11 . . . . (1900-01)
Conference Games Won . . . . .9 . . . . (1909-10)
. . . . .8 . . . . (1919-20)
Home Conference Games
Won . . . . 10 . . . . (1907-11)
. . . . .7 . . . . (1927-29)
. . . . .6 . . . . (1950-52)

Highest Scoring Illinois Victories

87-3	over Illinois Wesleyan	. . . .	1912
80-0	over Iowa	. . . .	1902
79-0	over Illinois College	. . . .	1895
79-0	over Illinois Normal	. . . .	1944

Largest Illinois Defeats

63-0	to Chicago	. . . .	1906
62-0	to Purdue	. . . . . ·.	1890
57-0	to Michigan	. . . .	1969

Lowest Scoring Illinois Victories
3-0

over 10 teams: Englewood H.S. (1901); Chicago (1910); Indiana (1910); Chanute Field (1918); Chicago (1920); Wisconsin (1922); Pennsylvania (1926); Northwestern (1933); Michigan (1935).

Lowest Scoring Illinois Defeats
3-0

to four teams: Michigan (1921, 1925, 1928); and Ohio State (1932).

ALL-TIME FOOTBALL LETTER WINNERS

"A"

Abraham, Geo. E., 1932
Acks, Ron, 1963, 64, 65
Adams, Paul, 1956, 57
Adsit, Bertram W., 1898, 99, 00
Agase, Alex, 1941, 42, 46
Agase, Louis, 1944, 45, 46, 47
Agnew, Lester P., 1922
Allen, Larry, 1970, 71, 72
Allen, Lawrence T., 1903
Allen, Robert, 1956, 57, 58
Allen, Steve, 1969
Allen, William M., 1965
Allie, Glen, 1964
Anders, Alphonse, 1939
Anderson, Harold B., 1909
Anderson, Kai, 1965, 66
Anderson, Neal, 1961, 62
Anderson, Paul T., 1921
Anderson, Wm. W., 1915, 16
Antilla, Arvo A., 1933, 34, 35
Applegate, Frank G., 1903
Applegran, Clarence O., 1915, 19
Archer, Arthur E., 1948
Armstrong, James W., 1891, 92
Armstrong, Lennox, F., 1913, 14
Ash, David, 1957, 58, 59
Ashley, Richard Jr., 1892
Astroth, Lavere L., 1939, 40, 41
Atherton, Geo. H., 1891, 92, 93
Avery, Galen, 1971

"B"

Bachouros, Peter F., 1950, 51, 52
Badal, Herbert, 1954
Baietto, Robert E., 1954, 55
Bailey, Gordon R., 1931
Bareither, Charles, 1967, 68, 69
Bargo, Ken, 1967, 68, 69
Barker, John K., 1891
Barter, Harold H., 1903
Baskin, Neil, 1969
Bassett, Denman J., 1947
Bassey, Ralph C., 1943
Batchelder, Robt. (Bo), 1964, 65, 66
Bateman, James M., 1905
Bates, Melvin B., 1953, 54, 55
Bauer, John A., 1930
Bauer, John R., 1951, 52, 53
Bodman, A. E., 1932
Boughman, James A., 1951
Baum, Benjamin F., 1907, 08, 09
Baum, Harry W., 1893, 94, 95
Baumgart, Tom, 1970, 71
Bauman, Frank, 1946
Beadle, Thomas B., 1895, 97
Beaman, Bruce, 1972, 73, 74, 75
Beaver, Daniel, 1973, 74, 75
Beckmann, Bruce, 1958, 59
Bedalow, John, 1970, 71, 72
Beebe, Charles D., 1894, 95, 96
Beers, Harley, 1902, 03
Bell, Frank E., 1936, 37
Bellephant, Joe F., 1957
Belting, Charles H., 1910, 11
Belting, Paul E., 1911
Bennett, Caslon K., 1930
Bennett, Ralph E., 1937, 38, 39
Bennett, Tab, 1970, 71, 72

Bennis, Charles W., 1932, 33, 34
Bennis, William F., 1937
Bergeson, C. H., 1928
Berner, John R., 1935, 36, 37
Bernhardt, Geo. W., 1937, 39, 40
Bernstein, Louis S., 1909, 10
Berry, Gilbert I., 1930, 31, 32
Berschet, Marvin, 1951
Bess, Bob, 1968, 69
Bess, Ronald W., 1965, 66, 67
Beynon, Jack T., 1932, 33, 34
Bieszczad, Bob, 1968, 69
Bingaman, Lester A., 1944, 45, 46, 47
Bishop, Robert E., 1952, 53
Blackaby, Ethan, 1959, 60
Bloom, Robert J., 1932, 33
Bodman, Alfred E., 1930, 31
Bodman, Stanley L., 1930
Boerio, Charles, 1950, 51
Bonner, Lory T., 1957, 58
Booze, MacDonald C., 1912
Borman, Herbert R., 1951, 52, 53
Bowen, Herbert L., 1890
Bradley, John J., 1905, 06
Bradley, Kendall R., 1935
Bradley, Theron A., 1943
Braid, Ken, 1971, 72, 73
Branch, James M., 1894, 95, 96
Bray, Edward C., 1943, 44, 45
Bremer, Lawrence H., 1908
Breneman, Amos L., 1915
Brennan, Rich, 1969, 70
Brewer, Melvin C., 1937, 38, 39
Briggs, Claude P., 1900
Briley, Norman P., 1899
Britton, Earl T., 1923, 24, 25
Broerman, John R., 1952
Brokemond, Geo. R., 1958
Bronson, Geo. D., 1902
Brooks, Carson C., 1966, 67, 68
Brooks, Richard A., 1906
Brosky, Alfred E., 1950, 51, 52
Brown, Charles A., 1923, 24, 25
Brown, Charles E., 1948, 49, 50
Brown, Gary W., 1959, 60
Brown, Horace T., 1909
Brown, James E., 1958, 59, 60
Brown, Jospeh A., 1937
Brown, William D., 1958, 59, 60
Brundage, Martin D., 1901
Bucheit, George C., 1918
Bucklin, Robert, 1969, 70, 71
Bujan, George P., 1943, 44, 45
Bundy, Herman W., 1901, 02
Burdick, Lloyd S., 1927, 28, 29
Burkland, Theo. L., 1896
Burns, Bob, 1968, 69, 70
Burrell, William G., 1957, 58, 59
Burris, Merlyn G., 1938
Burroughs, Wilbur G., 1904, 05, 06
Buscemi, Joseph A., 1946, 47
Bush, Arthur W., 1891
Butkovich, Andrew, 1941
Butkovich, Anthony J., 1942
Butkovich, William, 1943, 44, 45
Butkus, Richard M., 1962, 63, 64
Butler, Charles, 1954, 56
Button, Lyle A., 1947, 48, 49
Butzer, Glenn D., 1908, 09, 10

"C"

Cahill, Leo H., 1948, 49, 50
Callaghan, Richard T., 1962, 63, 64
Campbell, Robert A., 1939
Cantwell, Francis R., 1934, 35
Capel, Bruce, 1962, 63, 64
Capen, B. C., 1902
Carbonari, Gerald M., 1965, 66
Carney, Charles R., 1918, 19, 20, 21
Caroline, J. C., 1953, 54
Carr, Jr., H. Eugene, 1958
Carrithers, Ira T., 1904
Carson, Herbert M., 1934
Carson, Paul H., 1931
Carson, Howard W., 1934, 37
Carter, Donald H., 1911
Cast, Dick L., 1961
Castelo, Robert E., 1936, 37, 38
Catlin, James M., 1952
Cerney, Bill, 1974, 75
Chalcraft, Kenneth G., 1961
Chamblin, William J., 1953, 54
Chapman, Ralph D., 1912, 13, 14
Charle, William W., 1936
Charpier, Leonard L., 1916, 17
Chattin, Ernest P., 1930
Cheeley, Kenneth D., 1940, 41
Cherney, Eugene K., 1957, 58
Cherry, Robert S., 1940, 41
Chester, Guy S., 1894
Christensen, Paul G., 1916
Chronis, Tony, 1973
Chrystal, Jeff, 1973, 74, 75
Cies, Jerry B., 1944, 45
Ciszek, Ray A. C., 1943, 44, 45, 46
Clark, George, 1914, 15
Clark, Robt. M., 1922
Clark, Ronald, 1949, 50
Clarke, Edwin B., 1890
Clarke, Frederick W., 1890
Clayton, Clark M., 1898, 99
Clements, John H., 1929
Clements, Tony, 1968, 69
Clinton, Edgar M., 1896
Coffeen, Harry C., 1896, 97
Colby, Greg, 1971, 72, 73
Cole, E. Joseph, 1949, 50, 51
Cole, Jewett, 1935, 36
Cole, Jerry, 1969, 70
Coleman, DeJustice, 1957, 58, 59
Coleman, Norris, 1969
Coleman, Roger, 1974
Collier, Glenn, 1969, 70, 71
Collins, John J., 1962
Conover, Robt. J., 1930
Cook, David F., 1931, 33
Cook, James F., 1898, 00, 01, 02
Cook, James W., 1891, 92
Cooledge, Marshall M., 1925
Cooper, Norm, 1970
Cooper, Jr., Paul H., 1893, 94, 95
Correll, Walter K., 1941, 42
Counts, John E., 1959
Coutchie, Stephen A., 1922, 23
Cramer, Willard M., 1937, 38

315

Crane, Russell J., 1927, 28, 29
Crangle, Walter F., 1919, 20, 21
Craven, Forest I., 1932
Cravens, Robert D., 1961
Crawford, Walter C., 1923
Crum, Tom, 1968
Cummings, Barton A., 1932, 33, 34
Cunz, Robert W., 1945, 46, 47
Curry, Jack C., 1943
Custardo, Fred, 1963, 64, 65

"D"

D'Ambrosio, Arthur L., 1925, 26, 27
Dahl, Andres W., 1934
Dallenbach, M. Karl, 1909
Damos, Donn, 1970
Dadant, M. G., 1907
Danosky, Anthony J., 1958
Darlington, Dan, 1969, 70, 71
Daugherity, Russell S., 1925, 26
Davis, Chester W., 1910, 11
Davis, John, 1966, 67
Dawson, George, 1922
DeDecker, Darrel, 1959, 60
Deimling, Keston J., 1927, 28, 29
Delaney, Robert F., 1956, 57
Deller, Dick, 1961, 62, 63
Delveaux, Jack, 1956, 57, 58
DeMoss, Clarence W., 1952, 53
Depler, John C., 1918, 19, 20
Derby, Sylvester R., 1913, 14
DesEnfants, Robert E., 1954, 55
Dickerson, Jr., Charles F., 1961
Diedrich, Brian, 1974, 75
Dieken, Doug, 1968, 69, 70
Diener, Walter G., 1902, 03, 04
DiFeliciantonio, John, 1974, 75
Dillinger, Harry, 1903, 04
Dillon, Chester C., 1910, 11, 12
Dillon, David, 1939, 40
Dimit, George, 1946
Dobrzeniecki, Mike, 1971
Dobson, Bruce, 1971, 72, 73
Doepel, Robert F., 1920
Dollahan, Bruce E., 1957, 58
Donnelly, George, 1962, 63, 64
Dombroski, Jack, 1975
Donoho, Louie W., 1946
Dorr, Dick, 1964
Doud, William O., 1901
Douglass, Paul W., 1949, 50
Doxey, Samuel, 1891
Drayer, Clarence T., 1921
Driscoll, Denny, 1970
Dubrish, Bob, 1973
Dufelmeier, Arthur J., 1942, 46, 47
Dufelmeier, Jamie, 1969, 70
Duke, Austin L., 1952
Dundy, Michael W., 1961, 63
Duniec, Brian J., 1962, 63, 64
Durant, Philip S., 1921
Dusenberry, Marshall V., 1951
Dykstra, Eugene R., 1934, 35, 36
Dysert, Terry, 1970

"E"

Easter, Robert A., 1961, 62, 63
Easterbrook, James C., 1940
Easterbrook, John W., 1958, 59, 60
Eddleman, T. Dwight (Dike), 1946, 47, 48
Ehni, Ralph E., 1938, 39, 40
Eickman, Gary, 1963, 64, 65
Eliot, Raymond E., 1930, 31
Ellis, Donald C., 1949
Elsner, Bernard W., 1950, 52
Elting, Donald N., 1938, 39
Ems, Clarence E., 1917, 20
Engel, Elmer H., 1940, 41, 42
Engels, Donald J., 1949, 50, 51
Enochs, Claude D., 1897
Erb, Bruce, 1967, 68, 69
Erickson, Richard J., 1965, 66, 67
Ernst, Donald W., 1951, 52, 53
Evans, John C., 1930, 31

"F"

Fairweather, Charles A., 1901, 02, 03, 04
Falkenstein, Elry G., 1952, 53
Falkenstein, Robert R., 1940
Fay, Richard B., 1936, 37
Fearn, Ronald R., 1961, 62, 63
Feeheley, Tom, 1974
Fields, Kenneth E., 1928
Fields Jr., Willis E., 1965, 66, 67
Fischer, John A., 1934
Fischer, L. E., 1895, 96, 97
Fisher, Fred D., 1925
Fitzgerald, Richard J., 1963
Fletcher, Ralph E., 1918, 19, 20
Finis, Jerry, 1974, 75
Fisher, William, 1975
Fletcher, Robert H., 1918, 19, 20
Florek, Ray, 1946
Follett, Dwight W., 1924
Forbes, Stuart F., 1897
Ford, Brian, 1974, 75
Forst, Lawrence H., 1943, 45
Foster, Dale W., 1952
Fouts, L. H., 1893
Fox, Charles M., 1949, 50
Fox, Wylie B., 1962, 63, 64
Francis, Frank D., 1899
Francis, Gary, 1954, 55, 56
Franks, Willard G., 1946, 47
Frederick, George R., 1935
French, A. Blair, 1926, 27
Friel, Marty, 1974, 75
Frink, Frederick F., 1931, 33
Froschauer, Frank E., 1932, 33, 34
Fullerton, Thomas B., 1913
Fultz, Duane E., 1959
Furber, William A., 1890
Furimsky, Paul, 1954

"G"

Gabbett, William Todd, 1961, 62
Galbreath, Charles S., 1933, 34, 35
Gallagher, Thomas B., 1946, 47, 48
Gallivan, Raymond P., 1924, 25, 26
Gano, Clifton W., 1935
Gann, John , 1971, 72, 73
Gardiner, Lion, 1906, 07, 08
Garner, Donald S., 1930
Gartrell, Willie, 1974. 75
Gates, Andrew W., 1890, 91
Gaut, Robert E., 1892, 93, 94
Gedman, Stacy, 1967
Genis, John F., 1941, 42, 46
Geraci, Joseph L., 1959
Gerometta, Arthur L., 1943
Gibbs, Robert, 1940, 42
Glauser, Glenn L., 1961
Glazer, Herbert, 1935
Glosecki, Andy R., 1936
Gnidovic, Donald J., 1950, 51
Goelitz, Walter A., 1917
Golaszewski, Paul P., 1961
Gongola, Robert B., 1952, 54
Good, Richard J., 1940, 41, 42
Gordon, Louis J., 1927, 28, 29
Gorenstein, Sam, 1931
Gottfried, Charles, 1946, 47, 48, 49
Gould, Maurice, 1941
Gould, Dennis C., 1961
Gow, Mike, 1972, 73, 74
Grable, Leonard M., 1925, 26, 27
Grabowski, James S., 1963, 64, 65
Graeff, Robert E., 1955
Gragg, Elbert R., 1932, 33
Graham, John, 1970, 71
Graham, Walter, 1975
Grange, Garland A., 1927
Grange, Harold E. (Red), 1923, 24, 25
Graves, Perry H., 1913, 14
Greathouse, Forrest E., 1925
Greco, Dale, 1964, 65
Green, Howard S., 1906, 07
Green, Robert K., 1932
Green, Stanley C., 1946
Green, Vivian J., 1922, 23
Green, William J., 1925
Greene, Earl B., 1921
Greene, Steve, 1972, 73, 74, 75
Greenwood, Donald G., 1943,
Gremer, John A., 1955, 56
Grierson, Ray G., 1941, 42, 46
Grieve, Robert S., 1935, 36
Griffin, Donald D., 1941, 42
Grothe, Don, 1953, 57, 58
Gryboski, Edward, 1933, 34
Guenther, Ron, 1965, 66
Gumm, Percy E., 1908, 09

"H"

Hadsall, H. Harry, 1895
Halas, George S., 1917
Hall, Albert L., 1911

316

Hall, Arthur R., 1898, 99, 00
Hall, Charles V., 1928, 30
Hall, Harry A., 1923, 24, 25
Hall, Joseph W., 1950, 52
Hall, Orville E., 1944
Hall, Richard L., 1923, 24
Haller, Thomas F., 1956, 57
Halstrom, Bernard C., 1915
Hannum, Phillip O., 1903
Hanschmann, Fred R., 1915, 18
Hansen, Don, 1963, 64, 65
Hanson, Martin E., 1900
Hanson, Rodney, 1955, 56, 57
Happenney, J. Clifford, 1922
Harford, Doug, 1965, 66
Harmon, Ivan G., 1903
Harms, Frederick E., 1965, 66,
  67
Harper, William, 1965
Hart, R. W., 1890, 91, 92
Haselwood, John M., 1903, 04
Hatfield, Joe, 1972, 73, 74
Hathaway, Ralph W., 1938, 39
Hayer, Joseph C., 1949
Hayes, Bob, 1972
Hazelett, John, 1943
Hedtke, William A., 1931
Heinrich, Mick, 1972, 73
Heiss, Jr., William C., 1944,
  45, 46
Helbling, James L., 1943
Hellstrom, Norton E., 1920
Hembrough, Gary, 1959,
  60, 61
Henderson, William R., 1956,
  57, 58
Hendrickson, Richard W., 1957
Henry, Wilbur L., 1934, 35, 36
Hickey, Robert, 1957, 58, 59
Hickman, Robert Z., 1928
Hicks, Tom, 1972, 73, 74
Higgins, Albert G., 1890
Hill, Sam H., 1922
Hill, Stanley, 1912
Hill, W. Leron, 1957, 58
Hills, Otto R., 1928, 29, 30
Hinkle, Robert, 1947
Hinsberger, Mike, 1973
Hodges, James D., 1937, 38
Hoeft, Julius, 1932
Hoffman, James H., 1966
Hoffman, Robert W., 1912
Hogan, Mickey, 1967, 68
Hollenbach, Jeff, 1973, 74
Horsley, Robert E., 1931
Hotchkiss, R. J., 1894, 95
Huber, William W., 1946
Huddleston, Thielen B., 1930
Hudelson, Clyde W., 1912
Huff, George A., 1890, 92
Hughes, Henry L., 1920
Huisinga, Larry, 1970, 71, 72
Hull, Walker F., 1908, 09
Humay, Daniel M., 1966
Humbert, Fred H., 1927, 28, 29
Huntoon, Harry A., 1901,
  02, 03, 04
Hurley, O. Landis, 1940
Hurtte, Frank, 1944
Huston, William E., 1966, 67, 68
Hyinck, Clifton F., 1931

"I"

Ingle, Walden M., 1938

Ingwerson, Burton A., 1917,
  18, 19
Iovino, Vito J., 1956

"J"

Jackson, Dave, 1967, 68, 69
Jackson, Earl A., 1931
Jackson, Trenton, 1962, 65
Jacques, Virgus, 1973
Janecek, Bill, 1967, 68
Janicki, Nick, 1969
Jansen, Earl, 1935
Janssen, Donald, 1944
Jefferson, Harry, 1954, 55, 56
Jenkins, Eddie, 1971, 72, 73
Jenkins, Richard H., 1951
Jenks, Charles N., 1925
Jensen, Stanley C., 1930, 31
Jerzak, Edward, 1957
Jeske, Thomas, 1971
Johnson, Bob, 1972
Johnson, Carl, 1956, 57, 58
Johnson, Donald T., 1944
Johnson, Frank, 1974. 75
Johnson, Nathan E., 1939,
  40, 41
Johnson, Richard L., 1966, 67, 68
Johnson, William M., 1936
Johnson, Jr., Herschel E., 1966, 68
Johnston, Arthur R., 1897, 98,
  99
Jolley, Walter, 1927, 28, 29
Jones, Amos I., 1949, 50
Jones, Robert B., 1945
Jones, Tom, 1969, 70
Joop, Lester, 1943, 44, 45
Jordan, Larry E., 1965, 66, 67
Jurczyk, Gary, 1975
Jutton, Lee, 1901

"K"

Kaiser, John, 1969, 70
Kane, John F., 1943
Kanosky, John P., 1935
Karras, John, 1949, 50, 51
Kasap, George, 1951
Kasap, Mike, 1942, 46
Kassel, Charles E., 1924, 25, 26
Kasten, Frederick W., 1902, 03,
  04
Kavathas, Sam, 1974
Kawal, E. J., 1929
Kearney, Herschel P., 1943
Kee, Dick, 1963, 64, 65
Keith, Alvin, 1970, 71, 72
Kelly, Moe, 1969, 70, 71
Kennedy, Jr., John H., 1931
Kersulis, Walter T., 1944, 47
  48. 49
Kiler, William H., 1894, 95
Kimbell, Steve, 1965
King, Harless W., 1891
King, J. W., 1898
Kirk, Todd, 1904, 05
Kirkpatrick, Jesse B., 1918
Kirschke, John W., 1938, 39
Kirwin, Jim, 1975
Kittler, Bud, 1973
Kleber, Doug, 1973, 74, 75
Kleckner, Bill, 1972, 73, 74
Klein, J. Leo, 1915, 16, 17

Klemp, Joseph B., 1937
Klimek, Anthony F., 1948, 49,
  50
Kmiec, Kenneth K., 1965, 66,
  67
Kmiec, Tom, 1968
Knapp, Clyde C. G., 1926
Knell, Phil D., 1965, 66
Knop, Robert O., 1916
Knox, Carl W., 1937
Knox, Rodney, 1974
Koch, George W., 1919
Kogut, Chuck, 1971, 72, 73
Kohlagen, Richard M., 1952, 53
Kolb, Gary A., 1959
Kolens, S. William, 1940, 45
Kolfenbach, Edwin J., 1931

Kopp, William K., 1918, 19
Kowalski, August J., 1932
Kraft, Don, 1955
Kraft, Reynold R., 1915, 16, 17
Krakoski, Joseph, 1960
Krall, William E., 1945
Kreitling, Richard A., 1957, 58
Krueger, Bernard E., 1946,
  47, 48, 49
Kruze, John J., 1960, 61
Kuhn, Clifford,W., 1933, 35, 36
Kustock, Al, 1972, 73
Kwas, Eugene S., 1945, 46

"L"

Lange, Gary, 1969
Langhorst, Oliver M., 1928
Lansche, Oral A., 1913
Lantz, Simon E., 1894
Lanum, F. B., 1926, 29
Lanum, Harold B., 1910
Lanum, Ralph L., 1918
Larimer, Floyd C., 1917, 20
Lasater, Jr., Harry A., 1936, 37
Lavery, Larry R., 1959, 60
Laz, Donald R., 1950
Lazier, Murney, 1947, 48
Lee, Willie, 1971
Leistner, Charles A., 1943
Leitch, Neal M., 1918
Lenich, William, 1937, 38, 39
Lennon, J. Patrick, 1960
Lenzini, Robert E., 1951, 52, 53
Leonard, Marion R., 1924, 25
Lepic, Mike, 1974
Levanti, John, 1971, 72, 73
Levanti, Louis, 1947, 48, 49
Levenick, Stu, 1974, 75
Lewis, James W., 1928
Lewis, Joe, 1970, 71, 72
Lifvendahl, Richard A., 1919
Liitt, Leon B., 1907
Lindbeck, Emerit (Em) D.,
  1953, 54, 55
Lindberg, Lester L., 1933,
  34, 35
Linden, R. W., 1920
Lindgren, Justa M., 1898, 99
  00, 01
Line, Jerry, 1967
Livas, Steve, 1969
Lollino, Frank V., 1961, 62
Lonergan, Charles P. A., 1904

Pfeffer, John E., 1892, 93, 94, 95
Pfeifer, Myron P., 1940, 41, 42
Phillips, Jim (Chubby), 1973, 74, 75
Phillips, James E., 1938, 39, 40
Phipps, T. E., 1903
Piatt, Charles L., 1931, 33
Piazza, Sam J., 1948, 49, 50
Pickering, Mike, 1969
Pierce, Jack B., 1945, 47, 48
Piggott, Bert C., 1946
Pike, David R., 1962
Pillath, Jerry, 1968
Pillsbury, Arthur L., 1890
Pinckney, Frank L., 1905, 06
Pinder, Cyril C., 1965, 66
Pittman, Donald C., 1947
Pitts, R. L. 1902, 03
Pixley, Arthur H., 1893, 94, 95, 96
Plankenhorn, James, 1961, 62, 63
Pleviak, Anthony J., 1966, 67, 68
Pnazek, Karl, 1969
Podmajersky, Paul, 1943
Pogue, Harold A., 1913, 14, 15
Polaski, Clarence L., 1936
Popa, Elie C., 1950, 51
Pope, Jean A., 1904
Portman, C. P., 1933, 34
Potter, Phil Harry, 1916
Powless, Dave, 1963, 64
Price, Samuel L., 1963, 64, 65
Prince, David C., 1911
Prokopis, Alexander, 1944
Pruett, Eugene F., 1913
Prymuski, Robert M., 1946, 47, 48
Purvis, Charles G., 1939

"Q"

Quade, John C., 1893, 94
Quinn, Bob, 1969

"R"

Raddatz, Russ, 1968
Radell, Jr., Willard W., 1965
Railsback, Fay D., 1906, 07, 08
Raklovits, Richard F., 1949, 50
Ralph, Stanley, 1975
Rebecca, Sam J., 1950, 51
Redmann, Doug, 1967, 68, 69
Reeder, James W., 1937, 38, 39
Reeves, Harley E., 1892
Reichle, Richard W., 1919, 21
Reinhart, Rick, 1973
Reitsch, Henry O., 1920
Reitsch, Robert, 1925, 26, 27
Renn, Donald Dean, 1954, 55
Rettinger, Geo. L., 1938, 39
Rhodes, Ora M., 1896
Richards, Edward J., 1922, 23
Richards, James V., 1908, 09
Richie, James K., 1908
Richman, Harry E., 1927, 28
Riehle, John, 1968
Riggs, Jr., Thomas J., 1938, 39, 40
Ringquist, Clarence L., 1928
Roberson, Garvin, 1972, 73

Roberts, Chester C., 1909, 10, 11
Roberts, Gilbert J., 1922, 23, 24
Roberts, Jr., Clifford, 1958, 59, 60
Robertson, Robert, 1966, 67
Robinson, Darrell, 1969, 70
Robinson, Olaf E., 1929, 30
Robinson, Roy, 1972, 73, 74
Robison, M. W., 1922
Rogers, Randy, 1968
Rokusek, Frank E., 1922, 23, 24
Romani, Melvin C., 1959, 60, 61
Root, George H., 1893
Root, Clark W., 1930
Rose, Jerry, 1968
Ross, Steve, 1970, 72
Rothgeb, Claude J., 1900, 02, 03, 04
Roush, Wm. D., 1928, 29
Rotzoll, Dan, 1970
Rowe, Enos M., 1911, 12, 13
Royer, Joseph W., 1892
Rucks, Jim, 1970, 71, 72
Rue, Orlie, 1901, 13, 14
Rump, Charles A., 1905
Rundquist, Elmer T., 1915, 16, 17
Russ, Jerald B., 1945
Russell, Eddie L., 1963, 64, 65
Russell, W. Hunter, 1930, 32
Rutgens, Jos. C., 1958, 59, 60
Ryan, John (Rocky), 1951, 52, 53
Ryan, Mike, 1968, 69
Ryan, Jr., Clement J., 1955
Rykovich, Julius, 1946
Rylowicz, Robert A., 1950, 51

"S"

Saban, Joseph P., 1945
Sabino, Daniel F., 1950, 51, 52
Sabo, John P., 1918, 20, 21
Sajnai, Chester B., 1943
Samojedny, George, 1969, 71
Santini, Veto, 1969
Saunders, Don, 1964
Sayre, Elvin C., 1934, 35, 36
Schacht, Fred W., 1894, 95, 96
Schalk, Edward A., 1931
Scharbert, Robert D., 1961, 62
Schlosser, Merle J., 1947, 48, 49
Schmidt, Burton J., 1947, 48, 49
Schmidt, Gerald C., 1967
Schobinger, Eugene, 1912, 13, 14
Schoeller, Julies E., 1905
Schrader, Chas., 1956
Schultz, Arthur F., 1930
Schultz, Emil G., 1922, 23, 24
Schultz, Ernest W., 1925, 27
Schulz, Larry, 1974, 75
Schumacher, Gregg H., 1962, 63, 64
Schumacher, Henry W., 1930
Schustek, Ivan D., 1931, 32, 33
Sconce, Harvey J., 1894, 95
Scott, Robert E., 1952
Scott, Bob, 1975
Scott, Tom, 1967, 68, 69, 70
Seamans, Frank L., 1932

Seiler, Otto E., 1909, 10, 11
Seliger, Vernon L., 1946, 47, 48
Senneff, Geo. F., 1912, 13
Serpico, Ralph M., 1943, 44, 45, 46
Shapland, Eral P., 1912
Shattuck, Sr., Walt F., 1890
Sheppard, Lawrence D., 1904
Shively, Bernie A., 1924, 25, 26
Shlaudeman, H. R., 1916, 17, 19
Short, Wm. E., 1927
Shuler, Hugh M., 1897
Siebens, Arthur R., 1913
Siebold, Harry P., 1937, 40
Siegel, Kenneth C., 1944
Siegert, Herbert F., 1946, 47, 48, 50
Siegert, Rudolph, 1954, 55
Siegert, Wayne, 1949
Siler, Roderick Wm., 1901
Silkman, John M., 1912, 13
Singman, Bruce, 1962
Sinnock, Pomery, 1906, 07, 08
Skarda, Edward J., 1936, 37
Slater, Wm. F., 1890, 91, 92
Slimmer, Louis F., 1923, 24
Sliva, Oscar, 1969
Smalzer, Joe, 1974, 75
Smerdel, Matthew T., 1942
Smid, Jan, 1952, 53, 54
Smith, Charles J., 1944
Smith, Donald I., 1950
Smith, Eugene R., 1920
Smith, J. Dale, 1956, 57
Smith, James A., 1939, 41, 42
Smith, Kevin, 1975
Smith, M. Rex, 1950, 51, 52
Smith, Marshall F., 1948
Smith, Mick, 1965, 66
Smith, Stuyvesant C., 1919
Smith, Thomas D., 1965, 66
Smith, Willie, 1969
Smock, Walter F., 1900
Snavely, Edwin R., 1931
Snook, John K., 1932, 33
Sorey, Revie, 1972, 73, 74
Spiller, John, 1969
Sprague, Stanley R., 1945
Springe, Otto, 1909, 10, 11
Spurgeon, A. Lowell, 1935, 36, 37
Squier, George K., 1914, 15
Stahl, Garland, 1899, 00, 01, 02
Standring, Bob, 1973
Stapleton, John M., 1959
Starks, Marshall L., 1958, 59, 60
Stasica, Stanley J., 1945
Stauner, Jim, 1974, 75
Steele, James, 1890, 91
Steger, Kurt, 1975
Steger, Russell W., 1946, 47, 48, 49
Steinman, Henry J., 1929
Stellwagen, Joel, 1966
Stephenson, Lewis A., 1901
Sternaman, Edward C., 1916, 17, 19, 21
Stevens, Don, 1949, 50, 51
Stevens, Lawrence J., 1951, 52
Stewart, Baird E., 1952, 53, 54
Stewart, Charles A., 1905, 06
Stewart, David L., 1957, 58
Stewart, Frank, 1914, 15, 16

319